**This is Broomhall, Sheffield, UK
A Critical, Class & Qualitative Community Profiling to Analyse Community
Information Needs, and Providers**

Zapopan Muela

This is Broomhall, Sheffield, UK
A Critical, Class & Qualitative Community Profiling to Analyse Community
Information Needs, and Providers

By: Zapopan Muela
Copyright © 2016 Zapopan Martín Muela-Meza
All rights reserved.
ISBN: 149595546X
ISBN-13: 978-1495955464
Published by first time on 18 December 2016

Cover photographs of collage Copyright © 2016 by Zapopan Martín Muela-Meza, taken in Broomhall, Sheffield, UK by the author during 2005 and 2007, girl models of the photographs: the daughters of the author who accompanied him during his PhD studies in Broomhall, Sheffield: Carolina Muela (older) and Paulina Muela (younger). Cover design: special thanks to Francisco Ramiro Ruiz Medina who did the Photoshop of the cover. Also thanks to Eduardo Alejandro Diaz Ochoa, Maximiliano Diaz Ochoa, and Hector Salazar Hernandez for pixeling cover picture collage.

DEDICATION

This book is dedicated to my parents,

In Memoriam to my mother, Celia Montserrat Meza León (1943-2011), my beloved "gypsy" who happily was alive when she saw my PhD thesis *magnum opus* finished and my PhD degree conferred. It is edited on the 24th February 2016 as homage to the 73th anniversary of my mother the Gypsy Echincuele Montserrat poetess.

and

In Memoriam to my father, Everardo Muela Caballero (1938-2004), my beloved and immortal "open book" and "mark of fire" whose material body did not resist to be alive to see my PhD lifetime goal accomplished before it transformed and melted into another cosmic forms.

To my daughters,
Carolina Muela and Paulina Muela, whose love, friendship, and early *character* has been an inexhaustible source of motivation.

and
This is also especially dedicated with all of my love to mi fiancé Beatriz Adriana Ruiz Medina, who since 9 March 2013 has loved me and supported me like no other woman in the past.

"But ever since the dawn of civilization, people have not been content to see events as unconnected and inexplicable. They have craved an understanding of the underlying order in the world. Today we still yearn to know why we are here and where we came from. Humanity's deepest desire for knowledge is justification enough for our continuing quest. And our goal is nothing less than a complete description of the universe we live in."
— Stephen Hawking (1988: 13)

"The library connects us with the insights and knowledge, painfully extracted from Nature, of the greatest minds that ever were, with the best teachers, drawn from the entire planet and from all of our history, to instruct us without tiring, and to inspire us to make our own contribution to the collective knowledge of the human species. Public libraries depend on voluntary contributions. I think the health of our civilization, the depth of our awareness about the underpinnings of our culture and our concern for the future can all be tested by how well we support our libraries." –Carl Sagan, Cosmos (Sagan, 2001: 282)

"Twenty-one months I had the opportunity to become acquainted with the English proletariat, its strivings, its sorrows and its joys, to see them from near, from personal observation and personal intercourse, and at the same time to supplement my observations by recourse to the requisite authentic sources. What I have seen, heard and read has been worked up in the present book. I am prepared to see not only my standpoint attacked in many quarters but also the facts I have cited, particularly when the book gets into the hands of the English. I know equally well that here and there I may be proved wrong in some particular of no importance, something that in view of the comprehensive nature of the subject and its far-reaching assumptions even an Englishman might be unable to avoid; so much the more so since even in England there exists as yet not a single piece of writing which, like mine, takes up all the workers. But without a moment's hesitation I challenge the English bourgeoisie to prove that even in a single instance of any consequence for the exposition of my point of view as a whole I have been guilty of any inaccuracy, and to prove it by data as authentic as mine.
— Friedrich Engels
The Condition of the Working Class in England (Engels, [1845], 2000)

"Community / for Broomhall
Poem by Shirley Cameron

Community
you and me
a space / a time / where we live
a type of living
a timeless yearning
for unity
from indifference
to love of your difference
as you sense mine
so we can be known here
feel at home here
see and be seen
and somehow
be a community" (Broomspring Writers Group, 2002: 158)

"Wickerman"
"Just behind the station
before you reach the traffic island
a river runs though a concrete channel
I took you there once; I think it was after the Leadmill

The water was dirty
and it smelt of industrialisation
Little mesters coughing their lungs up
And globules the colour of tomato ketchup
But it flows
Yeah, it flows
Yeah, underneath the city
through dirty brickwork conduits
connecting white witches on the Moor
with Pre-Raphaelites down in **Broomhall**
Beneath the old Trebor factory
that burnt down in the early seventies
Leaving an antiquated sweet-shop smell
and caverns of nougat and caramel
Nougat
Yeah, nougat and caramel
And the river flows on..."
　　　The Wickerman, — The Pulp (Cocker, 2012)

PRESENTATION

The author of this book, *This is Broomhall, Sheffield, UK: A Critical, Class & Community Profiling to Analyse Community Information Needs and Provision*, **Dr. Zapopan Muela (MEXICO)**, obtained his PhD Degree at the University of Sheffield (UK, 2010). This book is the authentic monographic format of the author's PhD thesis entitled: *Community Profiling to Analyse Community Information Needs and Provision: Perceptions from the Residents of Broomhall, Sheffield, UK,* that you can download it full text and free of charge through his **E-LIS and UANL open access self archiving repositories,** or a pay-per-access through **The British Library,** with Document Supply DRT 527209, UIN: BLL01015935892, or through **The University of Sheffield Library,** with Record ID: 21176803160001441. It is published as monograph too in order to reach out those readers who prefer this format.

Zapopan Muela,
San Nicolas de los Garza, Nuevo Leon, Mexico, 18 December 2016.

CONTENTS

Dedication	iii
Presentation	Vi
List of tables	viii
List of figures	Ix
List of acronyms	X
Spanish-English translation note	Xi
1. Introduction	1
2. Methodology	7
3. Review of the literature	52
4. Historical and demographic background of the Broomhall neighbourhood	69
5. Analysis and discussion of findings. Perceptions of the issues and features of Broomhall, information needs, and provision	101
6. Conclusions and recommendations	145
7. Further research	153
Bibliography	157
Appendices	179
About the author	191

List of tables

Table 2.1 Conceptual scheme and its operationalization   9

Table 2.2 Libraries employed to review documental information for this thesis (2003-2007)   27

Table 2.3 Databases used to search documental information for this thesis   27

Table 2.4 Database fields of the working Broomhall directory of respondents   34

Table 2.5 Identification codes for interviewees   36

Table 2.6 General profile of all the interviewees (32 respondents in total)   36

Table 2.7 Profile of the individual interviewees. Long time neighbourhood residents (10 respondents)   36

Table 2.8 Profile of the individual interviewees. Information providers (8 participants)   38

Table 2.9 Profile of focus groups interviewees. Long time neighbourhood residents (3 focus groups with 14 participants)   39

Table 4.1 Density of dwellings per ground area in square meters of Section A (the Hanover Estates)   75

Table 4.2 Density of dwellings per ground area in square meters of the Broomspring Estate of Section B   75

Table 4.3 Density of dwellings per ground area in square meters of Section C   76

Table 4.4 Density of dwellings per ground area in square meters of Section D   76

Table 4.5 Incompatibilities amongst census Super Output Areas (SOA) or Enumeral Districts (EDs) levels and sections, A, B, C & D of Broomhall   77

Table 4.6. Comparative ground areas in square metres of the ex YMCA property on Broomhall Road and the Hanover Flats (section A)   107

Table 4.7 Broomhall Index and Domain Scores from 2001 census   94

Table 4.8 Broomhall 2001 Census Key Statistics compared with Sheffield   96

Table 5.1 Negative issues of Broomhall   102

Table 5.2 Positive (or less negative, controversial, and adverse) features of Broomhall   105

Table 5.3 Information provision through the letter boxes of Broomhall homes (at least in section C), from 16 September 2006 to 16 March 2007   107

Table 5.4 Community and voluntary sector documents collected at information providers' premises   110

Table 5.5 Statutory sector (central government) documents collected at information providers' premises   110

Table 5.6 Statutory sector (Sheffield City Council) documents collected at information providers' premises   111

Table 5.7 Documents from the private sector collected at information providers' premises   111

Table 5.8 Comparison of information providers' documents about their own organisation displayed at their premises   112

Table 5.9 Comparative ground areas in square metres of the ex YMCA properties on Broomhall Road (section D) and ex St. Silas Church (section C)   128

List of figures

Figure 4.1 Broomhall street map 74

Figure 4.2 Actual satellite map of Broomhall circa 2004-2005 as emerged from the data of this thesis 74

Figure 4.3 Map of Broomhall circa 1849 and 1899 according to the *Map of Derbyshire and Yorkshire, 1st ed. 1849-1899* 80

Figure 4.4 Map of Broomhall geographical limits according to the Broomhall Forum in 1999 99

Figure 4.5 Map of Broomhall geographical boundaries according to the Broomhall Forum in 2005 82

Figure 4.6 Map of Broomhall according to the Sheffield NHS (National Health Services), 2006 83

Figure 4.7 Map of the original proposal of the Broomhall Park Conservation Area, 1967 86

Figure 4.8 Map of the Broomhall Park Conservation Area as officially designated by the Sheffield City Council, 16 July 1970 87

Figure 4.9 Map of the Broomhall Park Conservation Area as officially enlarged by the Sheffield City Council, 5 July 1989 89

Figure 4.10 Map of Broomhall featuring the Havelock Housing Action boundaries 90

Figure 4.11 Map of Broomhall, c 1944, where the highly explosive bombs of the WWII Nazi Blitz were dropped on the 12th December 1940 92

Figure 4.12 Map of the plans for territorial expansion of Sheffield Hallam University within the Broomhall neighbourhood, c 1969 93

Figure 4.13 Map of Sheffield Hallam University Broomhall Park campus, section D, picture taken on 19 May 2007 94

Figure 4.14 Heptagram of Broomhall Index and Domain Scores from 2001 census 96

Figure 4.15 Broomhall Neighbourhood Locator Map within Sheffield from 2001 census 98

List of acronyms

BBC: British Broadcasting Corporation.
BCC: Broomhall Community Centre.
BCG: Broomhall Community Group.
BF: Broomhall Forum.
BME: Black and Minority Ethnic.
BPA: Broomhall Park Association.
CAB: Citizens' Advice Bureau.
CAQDAS: Computer-Assisted Analysis of Qualitative Data.
DII: Documental Information Institutions or Institutions of Information Recorded in Documents.
ED: Enumeral Districts.
EU: European Union.
FG: Focus Group (type of interview).
HMC: Hanover Medical Centre.
ICT: Information and Communication Technology.
IP: Individual interviews to information providers.
LIS: Library and Information Science.
NHS: National Health Service.
HMO: House in Multiple Occupancy.
PCT: Primary Care Trust.
RI: Individual interviews to residents.
SCAB: Sharrow Citizens' Advice Bureau.
SNIS: Sheffield Neighbourhood Information System.
SOA: Super Output Areas.
UANL: Universidad Autónoma de Nuevo León, México (Nuevo Leon Autonomous University, Mexico).
UNAM: Universidad Nacional Autónoma de México, México (Mexico National Autonomous University, Mexico).
YMCA: Young Men's Christians Association.

Spanish-English translation note

Unless otherwise noted, all Spanish to English translations are my own –Zapopan Muela.

1. INTRODUCTION

> "We humans are biased observers, with a vested interest in the answer. The cure for this disease is more data." —Carl Sagan and Ann Druyan, *Shadows of Forgotten Ancestors: A Search for Who We Are* (1992: 400)

1.1 Overview

This chapter will explain a) the research question, overall aim, and four objectives of the thesis, b) the structure of the thesis, c) the background of this study, and c) relevance of this research project.

The next section explains the research problem, aims, and objectives.

1.2 The research problem, aim, and objectives

1.2.1 The research question

The research question of this thesis was:

> What are the community information needs and provision of the residents of the Broomhall neighbourhood of Sheffield, UK according to their perceptions?

1.2.2 The overall aim

The overall aim of this thesis was:

> To analyse, through the application of a community profiling tool, the community information needs of the residents of the Broomhall neighbourhood of Sheffield, UK, and to evaluate to what extent information providers meet those needs.

1.2.3 Objectives of the thesis

This section explains the four specific research objectives that have been established to conduct this study and investigate the thesis research question and its overall aim. It also mentions the chapters where these objectives are analysed. These are the objectives:

1) To identify the community information needs of the residents of the Broomhall neighbourhood. This objective is analysed in the Chapter 5 (Analysis and discussion of the findings: perceptions of the issues and features of Broomhall, information needs, and provision).

2) To establish to what extent information providers satisfy the community information needs of the residents of the Broomhall neighbourhood. This objective is also analysed in the Chapter 5.

3) To explore the effectiveness of the community profiling tool to analyse community information needs and provision. This objective is analysed in the Chapter 3 (Review of the literature).

4) To understand the possible implications of this study for policy makers. This objective is analysed in the Chapter 6 (Conclusions and recommendations).

The next section explains the overall structure of the thesis.

1.3 The structure of the thesis

The thesis is structured into seven chapters. The present Chapter 1 forms the introduction to the thesis.

Chapter 2, "Methodology," analyses the research design to generate, analyse, and report this thesis.

This employs qualitative research methodology, particularly interpretivism or interpretivist approaches and methods of analysis of documents, observation and interviews (individual and in focus groups).

Chapter 3 presents a literature review about the three key elements of this project: *the community profiling tool, community information needs, and information providers.*

Chapter 4 presents a general historical and demographical background of the Broomhall neighbourhood, going as far as the 16th century until the year 2006, when the generation of data for this project ended.

Chapter 5 presents the analysis, and discussions of the major findings of the project. These findings are grouped in six major issues and two major features that emerged from the Broomhall neighbourhood.

These are the issues found:

1)Issues of territoriality or uses of the land (e.g. housing; expansion of Sheffield and Hallam universities becoming university student villages);
2)	Issues of poverty, social and economic inequalities (e.g. unemployment, debt, crime);
3)	Health issues (e.g. drug addiction, lack of: green public open space, playgrounds, and sports and leisure facilities);
4)	Political issues;
5)	Cultural issues (e.g. multicultural, ethnic, religious, and national issues);
6)	Communication issues.

These are the features found:

7)	Transport features;
8)	Educational features.

Those six issues and two features, at the same time, have been considered as the eight major community information needs as perceived by the residents of Broomhall and the information providers acting upon them. Hence, this chapter also analyses and discusses the interrelationships of those issues, features, and information needs, with the various ways that information providers tried to meet them.

Chapter 6, "Conclusions and recommendations," summarizes the major contributions to knowledge emerging from this thesis in this thesis, and the main conclusions and recommendations for: a) the Broomhall residents; b) LIS practitioners, and c) policy makers.

Chapter 7, presents the broad recommendations for further research that emerged from this project. These are some of the themes for further research that the author might follow (e.g. the creation of an *integral analytical model for Library and Information Science;* informal information networks of people who act like gateways to information; possible information provision of the unsolicited post people receive through their letterboxes; issues on the privatization of information provision in publicly funded institutions).

The next section explains the background of this thesis.

1.4 Background to the study

These sections will give an overview of the background to this study.

### 1.4.1	*Rationale for conducting research on Broomhall and how this doctoral research project was configured*

Unlike McGuire (1981), who conducted a community profiling research project in a middle class affluent neighbourhood of Sheffield, the author of this project thought from the outset to choose a deprived neighbourhood to do research about it. In the recent research, *Closing the Gap: a Framework for Neighbourhood Renewal in Sheffield*, it was shown that Sheffield has some of the most deprived Wards in England. Of the 29 wards Sheffield comprises, 10 of them are in the list of the top ten percent most deprived wards in England. Seven of these 10 are in the top five percent, and three are in the top one percent. Sheffield's poorest wards have more deprivation than those of Leeds, whilst being less deprived than those of Liverpool or Manchester. However, by contrast, Sheffield has some of the most affluent areas in England and Broomhall area is the number 10 most deprived neighbourhood according to Milne (2004: 5).

This research project began formally on the 30th of September 2003 when the researcher registered at the Department of Information Studies at the University of Sheffield. Originally the researcher's research problem was to find out about "some barriers such as economic, political, social, legal, cultural and others which hampered the free access to information resources in public libraries" with a global scope. Following the guidance of his first supervisor, he began reviewing the literature so as to narrow down and focus better his research problem, since it was far too ambitious. In doing so, by October 2003 he came across a tool of research called "community analysis" as employed in a community of Denver, Colorado in the USA in order to build a public library according to a "community analysis" of the actual information needs from the people in the community (Sarling and Van Tassel, 1999).

This idea attracted the researcher's interest, since part of conducting the PhD research project, as a Mexican student, was to learn methodologies to implement them to the Mexican LIS scenarios. When the researcher discussed it with his supervisor, he was told that it was a good idea to refocus the research proposal. In addition, the supervisor commented that in the British librarianship the U.S. "community analysis" concept was known as "community profiling." Moreover, the supervisor suggested to him to review the work of Beal (1985), *Community Profiling for Librarians,* who was a *community profiling* expert. The supervisor also suggested to him to review further the literature in the database of the Department of Information Studies at the University of Sheffield, because different LIS researchers and practitioners had already extensively conducted *community profiling* research for different LIS scenarios in that department for more than 30 years (e.g. Beal, 1976, 1979, 1985; Stone, 1985; Usherwood, 1992; 2003; Linley and Usherwood, 1998); with additional research by some postgraduate students from the same department (e.g. Curtis, 1972; Miller, 1977; Hall, 1981; McGuire, 1981; Hunter, 1998; Li, 1999; Ewart, 2004).

The author of this project began to be interested in the *community profiling* tool as a process to narrow down his initial doctoral research topic. In 17 November 2003 the author wrote the paper "An introduction to the applicability of qualitative research methodologies to the field of Library and Information Sciences" as an exploratory way to narrow down his doctoral research topic (Muela-Meza, 2003a); eventually this paper was published in a Peruvian peer review journal (Muela-Meza, 2006b).

Subsequently, an interesting article from the USA by Sarling and Van Tassel (1999): "Community analysis: research that matters to a North-Central Denver community," came to the knowledge of the author. The author as a Mexican grantee of the Mexican National Council of Science and Technology (CONACYT) [1] has as his overall aims to learn in the UK as a visiting scholar as many theories, methodologies, methods, and tools which could be implemented in Mexico according to the Mexican reality. Thus, the first impression from that paper was that *community analysis* was a tool that could matter to Mexico's reality. As far as the author knew, most LIS professionals were already aware of the classic librarianship conceptualization of *community of users' needs*. Librarians and other documental information professionals and practitioners need to be aware of this concept in order to effectively provide information services to any user community, any library or other documental information institution.

The author acknowledges that he had not been previously engaged in a major research project that required a knowledge of which theories, methodologies, methods, and tools would best help to fulfil that LIS "mantra" of satisfying all Mexican communities' information needs, issues, and problems. This is due to the fact that when he joined the Department of Information Studies at the University

---

[1] http://www.conacyt.mx/

of Sheffield, he was more interested in *information access barriers* in public libraries, not in *information needs*. However, before October 2003 he had made several literature reviews on public libraries since 1995 (Muela-Meza, 1995; 2001a; 2001b; 2002b; 2003b); on *freedom of information access* to global and Mexican governments (2001c; 2002a; 2004a); on *reference services* in academic libraries, including a brief review (1999a; 1999b; 1999c).

Furthermore, this flexible change of focus at the beginning of this project shows the reflexivity and open mindness adopted throughout the whole thesis by the author. When he came to the UK he came with some previous ideas, his and others', through a study of the literature. Thus, the idea of conducting empirical research on any LIS phenomenon which may help solve library and information problems in Mexico was a very exciting endeavour for the researcher to take.

Thus, at that time and in that context, when the author became aware of the *community analysis* term and all the immense reach it involved, he saw it as a candle in a sort of darkness (to paraphrase Sagan's book: *The Demon-Haunted World: Science as a Candle in the Dark (1997)*), because in those early days of this doctorate, the idea of narrowing the original "global" study the author had in mind was such a pressing task that at times it looked rather dark, fuzzy and blurred. When the author presented his paper (Muela-Meza, 2003a) to his first supervisor, and talked with him about *community analysis* as implemented by Sarling and Van Tassel (1999) the supervisor suggested to him that it was a very doable research project, but suggested to him a very slightly different term to use instead of *community analysis,* namely *community profiling*.

The phrase *"community profiling"* was not alien to the researcher. In LIS parlance, it is not alien either. In the Mexican LIS tradition where he obtained his B.A. degree in librarianship at the Nuevo Leon Autonomous University (UANL) since 1995 he already was aware of the concept of *community of users' profile* in any given library (as in Rendón Rojas, 2005: 116-117, or researched by many other Mexican LIS commentators even from earlier times as far back as the end of the 19th century (Sametz de Walerstein, 1991). In addition, while he was head of the Reference Section of the Central Library at the Ciudad Juarez Autonomous University (UACJ) in Ciudad Juarez, Chihuahua, Mexico, he built the first university-wide Profile of the Users' Community of the Reference Services at UACJ, which was described in a small paper at the UACJ university newspaper (Muela-Meza, 1999a; 1999b; 1999c).

However, the novelty, at least for the author, of *community analysis,* or *community profiling,* came twofold. On one hand, it came as an opportunity to research any community in terms of its collectiveness (collective group) or as a collectiveness of people belonging, living, working, etcetera in a geographically delimitated area. This idea was very attractive as a research topic because most of the LIS tradition has focused mostly on individuals, on an individual basis, not collectively.

On the other hand, it could be foreseen at the earliest stages of this project that *community analysis,* or *community profiling* could be researched for the sake of research itself applied on any community without having the necessity to do research by measuring its results against the aims, or objectives of any library, or any other documental information institution, as had been the tradition of library research since immemorial times, and more particularly since the advent of positivism applied to LIS.

Thus, these ideas of breaking up with some "well established" traditions in LIS and the potential of contributing something new to the universal commons of knowledge through empirical research were very exciting ideas. However, they also represented a great challenge, regardless of how small or big the eventual sample would be of people or geographical boundaries.

The next section will explain the relevant features that make this thesis distinctive within the library and information science (LIS) field.

1.5 Relevance of this doctoral research project

This is an overview of the features where this doctoral project might have a distinctive impact in the LIS field both: theoretically and methodologically:

• Whereas most of the LIS studies on *community profiling* have focused on the information needs of some particular groups of people, this study has also tried to analyse, in relation to the people included in the sample, their physical environment, where they live, work, study, etc.

• Whereas most of the LIS studies on *community profiling* have focused mainly on the information needs of individuals on an individual basis, this study has focused on *community information needs,* that is, by approaching the phenomenon as a collective phenomenon, not of standalone and isolated individuals; *community profiling* is about communities, not individual profiling.

• Whereas most of the studies have mainly profiled the communities in order to provide information services from existing or future libraries, this project has gone beyond that through several paths such as: discovering relationships among the people – the needs and issues affecting them in their material or immaterial context but materialistically determined – and their information providers; researching mainly for academic purposes to test the *community profiling* tool. If the project had informed any particular library, documental information institution, local or central government institution, agency, public policy, and so on, that would have been only done tangentially and only as a result of the overall thesis.

• Whereas most of the previous LIS studies on *community analysis,* or *community profiling* have relied mainly on quantitative research methodologies and methods, and some even applied positivism apparently in strict ways, this project has relied almost entirely on qualitative research methodologies and methods applied open-mindedly with flexibility, and reflexivity as to test their effectiveness when combined with *community profiling.*

The next section gives a summary of the introductory chapter of this thesis.

1.6 Summary

This chapter has presented a general overview of the thesis. It comprised these sections: a) the research question, overall aim, and four objectives of the thesis, b) the structure of the thesis, c) the background of this study, and c) relevance of this research project.

The research question, aim, and objectives have presented deductively the overall purpose of this research project, that is, going from the general (e.g. research question) to the particular (e.g. aim, and then objectives). Consequently, from the research question the aim was derived, and from this the objectives. Hence, the research question gives a synoptic view of the purpose of this study encompassing its key elements: an analysis of information needs from the perceptions of residents who are bonded as a community, and who live in a neighbourhood (Broomhall), located in Sheffield, UK, and an evaluation of the information provision they receive to meet their needs. The term *perceptions* implies that this is a study that employs qualitative research methodology.

The overall aim of this study operationalizes the research question as a clear affirmative statement of how, in general terms, this question is going to be responded to, throughout the study. The key elements mentioned in the research question remained, and another was added: the application of the *community profiling tool.* Hence, it is via the *community profiling tool* that the research question will be addressed, and how the study will be conducted (as a response to its overall purpose).

Hence, this overall aim is operationalized through four objectives. The first three comprise an analysis of the key elements of the overall aim: a) community information needs of these residents, b) information provided to meet these needs, and c) the effectiveness of the community profiling tool that was employed to analyse the first two objectives. The fourth objective was established to assess the possible implications of this study for policy makers.

The thesis was structured into seven chapters: Chapter 1, Introduction, Chapter 2, Methodology, Chapter 3, Review of the literature, Chapter 4, Historical and demographic background of the Broomhall neighbourhood, Chapter 5, Analysis and discussion of findings, Chapter 6, Conclusions and recommendations, and Chapter 7, Further research.

In the section of the background of the study was explained the rationale for conducting research on Broomhall and how this doctoral research project was configured. This background explained how the author began to be interested in employing the *community profiling tool,* in the qualitative research methodology, and how the Broomhall neighbourhood was selected to conduct this study.

In the section of the relevance of this doctoral research project, an overview was provided of the features that this study might have in terms of providing a distinctive impact for library and information science. Four features have made this study distinct from others: a) the application of the community profiling has focused not only on information needs of some groups, as other studies, but also on their physical environment, b) the application of the community profiling has focused on information needs of the community, on a collective basis, not individually as other studies, c) the application of community profiling in this study has been conducted for academic purposes for the sake of knowledge, not as other studies conducted for specific libraries or organisations.

Chapter 2 will explain the methodology employed in this project.

2. METHODOLOGY

"It is enormously easier to present in an appealing way the wisdom distilled from centuries of patient and collective interrogation of Nature than to detail the messy distillation apparatus. The method of science, as stodgy and grumpy as it may seem, is far more important than the findings of science. — Carl Sagan, The Demon-Haunted World: Science as a Candle in the Dark (1997: 39)

"In summary, the idea is to try to give all [sic] the information to help others to judge the value of your contribution; not only the information that leads the judgment in a particular direction or another." — Nobel laureate, Richard Phillips Feynman, *The Pleasure of Finding Things Out,* (Feynman, 2001: 210).

"Perception, without verification or grounds, is not sufficient guarantee of truth" — Bertrand Russell, *Mysticism and Logic*, 1929 (cited in Sagan, 1997: 320).

2.1 Introduction

This chapter presents the analysis of the qualitative research methodology and methods employed in this project, covering both the theoretical or conceptual scheme, and the pragmatic, or mechanical research design, and their interrelationships to the thesis' research question, main aim, and four objectives stated in the Introduction of this thesis (see Chapter 1).

The methodology and methods employed in this thesis are related to the research problem as has been stated by a commentator: "the research problem must determine the research approach and the methods employed" (Westbrook, 1994: 242). As stated in the Introduction (see Chapter 1), the research question was: What are the community information needs and provision of the residents of the Broomhall neighbourhood of Sheffield, UK according to their perceptions? In addition, the overall aim of this thesis was: To analyse, through the application of the community profiling tool, the community information needs of the residents of the Broomhall neighbourhood of Sheffield, UK, and to evaluate to what extent information providers meet those needs. As also mentioned in the Introduction (see Chapter 1), this overall aim was divided into four major specific research objectives: 1) the analysis of information needs, 2) the analysis of information provision, 3) the analysis of the effectiveness of the community profiling tool, and 4) the possible implications of this study for policy makers.

That is, from the Introduction (see Chapter 1) the reader can assess that this project has analysed the information needs and provision according to the perceptions of residents, who live in a given neighbourhood of Sheffield, UK (Broomhall), and of their information providers from within or outside Broomhall. Hence the reader can see at a glance that part of the sample from where this thesis generated its data, that it is geographically located (the Broomhall neighbourhood), and that the other part of the sample where also data were generated (that of residents and information providers also related to same neighbourhood). In addition, as the reader will assess later (see Chapter 4), Broomhall is a rather small neighbourhood. Hence, the reader at this stage might already have an idea of the nature of this research project relating to information needs and provision of a small neighbourhood, according to the perceptions of the residents and the information providers living or working from within or outside that neighbourhood.

Hence, the researcher of this project generated and analysed detailed data at a significantly deep level from the perceptions of few people who live (residents) in a given small neighbourhood (Broomhall), and those of their information providers. Simultaneously he made interrelationships of these data with the physical, natural, or material appraisal of the features of this neighbourhood, and with the literature related to those perceptions by using the community profiling tool to generate data. The community profiling tool will be analysed in Chapter 3 (literature review), but the prior methodology will be the subject of this chapter. Thus, the concepts, the qualitative research methodologies, and methods employed in this thesis, along with their favourable and competing views, are related to the research question, overall aim, and four objectives mentioned above.

This chapter is divided into these major sections:

1)Theoretical framework, which includes a) rationale for choosing a theoretical framework in qualitative research, b) discussion of the conceptual scheme and its operationalization, and c) the following concepts employed in this study: the concept of the materialist conception of history, the social class struggles concept, and the concept of configuration as an open structure of theory.

2)   Rationale for choosing a qualitative research methodology, which includes a rationale for choosing the qualitative research methods, this includes a) method of analysis of documents or literature review, b) method of non-participant observation, and c) method of interviews, individually and through focus groups.

3)   Design of the data generation, which includes: a) the rationale for the selection of the purposing sampling (which includes 1) selection of the purposing sampling, 2) selection process of interviewees –this includes a procedure to obtain a balanced sample, identification code of interviewees, and the composition of sample of interviewees–), b) the rationale of the pilot study, and c) the rationale of main study which includes the evolution of the interviews schedule from the pilot to the main study.

4)   Design of the data analysis.

5)   Procedures of validity (which includes the triangulation of methods), replicability (which includes the audit trail), neutrality, and generalization or transferability of the research project.

The next section analyses the theoretical framework.

2.2 Theoretical framework

The following sections will address: a) the rationale for employing a theoretical framework in qualitative research, and b) the discussion of the conceptual scheme and its operationalization (which includes the concepts of materialist conception of history, social class struggles, and the configuration as an open structure of theory). Each concept includes its rationale, and some views in favour and competing views.

The next section explains the rationale for choosing a theoretical framework.

2.2.1 Rationale for choosing a theoretical framework in qualitative research

The main methodology and methods for this research project belong to the qualitative research approach. Some commentators from this approach note that this approach does not employ any theory to be tested (this is a *deductive reasoning)*, but rather it generates a theory at the end of any research project (*inductive reasoning)*, such is the particular case of the advocates of the grounded theory (Strauss and Corbin, 1990; Glaser and Strauss, 1967). However, other commentators note that the qualitative research approach can underpin a theoretical approach aprioristically (*deductive reasoning)*, before the research project starts, e.g. to guide the initial stages of the literature or to interpret or understand events and observations (Gorman and Clayton, 2005).

The author of this research project has employed both the *deductive and inductive reasoning* of a theoretical framework, but following a third route. Building on the work of Mason (2002), this project has employed a theoretical framework where theory, data generation, and data analysis developed throughout the research project "simultaneously in a dialectical process." (Mason, 2002: 180). That is, it has moved "back and forth between data analysis and the process of explanation or theory construction" (Mason, 2002: 180). However, the author followed Mason's (2002) ideas as a process of explanation, instead of theory construction. That is, this project began with the idea to have a theoretical framework since the beginning, but this was employed with flexibility according to how the project developed, and going back and forth with the early theoretical statements to assess if later findings matched with earlier concepts. To this type of theoretical framework, according to her interpretivist approach in qualitative research, Mason (2002: 180-181) termed it *abductive or retroductive reasoning,* in clear distinction with the *deductive reasoning* (where theory comes first), or *inductive reasoning* (where theory comes at the end).

In this regard, some commentators who have conducted community profiling research on the health sector support the idea of having a theoretical framework (Moran and Butler, 2001). In addition, they also argue that when researchers who are doing community profiling research do not provide a theoretical framework they fall into difficulties of justifying their methodologies employed to generate or analyse data (Moran and Butler, 2001: 61). A major researcher of community needs profiling from the social work science (Green, 2000a; 2000c), and another commentator (Oliver, 2004), also agrees with Moran and Butler (2001).

Therefore, this research project maintains the idea that employing a theoretical background was a necessary step to be conducted in order to underpin the researcher's methodologies and methods before one begins the research project and during all its stages until the end. This theoretical framework was not comprised by a single theory, but by a series of different theoretical concepts, or concepts derived from different theories from philosophy, social and natural sciences following Mason's (2002: 180-181) *abductive or retroductive reasoning* by employing concepts since the beginning, during all the research process, and at the end, simultaneously in a "back and forth" process.

In this respect, some of the concepts that the author employed at the earlier stages of the project, such as the *critical and sceptical thinking* by Sagan (1997), and the *critical epistemology* by de la Garza Toledo (2001), were removed from the thesis. Because, when the author moved back from the final stages to the early stages, after the analysis and discussion of findings, conclusions and recommendations (cf. Mason's (2002) *abductive or retroductive reasoning),* those concepts could not longer be sustained, as their early insights did not match with the final findings.

The next section explains the conceptual scheme and its operationalization of the theoretical framework employed.

2.2.2 Discussion of the conceptual scheme and its operationalization

This section analyses the concepts employed in this thesis: a) the concept of the materialist conception of history, b) the social class struggles concept, and c) the concept of configuration as an open structure of theory, and the ways they were operationalized within the thesis.

On Table 2.1 below it is explained the conceptual scheme and its operationalization. In the first column the definitions of the concepts employed throughout this thesis are presented; this is referred to here as the conceptual scheme. In the second column are described the interrelationships of those concepts with other concepts, methods, terms, or key words that appear throughout the thesis. This is referred to here as the operationalization of the concepts, that is, the way they were actually employed. In order to clearly guide the reader to the interrelationships of the conceptual scheme with its operationalization throughout the thesis. A reference to the names of those other concepts, methods, terms, and keywords, and the chapters where they are located is included as well. Hence, whenever the readers find a major concept, method, term, or keyword in this or other chapters in the thesis they can return to Table 2.1 (below) and find the interrelationships of it with any of the three major concepts employed as a theoretical framework.

Table 2.1 is explained here.

Table 2.1 Conceptual scheme and its operationalization	
Definition of concepts	**Interrelationships with other concepts (including Chapters of localization)**
The concept of the materialist conception of history. "We must begin by stating the first premise of all human beings must be in a position to live in order to be able to "make history." However, life involves before everything else eating and drinking, housing, clothing and various and other things. The first historical act is thus the reproduction of the means to	Chapter 2 (the social class struggles concept; method of observation; cosmos); Chapter 3 (materialistic concept of need; "bottom up" concept of needs; information recorded in

satisfy these needs, the production of material life itself. In addition, indeed this is an historical act, a fundamental condition of all history, which today, as thousand years ago, must daily and hourly be fulfilled merely in order to sustain human life" (Marx and Engels, [1845-1846] 1976a: 41-42).	material documents; community profiling; spatial place where communities live in; human communities; labour; technology; territorial cosmic matter; cosmic evolution of nature; historic evolution of human society); Chapter 4 (material living conditions of people; territoriality); Chapter 6 (material and cosmic balance)
The social class struggles concept. Being human beings social mammals evolved from reptiles, they inherited the innate hierarchical drives of either dominance against the weak, or submission before the strong (at the beginning due to natural survival reasons, later and currently for institutionalized dominating motives) mainly to obtain valued resources (e.g. food, territories, properties, knowledge, information) (Sagan, 2001; 1980; 1978; with Druyan, 1992). However, "in societies with dominance hierarchies there will always be inequities in the distribution of valued resources. This is what defines dominance hierarchy" (Hauser, 2006: 394). Thus, these inequities have always prompted the dominated individuals or groups to challenge the dominant. These challenges are struggles (violent or non-violent), and they will continue as long as human social dominance hierarchy persists. "Though neither class nor race is a biological category, our mind is equipped with the hardware and software to pick out cues that identify the other... we can't erase the constraints that our mind imposes on our perceptions, and this includes dividing the world into dominant and subordinate, black and white" (Hauser, 2006: 212). Therefore, "the [written, recorded, Engels] history of all hitherto existing society is the history of class struggles" (Marx and Engels, [1848], 1976b: 482).	Chapter 2 (materialist conception of history; library and information provision); Chapter 3 (materialistic concept of need; "bottom up" concept of needs; information recorded in material documents; community profiling; spatial place where communities live in; human communities); Chapter 4 (working class revolts; cramped and unsanitary conditions of living of working class; territoriality; contrasting poorer and wealthier social classes); Chapter 5 (oppression; monopolization of knowledge and information; contradictions, tensions, and conflicts; to the findings of this project: issues of territoriality or uses of the land; issues of poverty, social and economic inequalities; health issues; political issues; cultural issues; communication issues; transport features; educational features); Chapter 6 (dominance hierarchies; hegemony; conflict)
The concept of configuration as an open structure of theory. A sociologist (de la Garza Toledo, 2006; 2002; 2001; 2000; 1999) notes that the concept of configuration as an open structure of theory takes a qualitative research approach by letting the different subjects configure their own world and reality as their subjectivities consider correct which not necessarily have to be free from contradictions, incoherencies, obscure sides, and so on. Another sociologist (Mason, 2002: 56, 178) has also researched a similar concept which she termed *constitution of meanings of people's own perceptions* as a central element of her qualitative research *interpretivist approach* to denote individuals crafting their own reality according to their own interpretations and perceptions.	Chapter 2 (qualitative research methodologies; opposed to positivism; data generation design (methods of documents analysis, observation, and interviews); data analysis; concept of the materialist conception of history; scientific knowledge (episteme); daily life knowledge (doxa); people's perceptions); Chapter 3 (empowerment; action participation; community development; information provision); Chapter 4 (territorial boundaries).

The next section will explain the rationale for choosing the concept of the *materialist conception of history.*

2.2.2.1   RATIONALE FOR CHOOSING THE CONCEPT OF THE MATERIALIST CONCEPTION OF HISTORY

These sections explain the rationale for choosing the concept of the materialist conception of history (see the definition above on Table 2.1) by presenting the views in favour of the concept, as well as the competing views.

This concept, as theorised and employed by German philosophers Karl Marx and Friedrich Engels ([1845-1846] 1976a: 41-42), was chosen, because this study supports the idea that the material conditions of living of people (e.g. of Broomhall) are the conditions that determine their intellectual, cultural, philosophical, and other types of intangible human conditions (e.g. information needs).

The next section addresses some views in favour of the *materialist conception of history*.

2.2.2.1.1   Views in favour of the materialist conception of history

This section explains some views in favour of the *materialist conception of history* (see its definition above in Table 2.1).

The concept of materiality is taken here as Marx and Engels ([1845-1846] 1976a: 41-42) configured it, as the first vital premise of all humans: they must first live and then do anything else, namely history. Materialist is considered here "in the sense of being anti-obscurantist and drawing attention to the role of material forces in the shaping of ideas" as one sociologist put it (Delanty, 2005: 71).

Thus, these social needs rely on a common foundation: they all depend of the first premise as in Marx and Engels ([1845-1846] 1976a: 41-42), that humans need to be alive in the material world in the first place. If humans are not alive in the material world, then it is impossible that their needs or anything else exist. On the other hand, like the ancient materialist Greek philosopher, Epicurus would put it: "nothing can exist from nothingness" (Reale and Antiseri, 2004a: 218). In addition, this concept of the materialist evolution of human life taken here is also supported by scientists such as Sagan and Druyan (1992) and Hauser (2006), who also emphasize that humans first need to exist in the material world to have human needs (e.g. information needs) and then seek or be looked after for their satisfaction (e.g. information provision).

Therefore, by analysing systematically those community information needs of Broomhall residents emanating from the grounded materiality of their living conditions, the researcher sought to understand them comprehensively: their issues, features, and information needs and provision within their neighbourhood. In addition, this materialistically rooted analysis set the basis for analysing how those needs translated into informational needs in terms of LIS scenarios, and how information providers, from LIS or others satisfied them or failed to do so.

The next section explains some competing views to the materialist conception of history.

2.2.2.1.2   Competing views of the materialist conception of history

This section explains some competing views to the *materialist conception of history* (see its definition above in Table 2.1).

The author of this project is cognizant of some possible discredit that the ideas of Marx and Engels, or Marxism might have in the academic discourse. Some of the reasons might have to do with the association of their ideas to some historical facts with an evident negative impact on large portions of population such as the repressive character of the Soviet Stalinist regime, or the Cold War, or other geopolitical issues. However, the discredit of the ideas of Marx and Engels might have been more grounded on the confusion between their ideas and the subsequent political implementation, by them or others. One thing is their ideas, and another thing is the political applications derived from those ideas.

There might be many critics to dispute Marxist ideas, but in this project, only a few were considered as competing views to illustrate this confusion of their ideas and a political application derived from their ideas. For instance, some authors (Reale and Antiseri, 2004b) reject and criticise the Soviet Stalinist regime as being oppressive (and so does the author of this thesis), but they reject and criticise Marxist ideas because allegedly they are the cause of Stalinism. Therefore, Marxist ideas, in their opinion, must be also oppressive. However, the author, in line with Reale and Antiseri (2004b), rejects the oppressive character of the Soviet Stalinist regime, but, unlike them (Reale and Antiseri, 2004b), he accepts Marxist ideas employed here on their own theoretical grounds, regardless of any politically oppressive application of those ideas. That is, Reale and Antiseri (2004b) do not criticise Marxist ideas on their own theoretical grounds, but influenced by their ideological and political beliefs, in this case of rejection of Stalinism. This idea is supported by a sociologist who notes that criticism against Marxist materialist ideas have generally been taken out of context (Delanty, 2005: 70).

When Reale and Antiseri (2004b) criticise the materialist conception of history they reject it by arguing that: "it results inacceptable the theory of historical materialism, as it was formulated by Marx. It cannot be accepted because to an empirical fact it makes it absolute and it gives it a metaphysical character" (Reale and Antiseri, 2004b: 194). However, metaphysics means "what comes after the physics, but it can also mean what lies beyond nature" (Mautner, 2000: 351). Hence, this poses the question: how can materialism be metaphysical, if materialism is rooted within physics, not after (meta) physics? That is not epistemologically possible. It might be only possible if some confuse both terms as Reale and Antiseri (2004b) do, but if some confuse the terms then the counter argument against the materialist conception of history would not be effective.

However, Marxist materialist ideas are taken in this study only on their own theoretical ground regardless of any controversial ideologies derived from them on the political arena (e.g. Stalinism). Moreover, by using them the researcher does not subscribe by any means to any political ideologies where allegedly these concepts were based on. Moreover, the author did not subscribe to any political ideologies or political agenda whatsoever in this thesis. In fact, some of the recommendations that emerged from this thesis (see Chapter 6) are that researchers should abstain from mixing ideological politics with science, because as a commentator from the natural sciences noted it, "politics is not a science" (Sagan, 1997: 433).

As for some competing views in LIS, the researcher of this project was also aware that the concept of information, as it has been argued by Rendón Rojas (2005), is not a materialistic one (as any concept is). It is an ideal one in the sense that it cannot be measured by any human-made physical material tool, e.g. a telescope, or microscope. Since it is simply a human abstraction, and reality becomes only real as humans through conventions agree to give meaning to the material cosmos. The author agrees with Rendón Rojas' (2005) argument about information as being an ideal concept. Nevertheless, concepts as any other ideas are also materially determined because the human body, and for this matter the brain, are constituted by organic matter, as a Russian materialist philosopher noted it (Ilyenkov, 1977; 1960).

The author is cognizant that there might be more competing ideas to the materialist conception of history, however it seemed a daunting task to include them all, because that goes beyond the scope of this project. However, the reader should bear in mind that this materialist concept worked better for this project due to its geographically rooted nature; hence, a material territory geographically delimitated. Thus, any competing concepts (namely idealist), were not adequate for this purpose.

The next section will explain the rationale for choosing the *social class struggles* concept.

2.2.2.2   RATIONALE FOR CHOOSING THE SOCIAL CLASS STRUGGLES CONCEPT

This section explains the rationale for choosing the *social class struggles* concept (see Table 2.1 above for its definition) by presenting the views in favour of the concept, as well as the competing views.

One of the political issues that emerged from the pilot study (see below in this chapter) was awareness that the residents from the four sections of the Broomhall neighbourhood were divided

by social class conflicts. These are some examples of this social class divide as perceived from two
residents of the first focus group interview:

> "because mainly the people who live here in those rich houses are students, lawyers,
> lecturers, but as for people they are working class people mostly live in this area [sections
> A, B and C] and they [are] enrolled in government benefits and the youngsters are being
> neglected" [a working class respondent from section C] [F.G.01.A]

> "I see like a divide in Broomhall, a divide in riches [sic] classes and poor in Broomhall, and
> the poor ones with families are neglected and that is what I see as the biggest problem
> right now" [a working class respondent from section C] [F.G.01.D]

Therefore, the author commented on this finding to his new supervisor, and suggested to him that
the *social class* issue should be addressed and included in the thesis. The supervisor accepted the
suggestion, and the researcher included the *social class* issue in the thesis. However, this inclusion
was not easy to conceptualise methodologically.

The next section addresses some views in favour of the *social class struggles* concept.

2.2.2.2.1   Views in favour of the social class struggles concept

This section explains some views in favour of the *social class struggles* concept (see its definition
above in Table 2.1).

Through the literature was found the concept of the social class struggles as attributed to Marx and
Engels (Marx and Engels, [1848], 1976a: 482; Delanty, 2005; Edgell, 1993). As defined by Marx and
Engels, "the [written, recorded, Engels] history of all hitherto existing society is the history of class
struggles" (Marx and Engels, [1848], 1976b: 482). The author is cognizant that such concept as
configured by Marx and Engels belongs to their *Manifesto of the Communist Party,* hence it leans
politically toward socialist and communist ideas. The author is also aware of the political
implications that pamphlet has had since 1848 when they wrote it.

However, this Marxist concept of social class struggles captured, at the beginning, some of the
perceptions of respondents in Broomhall as being divided by social class and that there were
conflicts at the time of the provision of social services derived from that social class divide. For
Marxism all societies were divided by social class, and the term *struggle* clearly states that those
social classes have been throughout history in conflict. That is a conceptual operationalization and
configuration of people's common language perceptions.

Nevertheless, the author was not content with the Marxist concept of *social class struggles,* as Marx
and Engels stated it, particularly because of its implicit political and violent agenda in favour of
socialism and communism against capitalism, however valid this concept was theoretically. That is
the reason why the author delved deeper in the literature in order to configure a concept that best
adapted to the Broomhall residents' perceptions of the early stages of this project, but avoiding any
relationship with the implicit Marxist political agenda towards violence. Furthermore, the role the
author played in this research project was not emancipatory, but mediatory (Delanty, 2005: 171),
and as an outsider non-participant observer towards the perceptions and actions of the respondents
of the Broomhall neighbourhood. In addition, the author has employed this Marxist concept, and
all the other concepts, based only on their theoretical grounds, and he has done so in a rigorous
manner, not simplistically.

The Marxist social class struggles concept has some underlying ideas. According to a sociologist,
"The key ideas underlying Marx's social science are the movement from *contradiction [sic]* to *crisis
[sic]* to *conflict [sic]* to *social change [sic]. ...* These contradictions derive from the class structure,
which is based on the exploitation of labour. ... The resulting inequality is a structural inequality
since there are two classes, those who work for wages and those who live from profit." (Delanty,
2005: 69).

First, Marxist theories and concepts have epistemological acceptance within the social sciences (e.g.

Delanty, 2005; Edgell, 1993), and as such they have been employed rigorously in this thesis. Second, the interrelationships of the ideas of contradictions deriving from the class structure based on the exploitation of labour, and the resulting structural inequality of the conflicts between the working class (who work for wages) and the capitalist class (who live for profit), gave theoretical clarity to a better understanding of the social conflicts amongst the residents of the Broomhall neighbourhood.

This social inequality as explained above affects different aspects of social life. For instance, a commentator from LIS made also a similar connection of social inequality as a cause of inequality of access to information and ideas, and a connection to class and power as part of the causes of that inequality:

> "Inequality in access to information and ideas cannot be explained fully without reference to its relationship to the primary dimensions of inequality; the patterns of class and power. It is part of a much broader social issue" (Usherwood, 1989: 22).

Thus, social inequality gives a general dimension between the relationships of class and the power each class has within itself and amongst others (e.g. working, middle and capitalist or bourgeois classes as employed here, see below for further explanation). A sociologist (Edgell, 1993: 52), in a book dedicated *ex professo* to the analysis of the social class concept, concluded that any member of society can be ascribed to any social class (even if he or she is going upwards or downwards in the social mobility from one class to the next) in relation to three major determinants:

1) By how much private property individuals own;
2) By how much knowledge individuals have (and for the case of this thesis, by how much information they have);
3) By how much physical labour they do (Edgell, 1993: 52).

That is, according to Edgell (1993), the more private property, knowledge and information any member of a class has, and the less physical labour she or he does for a living, the upper is the class she or he belongs to (e.g. capitalist or bourgeois class, and middle class), and vice versa (e.g. working class). Hence, the author agrees with Edgell's (1993) three major determinants of social class.

Edgell's (1993) three major determinants of social class are in line with the evolution of the social class concept since the earliest inception of the term. According to him:

> "originally the term class referred to the division of the Roman population on the basis of property for fiscal and military purposes. This pre-modern usage was a static one in the sense that classes were regarded as ascriptive groupings of people who inherited a shared rank in society. The modern vocabulary of class is inextricably associated with the total reorganization of society that followed the industrial revolution. ... Two of the major consequences of this momentous social change were the creation of two new classes in the transformed class structure and the tendency for class positions to be allocated on the basis of ability rather than birth" (Edgell, 1993: 1).

On similar lines, a psychologist notes that social class is "differentiated by occupational prestige, education, and income" (Jones, 1998: 146). Jones' (1998) occupational prestige, and income might be related to Edgell's (1993) physical labour, and Jones' (1998) education to Edgell's (1993) knowledge (and information added by the author).

Nevertheless, the commentators above (Delanty, 2005; Jones, 1998; Edgell, 1993; Usherwood, 1989), including Marx and Engels ([1848], 1976a), (whose concept is attributed to them), failed to explain the roots of *human conflicts*, *contradictions*, and *social inequality* associated with social class. These roots might be found (as mentioned above in Table 2.1 in the definition of *the social class struggles concept* as employed in this thesis) in the notion of "dominance hierarchy" from the natural sciences, namely materialistic evolutionary biology (Sagan and Druyan, 1992; Hauser, 2006: 394). That is the reason why the statement of Marx and Engels is included at the end of the working definition of this concept in Table 2.1 (see above).

As mentioned above in Table 2.1 in the working definition of this concept, the social class struggles concept emerged in the literature from the pamphlet *Manifesto of the Communist Party* by Marx and Engels written in 1848. Hence, by reviewing further the literature he found that the *dominance hierarchy* from biology (Hauser, 2006; Sagan and Druyan, 1992) explained better than Marx and Engels themselves their *social class struggles concept,* and without having the need to resort to a politically driven notion of violence of socialists and communists against capitalists as in Marx and Engels. As encapsulated in the definition above, the reader can assess at a glimpse a materialistic and evolutionary trail of the human genetic drive of *dominance hierarchy.* Sagan and Druyan (1992) even noted that submission from the subordinate to the dominant is more pervasive than dominance. Recently, a U.S. neurobiologist (Hauser, 2006) who has conducted research for several years about the genetic moral drives of human and non-human primates, has concluded that "in societies with dominance hierarchies there will always be inequalities in the distribution of valued resources" (Hauser, 2006: 394).

Therefore, Marxist political agenda towards the empowerment of the proletariat to make the socialist revolution to overthrow the capitalist or bourgeoisie class and seize power by military violence is not too far from the ideas of dominance hierarchy. The dominated classes would always challenge the dominant ones in order to obtain valued resources for the betterment of their material or cultural conditions (e.g. information recorded in documents). In addition, these challenges are struggles, either violent or non-violent, that will depend of the capability of negotiation of the dominant classes to satisfy the dominated classes' needs accordingly. The limitation of this Marxist conception is not that Marx and Engels foster violence of one class against others. That is already a socio-historic fact accepted by social science epistemology (e.g. Delanty, 2005; Edgell, 1993), and by the author of this thesis regardless that they have stated it bluntly in their pamphlet (Marx and Engels, [1848] 1976a). Their limitation might be found in their failure to explain that the proletariat or working class are also humans, and being humans, they carry genetically the drives for domination as noted by Hauser (2006). Hence, they failed to analyse the dominance hierarchy as explained by scientists from the natural sciences (Sagan and Druyan, 1992; Hauser, 2006).

After all that has been said, the *social class struggles concept* as complemented from philosophy (Marx and Engels, [1848] 1976a), and the natural sciences (Hauser, 2006; Sagan and Druyan, 1992), and as it is employed here, served the author to understand better the bigger dimensions of the underlying issues behind social class and human conflict. It served to understand better the contradictions amongst people, and how these intensify when these are interrelated with social class. Although Hauser (2006: 212) clarifies above in the working definition of this concept (see Table 2.1) that social class is not a biological category, it is noteworthy to learn that he also notes that human mind is hardwired to divide the world into dominant and subordinate. Hence, it is illuminating to know that humans have genetically inherited propensities to have contradictions, and to engage into conflicts, or struggles, regardless of their cultural, or socio-historic influences.

As for the library and information science field, the author wrote a book chapter relating to the ethical contradictions of the social responsibilities of LIS (Muela-Meza, 2007), where he made a comprehensive review of the major findings of Hauser (2006) from the past ten years. He concluded what has been explained above, that as long as humans live in societies shaped by dominance hierarchies (Hauser, 2006; Sagan and Druyan, 1992), which have taken the form of social classes (Marx and Engels, [1848], 1976a), then contradictions and inequalities will accompany human relationships, thus, conflicts, or struggles will always appear.

Hence, these contradictions (Muela-Meza, 2007), also affect information needs and provision in libraries and other institutions of information recorded in documents. Another LIS commentator approaches the analysis of the idea of idea of contradictions in LIS but only as related to community profiling by commenting that "what does not seem to have publicly acknowledged is that sometimes the needs and interests of different groups are mutually exclusive. Until we accept this librarians will struggle to meet these conflicting demands" (Roddy, 2005: 41). However, she does not explicitly mention that there are contradictions in her analysis of needs, and her ideas of "needs mutually exclusive" and "conflicting demands" do not relate to the social class concept, or with the *social class struggle* concept explained above. She does not explain either why the needs and interests of different groups of library and information users are mutually exclusive. Nevertheless it is noteworthy that a LIS commentator writing about community profiling in public libraries, although in a two page professional magazine article, approximates to the ideas of contradictions in LIS used by the researcher before (Muela-Meza, 2008; 2007; 2005c; 2004a; 2004b; 2003b), and throughout this thesis.

Another LIS researcher in a major PhD thesis applying community profiling to library services (Louie, 1976: 169-170) did not find contradictions *per se* in her study, however she found similarly to Roddy (2005) that "the concept of a metropolitan library serving *all* [sic] all members of its community is generally considered utopian." With utopian, Louie (1976) meant that public libraries could not serve equally every individual within the communities from the neighbourhoods where these libraries were established. However, Louie failed to analyse why it is utopian for libraries to provide all the information needed by all library users.

Hence, according to the concept of *social class struggles* employed here, the needs and interests of different groups of library users are mutually exclusive, and become conflicting demands, because all individuals in society belong consciously or unconsciously to different social classes (Jones, 1998). These are always in conflict (Edgell, 1993), or involve struggle (Marx and Engels, [1848], 1976b) amongst them. Since they live in a society organised through dominance hierarchy, the library and information needs, interests, and demands of everyone, despite the fact that each individual is different from the rest, would be mediated by the social class which they belong. As explained above, a society divided hierarchically through social classes which *per se* interact socially in constant contradiction and conflict, their members might bring consciously or unconsciously their social class interests (Jones, 1998) to their daily relationships with others (e.g. being information users, or information providers). As for being utopian for a library to satisfy equally all the needs of its users, it is utopian for LIS services and professionals, pretend to satisfy all users equally when they live in a society of inequality divided by dominance hierarchy, and within social classes in constant contradiction and conflict. A philosopher of the theory of needs elaborates this idea by noting that social groups (and classes for the interest of this study), may have attributed their needs equally in terms of quality, but their provision, in terms of quantity, would be different for all. She notes "needs are attributed to individuals according to their group [class] of affiliation, but these groups are now being produced by institutions. The attribution continues the [dominance] hierarchy within the social and political institutions. ... that is, to distribute in quality the same types of needs, but in a quantity entirely different [to each group or class]" (Heller, 1996: 89-90).

Nevertheless, the author is aware that this social class struggles concept alone might not explain effectively all the factors that make library and information provision an unequal service. There might be others regardless of users and providers belonging to a social class that might limit the capability of an equal information provision for all users through institutions of information recorded in documents (Documental Information Institutions, DIIs, like libraries). For instance, they might lack of enough budget to acquire all the information needed for everyone; they might not satisfy all information needs for the simple fact that there might not exist all the documents that satisfy them; they might not be the only information provider users choose to satisfy their needs; they might create collection development policies according to their budget, facilities, and staff which might limit them to satisfy all users' needs. Still, what is noteworthy about this concept is that users and information providers might not escape from such social class divide, and their implicit contradictions and conflicts, or struggles that may emerge when interacting with members of other classes, either consciously or unconsciously (Jones, 1998).

There are other examples from the literature that elaborate on the importance of the social class concept to analyse LIS phenomena. A study found evidence that public libraries are staffed mainly by middle class professionals, and that working class users were excluded to some extent from information provision (Muddiman, 2000a; Pateman, 2000). Another study found evidence of the impact of social class as determinant of some patterns of use of information agencies (e.g. libraries), where the upper classes (e.g. middle class professional/managerial occupations) are better informed and provided than the lower classes (e.g. working class unskilled occupations) (Marcella and Baxter, 2000). Another study found evidence that social class is a divider to access to Information and Communication Technology (ICT), where the upper classes had better access to ICT, whilst on the contrary the lower classes do not (Hull, 2003). Another LIS commentator suggested that the lower class newcomers to Canada might become a *class of information poor* who are "characterized by their difficulty or inability to obtain useful information" (Caidi and Allard, 2005: 304).

As for the different classes employed in this project, the author followed a three social class scheme as configured by a LIS commentator (Pateman, 2000: 28).

1. 1) The capitalist or bourgeois class comprises the owners and controllers of the means of production, distribution and exchange –the factories, banks, shops, land, etc. and their agents.
2. 2) The middle class includes middle grade management, small business, professional sections and middle ranks of the state apparatus who act to a considerable extent as agents of the capitalist class, but the degree to which they exercise control over the means of production is often limited, and their income is derived mainly from selling their labour power for a salary.
3. 3) The working class includes the great majority of the population, who sell their labour power, their capacity to work, in return for a wage or salary, and who work under the direction of the owner of the means of production and their agents (Pateman, 2000: 28).
4.

This research project has employed Pateman's class division in order to have an approximate idea that clarifies the social class position where the Broomhall residents or information providers stand concerning their social inter-relationships within this neighbourhood.

Operationalization of the social class struggles concept. As shown in the working maps of Broomhall (see Figures 4.1, and 4.2 in Chapter 4), in the section A of Broomhall is where most poor working class residents live. In section B, there is a mix of working and middle classes, yet the working class prevails. In section C, most of the residents are middle class with few working or capitalist classes. In section D, the Broomhall Park, which is almost homogenous, most residents belong to the middle class, and to some extent to the capitalist or bourgeois class.

Hence, below each interviewee's excerpt cited in the thesis is included a description of the social class, section (either A, or B, or C, or D), and a unique coding number assigned to each respondent (see these codes below on Table 2.5 in this chapter). All information providers, for this study, have emerged as belonging to the middle class.

Therefore, the *social class struggle* concept plays an important role in the analysis, and discussions of this study, because the reader can easily interrelate a social class status of a given respondent, with his or her territorial section within the neighbourhood (either A, or B, or C, or D). Thus, this gives an instant picture of territoriality linked with social class. Then the readers could assess the opinions of the respondents and compare them with others from the same or different classes within the same territorial section, or from a different section. In the case of information providers, the reader will still be able to distinguish marked differences amongst them depending of the section they work, or live and work. All the businesses are considered members of the capitalist or bourgeois class, either small, or medium (e.g. local shops, or local landlords), or big (e.g. construction developers).

The next section explains some competing views of the social class struggles concept.

2.2.2.2.2   Competing views of the social class struggles concept

This section explains some competing views to the *social class struggles concept* (see its definition above in Table 2.1).

The major competing views to the social class concept might be found in the views that consider that the capitalist society is not divided into social classes. For instance, a LIS commentator argues that most research in LIS relating to social issues, or social exclusion avoid deliberately using social class (Pateman, 2000). However, social class has been found to have a pervasive distinctiveness within capitalist society, and thus is an important concept with which to analyse LIS phenomena, as some LIS commentators have included it in their research (e.g. Caidi and Allard, 2005; Hull, 2003; Marcella and Baxter, 2000; Muddiman, 2000a; Pateman, 2000; Muela-Meza, 2008; 2007; 2005c; 2004a; 2004b; 2003b).

In psychology, a commentator who has conducted a PhD thesis relating to subjectivity and class consciousness to develop class identity has noted that most psychologists have neglected the social class analysis, and have preferred others instead such as race and gender to analyse individuals' identities (Jones, 1998). However, she has argued that it has been an error in psychological epistemology to pretend to homogenise people of the same gender, race, or ethnic group, thus obscuring their socio-economic differences which actually exist regardless of other features, and that the social class concept can shed light on those differences, and still be able to be employed with those and other concepts (Jones, 1998: 145). In a line similar to that of Jones (1998), an education scientist from the point of view of the Marxist educational theory elaborates further, arguing that the differences in gender, race, age, sexuality, etc. are "conditioned by social class and value production, with special reference to the struggle for economic and social justice" (Rikowski, 2002: 25). Hence, the author goes along with Jones' (1998) and Rikowski's (2002) arguments and has also employed the social class concept as a determinant to the differences of the different groups of people in Broomhall, regardless of their gender, race, age, sexuality, or other characteristics.

Other competing views have to do with the ideas that social classes, or groups, or individuals belonging to different classes, or groups, live or socially interact in harmony and cohesion, hence free from contradictions, conflicts, or struggles derived from the social class dominance hierarchy. These ideas fostering "community cohesion" have been found associated with the current thinking called post-modernism (Rikowski, 2002). These have also been found in literature specifically related to Broomhall. For instance, in capitalist class residential and business construction corporations doing business in Broomhall (these could be assessed in the studies of Cromar, 2003, and LDA Design, 2005), which have made capitalistic-driven short research projects to regenerate Broomhall into a market valuable zone which might benefit mainly the capitalist class development corporations. Cromar (2003) supported his study with the ideas of capitalist class or bourgeois commentators who underpin the idea of "social capital" (Putnam, 1999) where "social capital" would bring "community cohesion" and hence regeneration in the neighbourhoods with equal benefits for all social classes, without conflicts or struggles.

This post-modern idea of "social capital" has also been brought to the LIS discourse without the sufficient scientific rigor or criticism. For instance, some LIS researchers (Bryson, Usherwood and Proctor, 2003) mentioned that "social capital" emerged in their study as a theme from their empirical data (2003: 8). However, it is unlikely that the term "social capital" had emerged from a research of that nature, it rather seems that the authors brought it as an a priori theoretical framework and then built their research design upon it.

Another commentator (Pateman, 2006: 42) argues that by the post-modern term "social capital is meant the networks of interactions that we have with one another, that bind us together and act as a primary means of exchanging the information, skills and help we need in our day-to-day life." However, it is interesting to note that Pateman's (2000) earlier clarity on social class division, which is actually the working classification of social classes employed in this thesis, and Usherwood's (1989) notions of social class and power

as dimensions of social inequalities have been contradicted by their writings in more
recent years. Lately they have confused the capitalist or bourgeois class with the idea of the
"social capital" (Pateman, 2006; Bryson, Usherwood, and Proctor, 2003).

However, the post-modern terms "social capital" and "community cohesion" have not been
found as sound concepts validated by international social science epistemological
conventions (e.g. de la Garza Toledo, 2006; Delanty, 2005; Delanty, 2003; Edgell, 1993).
Furthermore, those commentators who supported the "social capital" idea (e.g. Pateman,
2006; Cromar, 2003; Bryson, Usherwood and Proctor, 2003; Putnam, 1999) have failed to
define the *capital concept* from the economic theory, which is clearly related to the
capitalist or bourgeois class, and hence have brought epistemological confusion to their
assertions. For instance, this is how Karl Marx, a philosopher who devoted more than 40
years conducting research about the *capital concept* and the overall capitalist system of
production, defined in 1867 the concepts of capital and capitalist (the individual) in his
multi-volume work, *Capital: A Critical Analysis of Capitalist Production*:

> "As capitalist, he is only capital personified. His soul is the soul of capital. But capital has one
> single life impulse, the tendency to create value and surplus-value, to make its constant factor,
> the means of production, absorb the greatest possible amount of surplus-labour. Capital is dead
> labour, that, vampire-like, only lives by sucking living labour, and lives the more, the more
> labour it sucks. The time during which the labourer works, is the time during which the
> capitalist consumes the labour-power he has purchased of him" (Marx, [1867], 1974: 224).

Marx's definition of capital and capitalist have been generally accepted by international
epistemological communities as a sound terminology for social science analysis (de la Garza Toledo,
2006; Delanty, 2005; 2003; Edgell, 1993), unlike "social capital,", "intellectual capital," "human
capital" and other post-modern terms which have not been accepted by epistemological
communities of the social sciences (de la Garza Toledo, 2006; Delanty, 2003; 2005; Edgell, 1993).
Those post-modern terms, instead of being theoretical concepts –either with theoretical or
empirical applications– to analyse socio-historic facts are merely ideologies (de la Garza Toledo,
2006) which only foster political values of dominance in line with the capitalist or bourgeois class
over subordinate classes (e.g. working class).

Furthermore, it is a daunting task to include all the competing views to the *social class struggles* as
configured in this thesis. Nevertheless, in this thesis attention has been given in maintaining an
epistemological and methodological rigor and consistency. Hence, however valid the post-modern
ideas for their theorists and practitioners, for this project they have not been considered because
they do not comply with the epistemological and methodological rigor and consistency of the social
sciences (de la Garza Toledo, 2006; Delanty, 2005; 2003; Edgell, 1993), which included library and
information science (Muela-Meza, 2008; 2007; 2005c; 2004b; Gimeno Perelló, 2007a; Rikowski,
2007; Rendón Rojas, 2005).

A sociologist elaborates on this idea in his epistemological book *Social Science: Philosophical and
Methodological Foundations*:

> "When it comes to methodology and philosophy for social science, postmodernism is
> limited. The value for social science of embracing vague concepts drawn from literary
> criticism and evocative images of power is limited. ... Its major failings are its inability to
> articulate critical normative foundation for social science on the one side and on the other
> it has deflected social science from the task of providing explanations for social
> phenomena" (Delanty, 2005: 118).

From the natural sciences, some authors agree with Delanty (2005) when they argue that
postmodernism has been found as a weak and obscurantist system of ideas that, instead of fostering
the advancement of science, instead tend to render it stagnant (Sokal and Bricmont, 1999).

Still, Delanty (2005) notes that one of the most important legacies of postmodernism is the
standpoint epistemology. Within this epistemology, social scientists take a political and ideological
position, similar to that of Marx and Engels in their *Manifesto of the Communist Party* (Marx and

Engels, [1848], 1976b). That is, from the standpoint epistemology, the role of social scientists is emancipatory, and the research process and findings are politically and ideologically partisan, providing an open set of guidelines for emancipatory political action against oppression or dominance (Delanty, 2005).

Nevertheless, as stated above, the only role the author of this thesis has played throughout this thesis is mediatory (Delanty, 2005: 171), and thus a role of an outside non-participant observer of the perceptions of the research settings or the ideological and political views and actions of the people who participated in the research project. Hence, however validated the postmodern standpoint epistemology may be in terms of social science epistemology, those ideas are beyond of the scope of this project.

The next section explains the rationale for choosing the concept of configuration as an open structure of theory.

2.2.2.3   RATIONALE FOR CHOOSING THE CONCEPT OF CONFIGURATION AS AN OPEN STRUCTURE OF THEORY

This section explains the rationale for choosing the *concept of configuration as an open structure of theory* (see the definition above on Table 2.1) by presenting the views in favour of the concept, as well as the competing views.

The author reviewed the literature to find out how to conduct interviews with the prospective respondents, and through this process there emerged an awareness of the concept of configuration, derived both from the need to conduct a community profiling research project by employing qualitative research methodologies and methods, and from the need to operationalize the interviews schedules to record the prospective respondents' perceptions.

After having adopted a suggestion by the author's second and final supervisor on June 2005, the author reviewed the work of British sociologist Jennifer Mason (2002), and found that it would become one of the epistemological bedrocks of this thesis. Related to the configuration concept is Mason's (2002) *interpretivist approach* (see below in this chapter a broader explanation). She noted that "An interpretative approach therefore not only sees people as a primary data source, but seeks their perceptions...but what an interpretivist would want to get out of these would be what they say about or how they are constituted in people's individual or collective meanings" (Mason, 2002: 56). When Mason (2002) mentions how the people's perceptions are constituted into individual or collective meanings (note particularly the term *constituted),* that then reveals the key concept of *configuration.*

The author, after reading Mason's (2002) insights of *people's interpretations of how they constitute the meanings of their perceptions,* delved deeper into the literature to find out similar approaches, and that is how he learnt about Mexican sociologist Enrique de la Garza Toledo (2006; 2002; 2001; 2000; 1999) and his *concept of configuration as an open structure of theory.* Mason (2002) did not provide a configuration of the concept of *constitution of meanings of people's own perceptions,* however de la Garza Toledo's (2006; 2002; 2001; 2000; 1999) *concept of configuration* did match fundamentally with Mason's (2002) insights. For instance, Mason (2002) in her chapter devoted to analysing qualitative data notes: "according to this broadly interpretivist view the role of the researcher is to understand everyday or lay *interpretation [sic],* as well as supplying *social science interpretation [sic],* and to move from these towards an explanation" (Mason, 2002: 178). On similar lines de la Garza Toledo (2006; 2002; 2001; 2000; 1999) agrees with Mason (2002) by stating that: "an open notion of configuration, in the sense to admit theoretical concepts and others from common language, but also as for the clarity of the meanings, in the relationships of the network, as for going from the more precise as deduction to the more obscure by passing through conceptual links which belong to the daily life reasoning with interpretivist and argumentative components, would allow us give a full account of a given reality and a reality in process of configuration, and of the articulations of subjects in a process of formation" (de la Garza Toledo, 2001).

The next section explains some views in favour to the *concept of configuration as an open structure to theory.*

2.2.2.3.1   Views in favour of the concept of configuration as an open structure of theory

This section explains some views in favour to the *concept of configuration as open structure to theory* (see its definition above in Table 2.1).

The researcher has analysed the concept of configuration as configured by de la Garza Toledo (2006; 2002; 2001; 2000; 1999), and Mason (2002: 56, 178), and adapted has adapted it to librarianship as a qualitative research concept (Muela-Meza, 2007; 2008). In addition, for this project that concept has been interrelated with the concept of the materialist conception of history of Marx and Engels ([1845-1846] 1976a) and Ilyenkov (1977; 1960), and with the concept of materialism of Sagan and Druyan (1992) mentioned above (see its definition above in Table 2.1 above).

Likewise, for this project this concept is of paramount importance since the researcher has observed (observation in the broadest sense of that term) and interpreted how some of the people of Broomhall have configured (from 19 October 2004 until March 2006 when the data generation from interviews took place) their material realities according to their own personal subjectivities, and hence, how their lives have been transformed, sometimes for the better, and sometimes for the worst. Hence, in the way the different groups or social classes of people have configured their individual and collective or social actions, and to that extent have transformed their social reality (individually or collectively, or both). In addition, some of the very interesting features of this concept of configuration are that it takes into account not only the cognitive or scientific knowledge (episteme) of people, but also their daily life or even incoherent or blurred knowledge (doxa) (de la Garza Toledo, 2002; 2001; Mason, 2002).

That is, it is a concept that allowed the inclusion of all respondents' different levels of knowledge or abstractions, but based on their concrete material reality, according to their interpretations and the author's interpretations. It helped the researcher to observe, qualitatively, how the different groups of people in the neighbourhood transform their individual and collective or social lives. Therefore, it helped the researcher to bring light on the conflicts, contradictions, and class struggles of those groups and to describe and analyse more adequately how the different groups or classes interacted within the Broomhall neighbourhood, without rejecting any lay or common language perception.

The next section explains some competing views to the *concept of configuration as an open structure to theory*.

2.2.2.3.2   Competing views of the concept of configuration as an open structure of theory

This section explains some competing views to the *concept of configuration as open structure to theory* (see its definition above in Table 2.1).

The concept of configuration as configured by sociologists de la Garza Toledo (de la Garza Toledo, 2006; 2002; 2001; 2000; 1999) and Mason (2002), as explained above, is a qualitative research concept.

The major competing views to this concept come from the positivistic or quantitative research paradigm. For instance, a foundational element of positivism is objectivism, which is "an objectifying attitude to nature by which nature [including people] is seen as existing outside science and can be neutrally observed" (Delanty, 2005: 11). That is, whereas the qualitative research concept of configuration allows the different subjects under research to configure their own world and reality, in the positivistic paradigm they should be seen as existing outside science, their perceptions excluded.

Whereas the concept of configuration takes also into consideration all people's levels of knowledge, including perceptions, opinions or daily life knowledge (doxa) (de la Garza Toledo, 2002; 2001), for the positivistic paradigm since Platonic times, only scientific truth (episteme) is considered as an absolute form of knowledge, and perceptions, opinions, or daily life knowledge (doxa) excluded (Delanty, 2005: 13).

21

The author is cognizant of more competing views to the qualitative research configuration concept, since there will always be competing views between qualitative and quantitative research paradigms. However, as mentioned above, this is a qualitative research study, and the research problem was precisely to find out about the community information needs and provision of the residents of Broomhall according to their perceptions. Thus, the qualitative research configuration concept was found adequate to assess those perceptions as respondents' configured them (regardless of their different cognitive levels of abstraction or expression), instead of other concepts, either positivist or not. In addition, the author is open to the possibility that there might be other concepts more adequate to analyse the aim and objectives of this thesis, however the concept of configuration was found adequate, and it proved to be highly instrumental for this study.

The next major section explains the rationale for choosing the qualitative research methodology.

2.3 Rationale for choosing the qualitative research methodology

These sections explain the rationale for choosing the qualitative research methodology in this thesis by presenting some views in favour, and some competing views.

During the early stages of this research project, the author embarked in a constant literature review, as suggested by his first supervisor, in order to finish his early PhD research proposal. Noteworthy is the research paper "An introduction to the applicability of qualitative research methodologies to the field of Library and Information Sciences," which the author wrote on 17 November 2003 (Muela-Meza, 2003a; 2006b) simply to clarify ideas, concepts, methodologies, and concepts. This was submitted to his supervisor for comments.

From these early stages of the research project there emerged from the literature, and through the guidance of the supervisor, the idea to conduct a community profiling research project geographically based (e.g. within a neighbourhood) and to employ qualitative research methodologies and methods to learn about the information needs and provision as perceived by the residents and information providers within that given neighbourhood.

Hence, the author chose the Broomhall neighbourhood, and he decided in agreement with his supervisor, to conduct a community profiling study by employing methods of analysis of documents, observation, and focus groups and individual interviews with residents to learn about their perceptions.

The next section explains some views in favour of the qualitative research methodology.

2.3.1 Views in favour of the qualitative research methodology

This section explains some views in favour of the qualitative research methodology.

One of the discussions in the social sciences lies on which methodologies and methods are most or least adequate to do analysis of social phenomena, whether quantitative or qualitative ones. Silverman (2000) argues that there is no such thing like best or worst methodologies and methods: "the choice between different research methods should depend upon what you are trying to find out." (Silverman, 2000: 1). As mentioned earlier, the research question of this project was to analyse the community information needs and provision of the residents of Broomhall according to their perceptions; accordingly, a commentator observed that "it is necessary therefore to profile the community and to be aware of the local perceptions and priorities [*of the residents of a given neighbourhood*]" (Usherwood, 1992: 34). More precisely, the type of qualitative research methodology employed for this thesis was interpretivism or interpretivist approaches (Mason, 2002: 56; Miles and Huberman, 1994: 7-8).

How then is a community profiler or researcher conducting community profiling to investigate the perceptions of the people from the perspectives of their communities and within their neighbourhoods or the geographical areas where they live? Through spoken language interviews is one of the most appropriate methods (either individually, or through focus groups or other group styles). Because people can orally express their world views and perceptions, and when these perceptions have been recorded on tape like in this thesis, or through video, or other recording methods, and then transcribed into text, then their perceptions by themselves or through the author's interpretation take form; written form.

A sociologist (Smith, 2002: 37) emphasizes that qualitative methods should be employed in community profiling, like ethnographic study of the community (mapping, walkabout, photography or video, collecting documents); in depth interviews with key professionals, activists or stakeholders; focus groups for specific sections of the neighbourhood (e.g. children, young people, women, minority ethnic communities, business people, etc.). He also suggests using census and official statistics and surveys from the residents (Smith, 2002: 37).

The next section explains some competing views to the qualitative research methodology.

2.3.2 Competing views to the qualitative research methodology

This section explains some competing views to the qualitative research methodology.

This is a qualitative research study, hence the major competing views to this approach come from the quantitative research paradigm.

For instance, some of the previous LIS studies, where community profiling has been conducted, have relied strongly on quantitative research methods such as questionnaires (Satyanarayana, 1997: 192; Sarling and Van Tassel, 1999; Kaniki, 1995). One of those (Kaniki, 1995), however, found some remarkable flaws on the use of quantitative methodologies to quantify some qualitative categories such as behaviour, gestures, postures, and others when he assessed information needs of some communities. He concluded that those categories were simply unquantifiable. In this regard, these unquantifiable categories can be better assessed with qualitative research methodologies and methods.

Along these lines, another LIS researcher (Penzhorn, 2002: 241) argues that in recent years LIS researchers have found dissatisfaction with the generalisation of quantitative methodologies and the depersonalisation of information provision and use. Hence, qualitative research is a more suitable approach to provide information according to a more personalised assessment of people's needs within their particular scenarios that might not be the same as others.

Other LIS commentators elaborate on this idea (Gericke 2000; Kalyane and Devarai, 1994). They address the issue that community profiling should employ qualitative methodologies, hence people in the neighbourhoods could be participative, engaged, and "empowered," and, therefore, information provision could be conducted according to their actual needs: to what they really felt, expressed, and requested, or even if they did not know how to articulate their needs. They also stated that LIS researchers, by doing community profiling in such ways, would be more likely to fill the gaps between people expressively or tacitly having information needs and their providers satisfying their actual needs.

Nevertheless, the author found several limitations in the qualitative research approach. For instance, one limitation is that this project turned to some extent into an anthropological or ethnographic-like project. That is, dealing with too much data from interviews transcripts, historic documents, and notes from non-participant observation on the field made the author become to some extent overwhelmed with data. The author has managed and coped well with this sort of overwhelming data, however if he could do this project all over again, he would at some point devise a questionnaire to complement even better the data pool. Hence, the questionnaire or various questionnaires would have helped the author to obtain information in a shorter period of time, then the author would have been better equipped to use the data generated from the questionnaire to more effectively conduct the interviews, observation, and document analysis.

Nevertheless, the reader should not assess this limitation in terms of epistemological or cognitive relativism, or lack of rigour, and objectivity. For instance, some physicists −at the heart of positivism− argue that a certain "relativist" attitude is methodologically natural in some social sciences such anthropology, because what matters in such studies is to understand culture in the way people perceive it (Sokal and Bricmont, 1999: 212). However, this was not an anthropological study, but the main aims of this project were to understand the Broomhall issues, features, information needs, and provision as people perceived them (through the own interpretations of interviewees and the author's of the data analysed through non-participant observation, documents, and interviews' transcripts).

The next section explains the rationale for choosing the qualitative research methods employed in this thesis.

2.3.3 Rationale for choosing the qualitative research methods

These sections explain the rationale for choosing the qualitative research methods employed in this thesis (documents analysis or literature review, non-participant observation, and individual and focus groups interviews), by presenting some views in favour, and some competing views.

The next section explains the method of analysis of documents (or literature review).

2.3.3.1   THE METHOD OF THE ANALYSIS OF DOCUMENTS (OR LITERATURE REVIEW)

The next section explains some views in favour of the method of analysis of documents (or literature review).

2.3.3.1.1   Views in favour of the method of analysis of documents (or literature review)

This section explains some views in favour of the method of analysis of documents (or literature review).

The literature review, according to Denscombe (2003: 212), is the first step to have a broad view of previous research and as a guide to design the instruments of generation and analysis of data. This has helped the researcher of this project to assess what, why, how, where and who have been doing research in the similar topics as to try to fill the gaps on what others have failed, or to improve the applicability of tools, methodologies or methods for the planning of the research, generation, and analysing data and writing of the thesis.

All investigations that lay claim to being 'research' should start with a literature review. The literature review, then tries to establish the existing state of knowledge in the area of proposed research and, drawing on this, to set out research questions that will help to advance our understanding of the topic (Denscombe, 2003: 212). The basic documents assessed which supported this thesis all along the way dealt with theoretical, ontological, and epistemological issues, and dealt with Broomhall situationally, considered as part of Sheffield, UK, both historically and contemporaneously from academic, government, and other independent sources such as organisations based on the neighbourhood.

The documents or publications reviewed included: indexes, abstracts, monographs, articles from journals, non-refereed articles in paper or from the Internet (sources available as pay-per-access, free-of-charge, or Open Access), these were in a variety of formats: maps, historic documents, photographs, audiovisual and multimedia resources, grey literature, etc. Emphasis was made on the grey literature as sources of data, since some of the printed information about the neighbourhood appeared in this format. In this project, several statistical sources from government and private providers were used in order to gain a wide view of the neighbourhoods under research as was suggested by another sociological expert on community research (Rogers, 2003).

The next section explains some competing views of the method of analysis of documents (or literature review).

2.3.3.1.2   Competing views of the method of analysis of documents (or literature review)

This section explains some competing views of the method of analysis of documents (or literature review).

The main competing views of the method of analysis of documents have to do with the fact that the interpretation of reality, or nature, or people's perceptions (either theoretically or empirically) is being made at a tertiary level of analysis (e.g. made by author of this thesis). This tertiary level of analysis is being done about secondary interpretations (e.g. the writers of the documents being reviewed by the author of this thesis) over primary interpretations (of the individuals –e.g. the respondents of the author's interviews–, or nature, or reality being studied, e.g. Broomhall neighbourhood).

In other words, to approximate to the empirical study of nature and reality (inclusive of humans) through the documents is necessarily sifted by two, or three or more levels or layers of interpretation through time and space. That means that through documents, depending on the subject, several or many individuals are interpreting a given piece of reality, nature, or population through time and space. Hence, given the composition of human nature, that documental information every time that it reaches a new reader (such the author of this thesis who analysed over 1000s of documents and the future readers of this thesis) is already sifted and mediated according to the different interpretations of the different readers/authors on the way through time-space. However, the risk posed for every new reader of past documental information is that all the previous interpreters since the origin of such documental chain might be wrong or limited in their interpretations. As a physicist put it, as a critical safeguard for present and future researchers, one should not exclusively depend on past experiences (Feynman, 2001).

Hence, to rely only on documental information in conducting empirical research is to risk an interpretation of erroneous past experience or considerably limited experience; thus, this documental past experience would limit the generation of new empirical knowledge, which will be in the future documental information of the past and so on. However, neither can it be suggested that only 'pure' present empirical research (without any review of the past experience or literature) can be more valid. Compare the comments that a researcher offered from within the qualitative research paradigm in LIS (Mellon, 1990).

Hence, if the analysis of documents alone cannot be the most adequate and comprehensive method of research, then other methods are needed to combine past and present experiences. That is one of the sound reasons for this project relying on different methods, like the analysis of documents, interviews and observation, in order to record present interpretations of the reality (the respondents' and author's interpretations of the interviews and the author's by means of observation).

In addition, the limitations of the analysis of documents methods have to do with the quality of the documents, such as validity, and reliability, and their implicit historical limitation, amongst some other limitations. For example, for this project, as mentioned above, different documents were analysed. In the case of census information, they appeared to have several limitations as to be considered as reliable sources for this project: namely, information was outdated in most instances (although some historical census information worked fine to some extent for the historical part of Broomhall, see Chapter 4 for a comprehensive assessment of Broomhall historical and demographic background).

The next section explains the operationalization of the method of analysis of documents.

2.3.3.1.3   Operationalization of the method of analysis of documents

This section explains the operationalization of the method of analysis of documents.

The author speaks and reads fluently in Spanish (his mother tongue) and English, his second language. Hence, the analysis of documents, other than those related to Broomhall, was conducted with an international scope, but using only English and Spanish as working languages. However, the author has used mainly English and focused his research based on British standards due to the influence of his first supervisor, and also because, as some authors suggest (Rugg and Petre, 2004), it is one of those unwritten rules that students, specially international students who have different academic standards back home like the author, when they register in British academic universities must comply with the British system.

The next section explains the search strategies of information when using databases.

2.3.3.1.4   Search strategies of information when using databases

This section explains the search strategies of information when using databases.

These were some of the elements included to create precise and pertinent search strategies: 1) logical Boolean operators AND & OR ("AND" reduces the search to cover only a small amount of information by combining two or more terms or phrases of several combined terms or sets of several combined terms and/or phrases and/or even larger sets, and the information retrieved is only the small portion where all sets meet together in intersection or juxtaposition; "OR" on the contrary expands a search to cover all the universe of elements to retrieve by combining two or more terms, or phrases, or sets and the information retrieved is the total of all the elements combined; the "NOT" was not employed for either was sought limited or wide combinations, not exclusions); 2) syntactical or proximity operators to create semantic phrases represented with quotes "", e.g. *"community profiling"* is a syntactical phrase where the quotes combined the terms *community* and *profiling* in a single meaningful phrase as if both were a single word.

The search strategies employed here are described synoptically and generically, but the author conducted many different combinations of strategies, not only these shown here. In addition, since the early stages until the final draft of the thesis the author kept abreast of the latest advances of the core content of this thesis thanks to many bibliographic alerts from pay-per-access databases from the University of Sheffield Libraries, from Google Scholar and Google.com, and from E-LIS. Hence, that has guaranteed that the literature review has been covered not only comprehensively at one single instance in time, but also constantly through time. Moreover, that is precisely one of the strongest assets of the qualitative research methodologies in a given project: they observe and assess small contextual phenomena, but comprehensively and constantly through time.

These are the search strategies to retrieve documental information. Strategies about the Broomhall neighbourhood from both controlled (e.g. Library and Information Science Abstracts database and using scientific descriptors) and uncontrolled vocabularies (e.g. Google):

> (Broomhall OR Havelock OR Hanover OR Spriengfield OR Broomspring OR Lynwood OR Sunnybank OR Gell OR Collegiate OR Exeter) AND ("Sheffield England" OR "Sheffield UK" OR "Sheffield South Yorkshire" OR "Sheffield Yorkshire" OR "Sheffield United Kingdom" OR "Sheffield Britain")

Strategies about *"community profiling," "information needs"* and *"information providers"* in LIS through controlled vocabularies, but from non LIS specialised databases:

> ("needs assessment" OR needs OR "social needs" OR need) AND (library OR information OR documentation) AND (LIS OR "library and information science" OR "information provision") AND (community OR "community profile" OR "community profiling" OR "community analysis")

The idea to use non LIS specialised databases was to discover authors from other disciplines who might have done similar research though applied to their disciplines, and thus to learn from them. Such is the case involving the work of a social work scientist Green (e.g. 2000a; 2000b; 2000c) who has been found to be the most prolific author doing research on community profiling, or *"community needs profiling"* as he has termed it.

In addition, it is important to note again as mentioned also in Chapter 3 (Review of the literature), that *"community profiling"* is not a descriptor from any of the controlled vocabularies employed in this project, whereas *"community analysis"* is indeed. However, the reader could assess seamlessly that both concepts are considered as *community profiling*. Even community profiling experts have used them interchangeably in the same way (Beal, 1985: 3). Hence, this project has adopted the terminology of the non-standardised and British practised *community profiling* tool instead of the internationally standardised *community analysis*.

Strategies about *"community profiling," "information needs"* and *"information providers"* in LIS through controlled vocabularies, but only from LIS specialised databases:

("needs assessment" OR needs OR "social needs" OR need) AND (community OR "community profile" OR "community profiling" OR "community analysis")

("community profile" OR "community profiling" OR "community analysis") AND ("English in LA" OR "Spanish in LA")

("needs assessment" OR needs OR "social needs" OR need) AND (library OR information OR documentation OR LIS OR "library and information science" OR "information provision")

It should be noted that *information needs* was not found as a descriptor, but only *"needs assessment,"* thus this is considered as a synonym of *information needs*.

Table 2.2 shows the libraries employed to review documental information for this thesis, either physically or electronically through Internet.

Table 2.2 Libraries employed to review documental information for this thesis (2003-2007)	
Name of library (libraries)	**Location**
British Library	London
British Library	Boston Spa, UK
Most libraries from Sheffield Hallam University	Sheffield, UK
Most libraries from the University of Sheffield	Sheffield, UK
Sheffield Central, Mobile, Broomhill, Highfield, & Upperthorpe public libraries	Sheffield, UK
UANL Raul Rangel Frías & University Library	Autonomous University of Nuevo Leon, Mexico

Table 2.3 shows the databases used to search documental information for this thesis

Table 2.3 Databases used to search documental information for this thesis	
Name of database	**Publisher**
Academic Search Premier	Ebsco Host
Amazon (from UK, US, France, Germany, & Canada)	Amazon, Inc.
ASSIA (Applied Social Science Index and Abstracts)	CSA
Bio Med Central	Bio Med Central
Books in Print	R.R. Bowker, Inc.
British Library book catalogue	British Library
DOAJ: Directory of Open Access Journals	DOAJ
Dissertation Abstracts	Proquest / UMI
E-LIS: E-prints in Library and Information Science	E-LIS
ERIC: Educational Resources Information Center	US Dept. Education
Google Scholar; Google.co.uk & Google.com	Google, Inc.
Horizon Information Portal catalogue	Sheffield City Council Libraries
Index to Theses	Index to Theses from UK and Ireland
ISI Web of Science & Web of Knowledge	Thomson Corporation
Library Catalogue	Sheffield Hallam University
Library catalogue Star	University of Sheffield Library
Library Literature & Information Full Text	The H.W. Wilson Company
LISA: Library and Information Science Abstract	Reed Business Information Ltd.
Newsbank British and international newspapers	Newsbank

REDALyC	Latin American Network of Scientific Journals in Open Access
SciElo	SciElo
Sheffield Today	*Star (Sheffield)* newspaper
Social Science Abstracts	CSA
Sociological Abstracts	CSA
UANL library catalogue & periodicals databases	Autonomous University of Nuevo Leon, Mexico
UNAM library catalogue & periodicals databases	National University Autonomous of Mexico

The next section explains the method of non-participant observation.

2.3.3.2   THE METHOD OF NON-PARTICIPANT OBSERVATION

The next section explains some views in favour of the method of non-participant observation.

2.3.3.2.1   Views in favour of the method of non-participant observation

This section explains some views in favour of the method of non-participant observation.

After the researcher had already an idea of the different groups of people and categories where data could be generated from, then the next step was to walk around the streets of Broomhall, with a diary in hand to physically observe people and things as they appeared to the researcher's sight. This is the method of observation.

The method of observation has more advantages than the method of questionnaires. For instance, if a researcher would be employing only questionnaires, she or he would generate the data at one single time, analyse them, report them, and not return to the community again. In addition, if someone conducted quantitative research triangulating quantitative with qualitative methods for small projects of less than a year, she or he would not assess, empirically, the major changes in a given neighbourhood. That would not be possible because the nature of quantitative research is to generate a vast amount of data in a given short period of time.

However, long qualitative research projects, such as this of nearly four years long, can detect the different major changes that take place in a neighbourhood, for instance by using observation method on a regular basis. In this case the researcher walked around and observed the Broomhall neighbourhood once every week or two weeks, or once every month at least in some cases.

The next section explains some competing views of the method of non-participant observation.

2.3.3.2.2   Competing views of the method of non-participant observation

This section explains some competing views of the method of non-participant observation.

Through the method of observation, the researcher can record people's actions as they happen, but this is conditional to the fact that he or she needs to be in the same time and place when people carry out their actions (Mason, 2002), and that was not possible in all events and circumstances for all the people of Broomhall who were under research. However, through observation many features of people's behaviour could be learned; by observing the materiality where people live, work, etc., e.g. houses, parks, open spaces, playgrounds, streets, pavements, trees, street lights, etc., a large amount data could be generated which in itself offered the researcher valuable features (cf. Forsetlund and Bjorndal, 2001).

The author is cognizant of some ideas that foster the inclusion of the researcher as an insider within the population and settings under research in qualitative research. For instance a commentator argues that participant observation (insider's view) has more advantages than non-participant observation (outsider's view), because the researcher could gain access to people, or resources to benefit the research process that outsiders could not, or that would be more difficult to reach

(Labaree, 2002). However, this competing view to the outsider non-participant observer has been
also challenged by the same author (Labaree, 2002), who notes that being an insider participant
observer poses some political risks for the researcher to gain access to people who might have
different political or ideological views who might decline their participation in the research project,
or if they participate might feel uncomfortable if the findings might not fit within their political
ideas (Labaree, 2007). Furthermore, being an insider participant observer has been found as having
inherently some methodological bias that might affect the objectivity of the data collection and
analysis (Breen, 2007).

The next section explains the operationalization of the method of non-participant observation.

2.3.3.2.3   Operationalization of the method of non-participant observation

The method of observation was employed in the form of non-participant observation. It was used to
draw direct evidence from the context where the events occurred exactly as they did, or as the
researcher interpreted (Denscombe, 2003: 192). Some commentators from the health sciences
(Forsetlund and Bjorndal, 2001) commented that researchers should use the non-participant
observation method when they assess people's information needs because they may capture some
unrecognized or potential needs just by simply observing the physical environment where people
perform any of their daily activities.

Non-participant observation means that the researcher observes people's actions, and events as he
or she perceives them in a unique given time or a series of instances through a short or large time
span, but without being involved in any participation with those people, or events (Breen, 2007;
Labaree, 2002). That is, completely detached from people, and from the events being observed.
Hence, the only role that the author played throughout the doctoral study and the thesis was a
mediatory role (Delanty, 2005: 171) towards the perceptions and actions of the respondents of the
Broomhall neighbourhood by acting only as an outside non-participant observer.

The next section explains method of interviews (individual and focus groups).

2.3.3.3   THE METHOD OF INTERVIEWS (INDIVIDUAL AND IN FOCUS GROUPS)

The next section explains some views in favour of the method of interviews (individual and focus
groups).

2.3.3.3.1   Views in favour of the method of interviews (individual and focus groups)

This section explains some views in favour of the method of interviews (individual and focus
groups).

The use of interviews normally means that the researcher has reached the decision that, for the
purposes of the particular project in mind, the research would be better served by getting material,
which provides more of an in-depth insight into the topic, drawing on information provided by
fewer informants. (Denscombe, 2003: 163). Thus, the interviews were employed formally and
informally in order get in-depth insights from the interviewees on the questions being asked which
led to an understanding of the phenomena under research (Denscombe, 2003: 163). A LIS
researcher (Nicholas, 2000: 111-112) considers that interviews have many advantages over other
types of research methods, since researchers are thereby enabled to make few but key questions to
interviewees and these can give as extensive, free and abundant answers to those few questions as
their time allows it, both theirs and the researchers', and therefore generate plenty of valuable data
for the researchers' projects.

For this project, the focus group method is simply considered as part of the method of interviews,
but conducted in a group fashion (Arksey and Knight, 1999). Hence, it is considered in this project,
after Arksey and Knight (1999), that there is not a major difference between individual and focus
groups interviews (and for that matter of any other different type of interviewing). That is, the
participants of focus groups interviews are simply interviewees, but arranged in a group form. They
follow the mechanics and dynamics of a focus group developed over the years by many

commentators (e.g. Huberman and Miles, 2002; Mitchell and Branigan, 2000; Glitz, 1998; Krueger, 1998; Krueger and King, 1998; Morgan and Scannell, 1998; Kitzinger, 1995; Morgan, 1988), not as a very special type of method, but simply as any other type of interview, conducted in a focus group style. That is, by a group of interviewees focused on certain topics or themes; in this case, the same ones this project conducted for both group and individual interviewees.

The focus group is a qualitative research technique, originally developed by social scientists, to gather data on the opinions, perceptions, knowledge, and concerns of small groups of individuals about a particular topic. The technique involves questioning and listening within the small group setting, to allow participants to describe their experiences in their own words, (Glitz, 1998:1). Some commentators mention that holding focus groups allow data to be obtained from a larger number of respondents and for people to develop their original responses after they heard other people's views, (Patton, 1990; Morgan, 1988).

A sociologist (Kitzinger, 1995) comments that this method is particularly useful for exploring people's knowledge and experiences and can be used to examine not only what people think, but how they think and why they think that way. Focus groups can answer certain types of questions better than others can. They are particularly good at exploring concepts, generating ideas, eliciting opinions and measuring the degree of consensus on a topic. This is because group interaction is used to generate data. Group members stimulate each other to think and express opinions that in turn stimulate more thought (Mitchell and Branigan, 2000).

In this project, focus groups interviews were used after the literature review and observation, but before individual interviews, because as some LIS researchers have observed, when assessing information needs, focus groups can establish some of the crucial issues which would be important to follow up in subsequent interviews, from those opinions can also be established to whom interview later on (Williamson, Schauder and Bow, 2000).

The next section explains some competing views of the method of interviews (individual and focus groups).

2.3.3.3.2   Competing views of the method of interviews (individual and focus groups)

This section explains some competing views of the method of interviews (individual and focus groups).

The major limitation of the interviews method (either individually or through any group modality, e.g. *focus groups*) is that it only captures interviewees' experiences expressed in their own words; what the interviewees think *they have done, they do or will do* (Silverman, 2005; Arksey and Knight, 1999; Deacon and Golding, 1991). That is, their actions are mediated by their own world view, subjectivities, and ideologies (e.g. like actually all human beings behave indeed, after Lenin, [1908], 1964 and Ilyenkov, 1960; 1977), hence what they say (orally, because if written it would then be a questionnaire, but not an interview) through the interview process that they have done, do, or will do, does not necessarily have to be exactly how they express it.

Silverman (2005) has even criticised further what he argues has become an *interview society* in qualitative research, where practitioners, when using interview methods, should not take them as a 'gold standard': "the pursuit of people's 'experience' by no means constitutes an adequate defence for the use of open-ended interview" (Silverman, 2005: 240).

This project has focused mainly on the residents' perceptions of the research question, aim, and objectives at stake, and accordingly, their own perceptions are precisely their main limitation. So that, building for instance on Green's (2000a; 2000b) "bottom-up felt needs" concept (see Chapter 3) and de la Garza Toledo's (2002; 2001) "configuration" concept, already explained above in this chapter (see Table 2.1 for its definition), they do indeed precisely consider individuals' perception and their experience —in this case captured through the interviews method, as an important source of evidence to support research findings, discussions, conclusions, and recommendations. However, as it is being explained here, people's perceptions of their past, present or future experiences, are precisely limited, when considered as the only source of evidence.

There proved to be no homogeneous background for the interviewees, e.g. social class; ethnicities. However, in terms of the different focus groups' participants, most of them were from working class, unemployed, or poor backgrounds. Therefore, that means that to set up these types of focus group was to some extent a difficult task. For instance the first focus group interview with young and adult working class people was also in the open, but it was more homogeneous, although at times impressions between the young people and adults clashed. The set-up of the second focus group with young adult student women was perhaps the most difficult of all because some of them were not allowed to talk to men due to barriers relating to their BEM (black and ethnic minority) cultural backgrounds. Hence, that focus group alone took about seven months to obtain access through a very intricate, but nonetheless, rewarding process of trust building through gatekeepers. In the case of the third focus group with unemployed elderly participants, it was conducted under circumstances to some extent difficult. These respondents gathered in a place where privacy was interrupted constantly.

Another limitation of all the focus group interviews was that some respondents were more articulate than others were, and although the researcher tried as much as he could to try to engage in a balanced participation with all the respondents, that could not be fully achieved. This limitation is reflected in Chapter 5 where not all respondents' perceptions could be incorporated throughout the findings, because not all of them responded to all the questions as some did. However this limitation did not limit the overall soundness of the focus group interviews, because as a commentator explains, there is the caveat that the success of this type of interviewing depends of the types of respondents and their contexts (Kitzinger, 1995). In addition, those limitations from the focus group interviews were compensated by the individual interviews where all individual interviewees responded fully to all questions, as is expected from individual interviews.

The next section explains the operationalization of the method of interviews.

2.3.3.3.3 Operationalization of the method of interviews

The formal interviews with residents and information providers were both tape recorded and notepad recorded, but from the informal ones only notes were taken. Some of the reasons for doing this were that the settings for the formal interviews were well planned in advance, with all the ethical considerations well planned and actually conducted accordingly, but in the case of the informal interviews or chats with many people from the neighbourhood, these were always unplanned and spontaneous, and for the most part conducted at the street level (e.g. passing by the Broomhall allotments; at shops). Hence the researcher could not be carrying a tape recorder all the time or be tape recording people without their consent and besides, the informal interviews were not strictly a part of the planned interviews.

Furthermore trust was also at stake. Most of the time those notes from informal interviews or chats were taken in a very small pocket notepad (detective style) always after and away from the different scenarios. This was done because whenever people saw the researcher taking notes (particularly in section A and the areas C and B near section A) they felt uncomfortable and made him also feel uncomfortable. Perhaps they would feel like being 'questioned by the police', hence that could hamper the trust built by the researcher, the data generation process, and most of all it might have hampered the whole research process on un-ethical grounds.

The next section will explain the design of data generation.

2.4 Design of data generation

The next sections will explain the design of data generation as employed in this thesis, which includes: a) the rationale of the selection of the sample, b) the rationale of the pilot study, c) and the rationale of the main study.

The next section explains the rationale of the selection of the sample for this research project.

2.4.1 Rationale of the selection of the sample

The next section explains the selection of the purposing sampling employed in this research project.

2.4.1.1 THE SELECTION OF THE PURPOSING SAMPLING EMPLOYED IN THIS RESEARCH PROJECT

This section explains the selection of the purposing sampling employed in this research project.

As already explained in the background to the study in section 1.4 (see Chapter 1 of the Introduction), the author conducted community profiling research in the Broomhall neighbourhood in order to analyse information needs and provision through the perceptions of residents and information providers. Hence, the sampling of this study comprises two integral parts: a) people (that is, long-term residents living in the Broomhall neighbourhood, and as well the information providers from within or outside the neighbourhood but who serve those residents), and b) the geographically delimitated Broomhall neighbourhood (see Figures 4.1 and 4.2 in Chapter 4 to assess the working maps).

For this project, purposing sampling models were employed instead of random sampling ones, because what it is being sought, as Denzin and Lincoln (2000: 370) suggest, "are the groups, settings, and individuals where and for whom the processes being studied are most likely to occur." Alternatively, like Wengraf (2001: 102) puts it when building on Patton, purposeful sampling: "Selects information-rich cases for in-depth study. Size and specific cases depend on the study purposes." In this respect, Silverman (2005: 129) suggests that when choosing the purposive sampling model, "we think critically about the parameters of the population we are studying and choose our sample case carefully on this basis."

The type of purposeful sampling employed in this project was the type of snowball or chain sampling (Hall, 1981: 27), which "identifies cases of interest from people who know people who know what cases are information-rich; that is, good examples for study, good interview subjects" (Wengraf, 2001: 102).

The next section explains the selection process of the interviewees that took part in this research project.

2.4.1.2 THE SELECTION PROCESS OF THE INTERVIEWEES THAT TOOK PART IN THIS RESEARCH PROJECT

This section explains the selection process the interviewees that took part in this research project.

Following the purposing sampling through the type of snowball or chain sampling, the author interviewed only 32 individuals: 24 residents, and 8 information providers. Of these: 18 individuals were interviewed individually (10 residents and the 8 information providers), and 14 distributed in three focus groups (two focus groups were conducted through the pilot study, and the other two through the main study, see below for further explanation of these).

The beginning of the selection process of interviewees through the snowball sampling process emerged from four circumstances: a) the author needed a population to generate data from a sample, b) the author when first arrived to Sheffield used to live in the Broomhall neighbourhood, c) the first supervisor of the author suggested to him that since the author was already a foreigner in the UK, that any neighbourhood would be feasible to conduct research about it; hence, the author suggested his supervisor that if Broomhall was a suitable neighbourhood, then that would be how the Broomhall was selected; and d) the author in the first days when he arrived to Sheffield met a Mexican research student at the University of Sheffield who already lived in Sheffield with her husband and family, and after the author and the supervisor agreed on selecting Broomhall as a research neighbourhood the author told this Mexican student about his research project, and this lady put him in contact with a key information provider within Broomhall whom this student knew for few years and with whom she had a good level of trust.

Hence, the researcher made an informal request to this student to arrange a meeting with this information provider at her premises. This meeting took place at the information provider's premises in late October 2003 (that is, in the first three of four weeks since the researcher had arrived to the UK by first time). At this earliest stage of the research, as explained below in the pilot study, the methodologies and methods to be employed and the methodological instrumentation was not yet designed. Nevertheless, the meeting with this key information provider, who had great influence in the communities of the Broomhall neighbourhood, was of paramount importance for the researcher. Thus, this first information provider and key respondent of the research project was very friendly and cooperative with the author and gave him many ideas, hints, clues, and most of all referred him to other residents and information providers from the neighbourhood. This respondent was then the beginning of the snowball sampling process. From the individuals this respondent referred to the author, some became actual respondents and these afterwards referred the author to further prospective respondents; and the snowball sampling grew in that way.

Nevertheless, the author did not approach all the prospective respondents referred simply because they were referred by others. The author had to design a rigorous procedure to guarantee a balanced sample of the different communities comprising the Broomhall neighbourhood. This procedure is explained in the next section.

2.4.1.2.1   Procedure to obtain a balanced sample that reflects the different communities of Broomhall

As explained above in the section of the *social class struggles concept* (see also Table 2.1), as long as there exists a dominance hierarchy of social class contradictions, then conflicts, and struggles will constantly emerge. This project tried to obtain a balanced sample that reflects the different communities of Broomhall, however that task was not completely accomplished. Much of it was due to this social class divide found in Broomhall at the early stages of the research. For instance, the three working classes of this project are working class, middle class, and capitalist or bourgeois class, however some members from the latter, who were referred to the author from respondents of sections A, B, or C, were invited to take part in this project, but they declined their participation.

Furthermore, Broomhall emerged as divided in four sections (A, B, C, and D), being A the most deprived where most working class residents live, B less deprived than A, but less affluent than C, this more affluent than B, but less affluent than D, and this the most affluent of all where most middle and capitalist class members live (see Figures 4.1 and 4.2 for the working maps in Chapter 4), however as shown below in Table 2.6, only one respondent participated from section D. That is, capitalist class residents from all sections, but in particular from section D, they all declined to take part in this research project; likewise, middle class residents from section D declined too.

In addition, as analysed in chapters 4 (historical and demographic background of Broomhall), and 5 (where the findings of this project are analysed and discussed), it emerged that the section D, the Broomhall Park, was not part of Broomhall, but a different neighbourhood. Nevertheless, since within section D is located the historic and Manor type Broom Hall mansion which historically gave name to the Broomhall neighbourhood, the author tried to include residents from that section in the sample, but without success.

To try to overcome that limitation of the snowballing sampling, the author collected several names of capitalist or bourgeois class residents from section D publicly available in the literature (e.g. Cromar, 2003; Sheffield City Council, 2006a; *Star (Sheffield)*, 2002a; 2002b; 2004b), and invited them to take part in the project, but they also declined. That is the main reason why the residents of the capitalist or bourgeois class throughout the four sections of Broomhall were absent from the sample.

What steps did the author take to assure a rigorous and consistent procedure of selecting prospective respondents? As explained below in the audit trail process as part of the replicability procedure of this project, this project generated an impressive amount of data of all types. The sampling process also generated a daunting amount of data: 62 pages A4 size in digital format listing the 1,860 e-mail messages relating the process of contacting the more than 200 prospective respondents. That is, the author in order to gain access and most of all trust with the actual participants exchanged with them many e-mails, but to get in touch with them he sent 1,860 messages during the time span the data generation took place. Besides the e-mail communications, the author also made many telephone calls and paid many visits to prospective respondents, or individuals who would serve as a reference to contact prospective respondents. This process of selection generated an overwhelming amount of data.

Hence, in order to maintain a tight control of the avalanche of data that the author compiled for about four years, he created a relational database for his own use. As shown in Table 2.4 below the reader can assess the various database fields of the working *Broomhall directory of respondents* that the researcher created (with the free software Open Office database suite) since November 2003 and maintained and updated until March 2006 when the generation of interviews data finished. The table is divided into three columns: a) personal data, b) job data, and c) research data. The creation of this database began on November 2003 but it was constantly improved as the project advanced and new fields were included.

With this database the author coped with the avalanche of data generated to select the sample of prospective respondents from beginning to end. The most important field of this database was the *Follow-up notes* that the researcher kept with the more than 200 prospective respondents. That is, in order to obtain the most balanced sample to cover as much as possible the different respondents from the three working classes of this project, from the four sections, from both genders, from different groups of age, ethnic backgrounds, and economic status, the author made in his database the most comprehensive profile of each prospective or actual respondent. The database included real names of people: contacts, of referral contacts, actual or prospective respondents, names from the literature (included actual bibliographic or full text records).

Selecting the sample alone became as important as reviewing the literature. The process, same as with all the procedures that help accomplish this research project, was conducted scientifically, professionally, rigorously, ethically, with discipline, and most of all with too much patience. Through the *Follow-up notes* field of the database the author recorded in the database as a log or blog the daily communication relating to the more than 200 prospective respondents: e-mails, telephone calls, and visits, including dates and time. The only purpose of this database was simply to obtain a balanced sample and a pool of actual respondents. All the notes in the *Follow-up notes* field stopped when either a contact accepted to take part in the interview by stating the date and time when the interview took place, or if they declined after being contacted, or if the author declined any follow-up, as it happened with hundreds of prospective respondents who never responded to the researcher despite the fact that he contacted them many times over months and even more than a year.

Furthermore, none of the respondents knew that the researcher was creating a detailed profile of each of them for several months or years, only the author's supervisors knew about this directory. However, due to the ethical statement made by the researcher to the actual or prospective respondents to guarantee confidentiality to all the respondents, nobody except the author had access to this database. This is the reason why on Table 2.4 below only the names of the fields, and an explanation of each is presented in order to comply with this ethical consideration regarding confidentiality, but the actual profiles of the prospective and actual respondents were on ethical grounds withheld.

Table 2.4 is shown here.

Table 2.4 Database fields of the working Broomhall directory of respondents		
Personal data	**Job data**	**Research data**
Contact ID (an arithmetic consecutive number)	Organization name (where residents or information providers work)	Respondent code
Title (if Mr., Mrs., Ms.)	Position	Type of respondent (if resident or information provider)
Gender	Address	Method (if individual or focus group interview)
Surname	City	Interviewed? (yes or no)
First name	Postal code	Social class (if member of the working, middle, or

		capitalist class)
Home address	Work telephone 1	Section of Broomhall where the respondent live or work (A= Hanover flats, B= Broomspring, C= Havelock, and D= Broomhall Park)
City (some information providers live outside Sheffield, but worked in Broomhall)	Work telephone 2	Economic status (if employed, unemployed, homeless, pensioner, student, in government benefits)
Postal code (to find out to which of the 4 areas of Broomhall classify them)	Work fax	Age
Home telephone	Work e-mail	Ethnicity
Mobile telephone	Work web page	Referred by (person or persons who referred this person as candidate to be respondent following the snowball sampling)
Personal e-mail		Respondent's name found in the literature (yes or no; some respondents were not referred by others but found on the literature)
Personal web page		Follow-up notes (a constant follow-up of the actions of the researcher towards gaining access and trust with the prospective respondents until they accepted or declined to be interviewed, or the author desisted to interview them after a constant lack of response)

Therefore, the author by employing his own database had the chance to select and discard prospective respondents in order to obtain balance in most of the fields of the database, e.g. social class, section where they live or work in Broomhall, gender, age, economic status, and ethnicity. The main idea was to obtain a balanced sample comprising the three working classes from the four sections of Broomhall.

This was achieved as follows. As mentioned above, capitalist or bourgeois class members could not be integrated as respondents in the project. However, as analysed in Chapter 5 (where Findings are analysed and discussed), most capitalist or bourgeois class members emerged mainly related to the construction industry. Hence, to circumvent this limitation, the participation of this class was included as a literature review along with the perceptions of working and middle class interviewees (e.g. Exposed, 2007; LDA Design, 2005; Star (Sheffield), 2002b; 2004b; Broomhall News, 2004a; Cromar, 2003). The construction industry in Broomhall emerged as having the most adverse impact to the different communities. Hence, the inclusion of literature addressing some of the construction industry plans underway in Broomhall was remarkable.

Thus, despite the fact that no capitalist or bourgeois class members could be interviewed, the sample comprising the respondents selected from working and middle class backgrounds and the literature reviewed relating to capitalist class members gave the author a balanced sample considering the three working classes from the four sections of Broomhall. See below in this chapter the actual composition of the sample of interviewees.

In addition, from this database (see above Table 2.4) several other operationalization procedures were derived. For instance the application of an identification code to distinguish each interviewee. This is explained in the next section.

2.4.1.2.2   Identification code of interviewees

This section explains the identification code assigned for interviewees who took part in this research project.

Every interviewee who took part in this research project was assigned a unique identification code added at the end of each transcript excerpt textually cited in chapters 4 and 5 (but mainly in the later which is devoted to the analysis and discussions of the findings of this thesis mainly through the perceptions of respondents). This was done to guide the reader to unequivocally distinguish the different perceptions of all the interviewees.

These codes were conformed as follows. For resident individual interviewees the abbreviation R.I. was given, and after it a subsequent arithmetic number was given according to how they were being interviewed in chronological order. For instance, R.I.01 means the first individual resident that was interviewed. For focus group interviewees the abbreviation F.G. was given, after it a subsequent number was given to distinguish each focus group, and after it a capital letter in alphabetical order was given to distinguish each respondent since focus groups comprised several respondents. For instance F.G.01.A means that A was the first respondent who spoke within the first focus group. For information providers the abbreviation I.P. was given, and after it, same as with R.I.s above, a subsequent number was given to distinguish each respondent. For instance, I.P.01 means the first information provider that was interviewed.

See Table 2.5 below to assess at a glance the identification codes that were given to each respondent.

Table 2.5 Identification codes for interviewees	
Type of respondents	**Identification codes**
Focus groups (FGs) interviews to residents	3 FGs. FG 1: 6 respondents (F.G.01.A, F.G.01.B, F.G.01.C, F.G.01.D, F.G.01.E, F.G.01.F). FG 2: 3 respondents (F.G.02.A, F.G.02.B, F.G.02.C). FG 3: 5 respondents (F.G.03.A, F.G.03.B, F.G.03.C, F.G.03.D, F.G.03.E)
Individual interviews to residents (RIs)	10 RIs: R.I.01, R.I.02, R.I.03, R.I.04, R.I.05, R.I.06, R.I.07, R.I.08, R.I.09, R.I.10.
Individual interviews to information providers (IPs)	8 IPs: IP.01, IP.02, IP.03, IP.04, IP.05, IP.06, IP.07, IP.08.

In addition to the identification code of each respondent, the author also added the social class that respondents belong to, according to the author's analysis, and the section of Broomhall (A, B, C, or D) they belong to according to them, either as a resident or information provider. Hence, the reader can assess in each excerpt the respondents' perceptions according to the social class and section within Broomhall to which they belonged. From this assessment the readers might obtain interrelationships of how belonging to working class makes a significant difference than belonging to a middle class, or how living in section A, the most deprived, makes also a significant difference than belonging to more affluent sections such as B, or C, or D (this the most affluent).

2.4.1.2.3   Composition of the sample of interviewees

For this project, 32 individuals were interviewed: 18 individually (10 residents and 8 information providers), and 14 through 3 focus groups. See Tables 2.6 through 2.9 to assess the specific profiles of all the respondents who took part in this project. As derived from the *Broomhall directory of respondents* created by the author as a personal and non-public organizing tool (see above Table 2.4), through Tables 2.6 to 2.9 the readers might find a sample reflecting a balance of residents and information providers, living or working in Sections A, B, and C of Broomhall, with working and middle class, economic status, gender, age, and ethnicity. For capitalist or bourgeois class in general and from section D in particular it was discussed above that all the prospective respondents declined to take part in the research, hence this balance only applies to working and middle class with the actual Broomhall (sections A, B, and C).

See Table 2.6 below to assess at a glance general profile of all the interviewees.

Table 2.6 General profile of all the interviewees (32 respondents in total)					
Social class	Location within Broomhall	Economic status	Gender	Age	Ethnicity
15 working class members 17 middle class members	8 from Section A 5 from Section B 17 from Section C 1 from Section D 1 from Broomhill closest neighbourhood	2 homeless 2 unemployed 2 on government benefits 2 pensioners 3 students 12 employed 3 physical labour occupation 2 low managerial occupation 2 school teachers 2 university lecturers	16 female 16 male	7 youngsters 17 adults 8 elderly	12 BME 20 British Caucasian

The general profile of the residents individually interviewed is shown in Table 2.7 below.

Table 2.7 Profile of the individual interviewees. Long time neighbourhood residents (10 respondents)					
Social class	Location within Broomhall	Economic status	Gender	Age	Ethnicity
3 working class members 7 middle class members	1 from Section A 1 from Section B 8 from Section C	3 physical labour occupation 1 pensioner 2 low managerial occupation 2 school teachers 2 university lecturers	5 female 5 male	8 adults 2 elderly	1 Black Minority Ethnic (BME) 9 British Caucasian

The general profile of the information providers individually interviewed is shown in Table 2.8 below.

Table 2.8 Profile of the individual interviewees. Information providers (8 participants)					
Status within their middle class	Location within Broomhall	Economic status	Gender	Age	Ethnicity
3 low managerial with no university degree	2 from Section A 1 from Section B 3 from Section	8 employed	4 female 4 male	7 adults 1 elderly	2 BEM 6 British Caucasian

1 school teacher 9 middle-top managerial with university degree (4 of them library or information management related)	C 1 from Section D 1 from Broomhill closest neighbourhood				

The general profile of the residents interviewed through focus groups is shown in Table 2.9 below.

Table 2.9 Profile of focus groups interviewees. Long time neighbourhood residents (3 focus groups with 14 participants)					
Social class	Location within Broomhall	Economic status	Gender	Age	Ethnicity
12 working class members 2 middle class members	5 from Section A 3 from Section B 6 from Section C	2 homeless 2 unemployed 2 on government benefits 1 pensioner 3 students 4 employed	7 female 7 male	7 youngsters 2 adults 5 elderly	9 BME 5 British Caucasian

The next section explains the rationale of the pilot study.

2.4.2 The rationale of the pilot study

This section explains the rationale of the pilot study.

The pilot study was a preliminary study to the main study, which lasted from 30 September 2003 until 18 October 2004. Its main purpose was to test in some degree the different methodologies and methods for both the generation and the analysis of data, but in a very short time span.

This pilot study generated a 60 pages MPhil/PhD Transfer report, entitled: *Broomhall community profile*. When it was decided by the end of 2003 to focus on a community profiling of Broomhall and with qualitative research methodologies, the idea back then was to conduct the pilot study there in Broomhall and then in the main study compare it with another neighbourhood, which by the end of 2004 was decided to be Broomhill. However, by September 2005 it was decided with the researcher's new supervisor that due to the researcher's lack of sufficient resources: funding and time, the main study would be conducted only in Broomhall.

In such a case, the pilot study served to depict some of the main features of the neighbourhood, which would serve as the basis to find out about the Broomhall residents' information needs and to which extent information providers would meet them. These were the main features profiled as of 18 October 2004 (Muela-Meza, 2005a):

1. Housing development (e.g. demolishing & building; local residents being moved out).
2. Unemployment (e.g. abandonment of neighbourhood; drug addiction).
3. Health – heart and respiratory diseases (e.g. drinking, smoking, unhealthy food).
4. Multiculturalism – social exclusion (e.g. social class divides and conflicts).
5. Educational exclusion – due to linguistic barriers (about 60 languages were spoken in Broomhall).

Most of those features, or issues were configured or generated as the research moved along inductively, especially through observation and the transcripts of the two first focus group interviews. However, for the design of the focus groups guide some issues were proposed deductively as prompts to the participants as needed.

These are the questions used for the focus groups and the pre-selected themes as prompts:

A. What are the major features of the community? (prompts: population, transport, communications; cultural, traditions (local festivals, working men's clubs, ethnic traditions etc); land usage (industry; Shops etc); housing; communications in the community (local newspapers, free sheets, radio TV, etc); local authority policies (with the local community).
B. What is the best and what is the worst thing about living in this community?
C. What are and have been the major issues facing the community?
D. Where do you go to find facts and/or to have better understanding of your issues? (Prompts: or whom do you ask for help?).
E. Is there anything else you would like to add?

See the next section to compare the evolution of questions guide from the pilot to the main study.

The data of the pilot study were generated from not only the previous literature review, and non-participant observation, and informal chats with people in the neighbourhood, but also from two focus groups with residents. In consultation with the research supervisors it was decided that those focus groups were well conducted and relevant, and could appropriately be included in the main study.

The next section explains the rationale of the main study.

2.4.3 The rationale of the main study

This section explains the rationale of the main study.

The generation of data from the main study lasted from 19 October 2004 until March 2006. In fact, it is better said that it lasted from the very beginning of the program on the 30th of September 2003 until the very final correction of the thesis before the *viva voce,* since the data from the pilot study served the thesis as the main foundation to build on, and although the generation of data from individual interviews and focus groups had finished by March 2006, the updating of documental sources continued until the end of August 2007, just before the final submission of the thesis.

Also, as for other sources of data generation, the research diary note taking of the researcher from 30 September 2003 up to 15 December 2006 amounted to more than 1, 000 pages of notes: field notes; bibliographic records; hints; vague ideas; draft phrases or ideas; "spark" ideas; that is, all kinds of writings, and ideas which served well to what some commentators call in qualitative research the "audit trail" (Rice-Lively, 1997: 186; see also below the audit trail conducted by the author as part of the replicability process).

The next section explains the evolution of the interview schedules.

2.4.3.1   EVOLUTION OF THE INTERVIEW SCHEDULES

This section explains the evolution of the interview schedules from the pilot study through the main study.

There were no major changes from the pilot focus groups interview schedule to the main study. The major thing added was a schedule for the information providers, and as mentioned in the interview method section above, here the individual interviews, and focus groups are considered both as interviews, thus,   at the end, only two interviews schedules were developed: one for full time residents and one for information providers.

Comparison of the interviews schedules between the pilot and main studies. By comparing questions from the pilot and main study, the question A and B remained the same, for both residents and providers, but only in B were prompts added in the main study:

A. What are the major features of the community? (prompts: population, transport, communications; cultural traditions (local festivals, working men's clubs, ethnic traditions etc); land usage (industry; Shops etc); housing; communications in the community (local newspapers, free sheets, radio TV, etc); local authority policies (with the local community).

B. What is the best and what is the worst thing about living in this community?
Prompts: Either they would be best or worst these issues could be:
Safety; Transport; Housing; Health

Question C is very similar but was substantially improved. For residents it was:

C. What are and have been the major needs, or issues or concerns you face in the community?
Prompts: For example: Health issues; Social and economic issues; Employment opportunities; any other?

For information providers was:

C. What are and have been the major needs, or issues or concerns you think people experience, or face in the community?

Question D was the same but more prompts were added. For residents was:

D. Where do you go to find facts, or to have a better understanding, or to find solutions to your issues or concerns?
Prompts: Or whom do you ask for help? For example: Relatives; Friends; Community leaders; Church leaders; Advice centres; e.g. Citizen's Advice Bureau
Libraries; Any other?

For information providers was:

D. How do you (or does your organisation/institution) contribute with those people to find facts, or to have better understanding, or to find solutions to their needs, or issues, or concerns?

Two new questions were introduced. For residents:

E. How well your needs are satisfied from the people or institutions you sought for help?

For information providers:

How well their needs are satisfied or their issues alleviated with your help (or with the help from your organisation/institution) when they have sought you (them) for help?

For both, to assess how the residents felt about the service they received from information providers, and how the latter thought that residents felt of their service.

And, for both:

F. What has worked and what hasn't worked and why?

To have a self assessment from the respondents of possible causes of satisfaction or dissatisfaction, in both obtaining and providing information services.

The final question in both studies remained the same, and in the main one the same for providers too:

G. Is there anything else you would like to add?

The next section explains the design of data analysis.

2.5 Design of data analysis

This section explains the design of data analysis.

2.5.1 Theoretical and methodological analysis of data

The findings, discussions, conclusions and recommendations of this thesis were deliberately arranged and presented from the most negative (or controversial, or adverse) issues to the positive (or less negative, or controversial, or adverse) features; issues are seen as negative and features more positive. This order was chosen not only because it embodies the intrinsic analytical logic of the *social class struggle* concept where theoretically and generally the poor working class people (including the destitute, asylum seekers, refugees, homeless, jobless and other poor people alike) are more prone to be deprived in every sense, but also because it emerged from the data that the working class people were precisely the most deprived from Broomhall neighbourhood. Hence, where information needs were perceived as having the most adverse effects.

In line with the qualitative research methodology of interpretivism or interpretivist approaches (Mason, 2002: 56; Miles and Huberman, 1994. 7-8) employed in this study to generate data, the same methodology has been used to analyse data.

From the literature reviewed, Mason's (2002) analysis of qualitative data was found the most suitable for this project. She (Mason, 2002: 148-149) notes that that three levels of analysing qualitative data can be employed by researchers: 1) literally (e.g. if it is interview transcripts, then they should be transcribed literally); 2) interpretatively (following the same interview example, then the researcher may try to make her or his own interpretations of the transcripts and not include literal extracts); and 3) reflexively (where the researcher's world view would be part of the data generated).

This project employed only levels 1 (literally) and 2 (interpretatively) of Mason (2002). The author cited excerpts from data of the literature and interviews (both of individuals and focus groups) which are considered the *literal* level of analysis by Mason (2002), thus every time the reader assesses a citation from either the literature or interviews he or she would be assessing a *literal* level of analysis. However, the author made an interpretation of each excerpt of data cited, and then he employed Mason's (2002) second level of analysis of *interpretation* of the data.

Moreover, in the literature, Mason's (2002) interpretivist approach to analyse data has also been similarly employed by other researchers. For instance, a commentator notes that the observation that research reports is "written on the basis of the active interpretation of the reader" (Porter, 2007: 80). Along these lines, another commentator notes that it is precisely through the interpretation of the information how the research thesis or new knowledge is constructed (Cisterna Cabrera, 2005: 63). Nevertheless, some commentators present a caveat that "qualitative researchers are often at risk of merely categorising and illustrating participants' accounts rather than developing 'provocative and insightful' interpretations that could contribute to meaningful theory-building" (Rizq and Target, 2009: 68). Another commentator notes that the interpretation of data to be more than descriptive "relies ultimately on the researcher's interpretation of data" (Jootun, et. al, 2008: 43).

Hence, in this project the data has been analysed with the same logic as how it was generated, by using triangulation of methods. That is, through the generation, analysis, and writing of data blended into one another (Linley and Usherwood, 1998: 15). In addition, some experts of qualitative research data analysis emphasize that the analysis of data most of the time is done with words: "The words can be assembled, sub clustered, broken into semiotic segments. They can be organized to permit the researcher to contrast, compare, analyse, and bestow patterns upon them" (Miles and Huberman, 1994: 7).

Accordingly, the data generated with the methods of analysis of documents, observational field notes, and interview transcripts were read seeking interrelationships and themes; as a researcher has suggested:

"This analysis was first done through a 'floating reading', somewhat akin to the psychoanalysts floating attention, which allowed us to identify unexpected themes or surprising words, and to spot certain connections. Another reading more systematic was based on different data: tables with a nominative entry and several thematic entries which summarize a certain number of characteristics and which bring out the relationships between them; a list of quotes by themes" (Petit, 1998).

Then, "excerpts of data are classified –words, sentences, and paragraphs—into intuitive and anonymous categories" (Saquilán, 2005: 44), "in such a way that patterns in the data are made clear" (Bradley, 1993: 445). In addition, all of these data once analysed have been intertwined, or collated, or threaded throughout the whole doctoral thesis in the form of text following in order to obtain a triangulation of the findings obtained from the different methods employed through a triangulation process too: analysis of documents, observation, and interviews.

However, being this thesis underpinned by interpretivism or interpretivist qualitative research methodology (e.g. Mason, 2002: 56; Miles and Huberman, 1994. 7-8; Porter, 2007: 80; Cisterna Cabrera, 2005: 63; Jootun, et. al, 2008: 43), the author was not concerned in theory-building as some note (Rizq and Target, 2009: 68; Strauss and Corbin, 1990; Glaser and Strauss, 1967). However, this could not be considered a lack of rigour, because the author was concerned in interpreting critically and analytically the interpretations made by people through documents or interviews as well as by data generated by the author.

2.5.2 Limitations of the analysis of data

A possible limitation to the analysis of data might be that, the author did not follow the methodology of interpretative phenomenological analysis (IPA), or hermeneutics in order to analyse data as some commentators suggest (Rizq and Target, 2009: 68; Standing, 2009; Quinn, et. al, 2008; Larkin, Watts and Clifton, 2006; Smith, 2004). This might seem as a limitation to some extent because the author has employed interpretivism or interpretivist approaches (e.g. Mason, 2002: 56). However, Mason's (2002) interpretivist methodology have been employed on broader terms and interrelated with the working concepts employed in this thesis: *the materialist conception of history, the social class struggles,* and *the configuration concept as an open structure of theory* as well as other concepts such as *configuration*. Hence, the interpretative phenomenological analysis methodology was not found suitable to be interrelated with those concepts. Furthermore, there is a sound critique from social science epistemology that "interpretation [*within the interpretative phenomenological analysis, and hermeneutics methodologies, MUELA-MEZA, Z.M.*] does not involve critique but mere understanding" (Delanty, 2005: 61). Thus, the interpretivist methodology employed in this thesis sought not only a mere understanding of the phenomena researched, but also critique.

Another possible limitation to the analysis of data might be that the author did not employ *strictly speaking* any specialised software package called Computer-assisted Analysis of Qualitative Data (CAQDAS), like ATLAS or ETHNOGRAPH. A commentator noted that qualitative research emerged as a response to the quantitative research which was more concerned with technology (including computers), than with pressing social or political issues (Silverman, 2005).

However, that was not the reason why the author did not employ any specialised CAQDAS. The author does employ computers since many years to conduct his academic work. Hence, he did not conduct the analysis of data fully 'manually' without the help of a computer software. He did use the MS-Word word processor suite throughout the doctoral program, and to some extent to find the occurrences of some analytical categories already designed from the onset through the interview schemes.

In addition, the author was cognizant of the commercial CAQDAS called ATLAS. The author had access to the full version CD-ROM of the ATLAS software at the Department of Information Studies at the University of Sheffield, but in agreement with his supervisor it was decided not to employ it because only 32 interviewees were recorded, hence being this research project of a small scale, the amount of data generated from transcripts did not represent a problem as to be analysed with ATLAS, or with any other CAQDAS packages. This argument is also noted by some commentators (Silverman, 2005; Mason, 2002). That is, more than an advantage it represented a disadvantage, because for a small scale project such as this, a non-CAQDAS analysis was more suitable (Silverman, 2005), or epistemologically effective (Mason, 2002: 164).

In addition, before the analysis of data, the author also reviewed the demo version in CD-ROM of the only software package found in the literature related specifically to community profiling: the *Compass for MS-Windows. The Community Profiling Software,* developed by the Policy Research Institute of the Leeds Metropolitan University, UK (Policy Research Institute, 2004). He commented about this software package with his supervisor after thoroughly reviewing the actual pool of 463 sample questions included in the CD-ROM for researchers to choose in order to tailor their own questionnaires. However it was also agreed not to use the full version of this package for these reasons: 1) because the interviews were already conducted by the time the candidate was aware of this package, hence it was not necessary to use or tailor any of the 463 sample questions of the software; 2) *Compass* was not a CAQDAS package, and if ATLAS which was an actual CAQDAS was already rejected, *Compass* could not suit the needs for computer-assisted analysis of qualitative research data because it entirely favoured the quantitative research approach by using a fixed questionnaire; and 3) this research project conducted community profiling entirely with qualitative research methodology and methods.

Thus, the choice for not using *strictly* a CAQDAS or any other specialised software package could not be seen as a major limitation for this project.

The next major section explains the procedures to obtain validity, replicability, neutrality, and generalization in this study.

2.6 Validity, replicability, neutrality, and generalization of the research project

These sections explain the various procedures that were considered in this thesis to assure validity, replicability, neutrality, and generalization or transferability.

The next section explains the procedure of validity.

2.6.1 Validity

Some views about validity are related to the operationalization of concepts, as a commentator from the qualitative research paradigm notes: "if your research is valid, it means that you are observing, identifying, or 'measuring' what you say you are. ... Validity is often associated with the 'operationalization' of concepts, a term more commonly associated with quantitative and experimental forms of research, but nevertheless one which encapsulates the idea that you need to be able to demonstrate that your concepts can be identified, observed or 'measured' in the way you say they can. You therefore need to work out how well a particular method and data source might illuminate your concepts, whatever they are" (Mason, 2002: 39).

In this sense, the three major concepts employed in this thesis: *the materialist conception of history, the social class struggles,* and *the configuration concept as an open structure of theory,* as has been explained above, identified, observed, and 'measured' other concepts, methodologies, methods, findings, conclusions, and recommendations as the author mentioned they would.

As for the *materialist conception of history* (see definition in Table 2.1 above), by researching about the materiality of the living conditions of the people of Broomhall (e.g. housing, parks, green spaces, playgrounds, shops), this concept helped the researcher to identify, observe, and 'measure' the major material features and issues which determined people's information needs.

As for the *social class struggles concept* (see definition in Table 2.1 above), it helped the researcher to identify, observe, and 'measure' how the people of Broomhall were divided by social classes, why conflicts and struggles emerged as derived from that division, and the implications this division had for people's information needs and their provision.

As for the *concept of configuration as an open structure of theory* (see definition in Table 2.1 above), it helped the author to identify, observe, and 'measure' the perceptions of respondents according to their own interpretations, and the author's interpretation. Likewise, the idea of beginning an open concept also helped the author to consider the procedures of data generation and analysis as a constant and open process of configuration of interpretations, analysis, discussions, findings, and ultimately conclusions and recommendations throughout the thesis.

Other views about validity are interrelated with reliability. A commentator has found this interrelation in this way from the quantitative or positivistic research paradigm: "a proof [or assessment, Muela-Meza, ZM] can be reliable, but not valid, but a proof cannot be valid if it is not reliable. In other words, reliability is a necessary condition, but not sufficient, for validity" (Salking, 1999: 129). Another elaborates on this interrelation, also from a positivistic paradigm: "It is, though, no good producing results which are reliable but wrong; the data need to be reliable *and right [sic]*. Only if they are right can the data be deemed *valid*" (Denscombe, 2002: 111).

In this sense, the data generation, and analysis, and the findings and overall presentation of the thesis, are therefore valid and reliable. However a commentator from the qualitative research paradigm argues that validity and reliability could not be assessed in the qualitative research paradigm in the same way as in the quantitative research or positivist paradigm, and that the process of *triangulation of methods* is a more adequate way to obtain validity and reliability in qualitative research (Golafshani, 2003).

In this sense, the next section will explain the *triangulation of methods* the author also employed in this thesis to obtain validity and reliability.

2.6.1.1   TRIANGULATION OF METHODS

A LIS researcher expert in community profiling (Beal, 1985: 47) observes that due to the nature of community profiling research, a single method will not be enough to capture sufficient and adequate data to come up with a sound and systematic analysis of the problems to be assessed. Thus, several methods have been applied in this project to bring about a rigorous validity and reliability. The lack of validity and reliability has often been criticised as a weakness of the qualitative research as some sociologists have pointed out (Smith, 2002: 37; Denscombe, 2003: 134). Thus, triangulation of methods extends the breadth of projects and improves the quality of the research; obviously, conclusions arrived at by using several different means are more likely to be correct, and accepted as such (Gorman and Clayton, 1997: 32).

Hence, one single method for data collecting or generation will not be enough to get valid results to support a research project, and therefore several methods should be used instead (Smith, 2002: 37; Denscombe, 2003: 134). This is called triangulation or the use of multi-methods or several methods in a kind of triangulation fashion as to obtain validity of the data collected for a research project. A social scientist (Green, 2000b: 27) called it *mixed method approach*. However, in itself the use of triangulation or multi-methods is not another type of method. Some commentators elaborate further mentioning that when conducting community profiling the use of triangulation of methods could breach the gap between the profilers and the people being 'profiled' (Moran and Butler, 2001: 72).

In this sense, as already explained above in this chapter in the section of *Rationale for choosing the qualitative research methods,* this study employed through this process of triangulations these methods: analysis of documents, non-participant observation, and focus groups and individual interviews.

The next section explains the procedure of replicability.

2.6.2 *Replicability*

Verification equates to the replicability found in a number of texts on qualitative research methodology. This relates essentially to the extent to which the research can be replicated, or verified.

Replication can be facilitated by the provision of a clear and transparent audit trail detailing the research processes and decisions taken by the researcher.

The next section describes the audit trail.

2.6.2.1   AUDIT TRAIL

The audit trail helps the reader to assess if the data generated are the genuine data. The audit trail is a trail that qualitative researchers leave so if they need to be audited for objectivity purposes, anyone in a given case could resort to check on it. In qualitative research it is inappropriate to talk of complete objectivity. Thus, what qualitative researchers can do, as Rice-Lively (1997) argues, is to build trustworthiness by "controlling the researcher's bias" through a well kept and thorough record keeping, the "audit trail."

Hence, this research project did actually take place and the data generated are genuine. All the documents employed in this thesis do actually exist, they were properly cited in the body of the thesis, and their actual bibliographic records are accessible in the Bibliography section. Most of them are accessible in libraries, or online (either on a pay-per-access, or free-of-charge Open Access), and those that belong to community centres include the names and addresses of those centres for actual further access.

As for the observation method, the author filled more than 1,000 pages of hand written diary notes. Furthermore, most of the observation outcomes are also recorded in 600+ pictures which are accessible online at the author's master PhD file free to everyone to see, download, copy, store, and print, without any copyright barrier (see Muela-Meza, 2003-2006). Hence, the reader can access free-of-charge this file (Muela-Meza, 2003-2006) and contrast the interpretations made by the author with the actual pictures taken. Furthermore, the reader can go to the actual places where the pictures were taken and corroborate that they are genuine.

Furthermore, the author has kept an electronic record of all the documents used as evidence or generated by him. This record has been backed-up in his laptop, in an external massive storage disk, and DVDs (amounting altogether more than 50 GB of documental information including the pictures). All the documents except the pictures are also backed-up printed on paper.

As for the interviews, the author has in his possession all the cassettes that show the evidence that the interviews took place and he has a copy of all the transcriptions and a detailed database with a comprehensive directory (*Broomhall directory of respondents*) with the profiles of each of the 32 respondents who actually took part in the research, but also of others who did not (see above in this chapter the section of *Procedure to obtain a balanced sample that reflects the different communities of Broomhall*, and Table 2.4 to assess the importance of this directory and the database fields).

Furthermore, the author accumulated 62 pages A4 size listing all the 1,860 e-mail messages of communication related to the data generation with actual and potential respondents through the University of Sheffield mailer, Yahoo, and Gmail. However, the actual communication is accessible online, but only by the author in order to keep the ethical consideration of data confidentiality and anonymity promised to respondents. Each message is on average 1 page long A4 size, so on average all of these messages amounted 1,860 pages long, but many included attachments. Thus, the cassettes containing the interviews, the transcriptions, and the private communication related to the research cannot be accessible to just anyone, but only to the author (not even to the respondents) on ethical grounds and the written promise of strict confidentiality and anonymity of the respondents, also on the grounds of security for all the stakeholders involved: respondents, supervisors, the University of Sheffield, and the author.

The audit trail can also facilitate checking of the accuracy and honesty of the research. This thesis can be accessed and read by anyone because the data and findings are reported genuinely and honestly without falling into logical fallacies such *ad hominem (*where persons are addressed personally instead of their arguments*). In this thesis only arguments were analysed, discussed, and reported but all respondents' identities and privacy were honestly protected and their perceptions were kept anonymous.

By doing all of that is how the choice of qualitative research methodologies became configured in the context and in the way that events happened. The people conducted the events, or how they said they did, or how the researcher interpreted they all did, or how a mix of all of them were configured, or combined through a sound triangulation of methods.

Thus, the generation of data was designed and actually conducted in two stages: the first was the pilot study (see above in this chapter), which lasted from 30 September 2003 until 18 October 2004, and the second was the main study (see above in this chapter), which lasted from 19 October 2004 until March 2006 .

The next section explains the neutrality process.

2.6.3 Neutrality

This section explains how the researcher obtained neutrality in the research project.

One historic debate at the core of social sciences lies on the objectivity of research; on how impartial, neutral, and unbiased it is. Whereas objectivity may be easy to be obtained in the natural sciences, in the social that is not case. That may be due in part to what Ford (1987: 23) points out that the phenomena in the social research could not be controlled in the same way as the ones of the natural sciences. Alternatively, it may be due also to the fact that in the social sciences, as Frías and Borrego (2004: 204) argue, "it is not possible to separate completely the subject –the researcher—from the object –the research phenomena."

Some commentators elaborate those ideas further by arguing that in the social sciences research can never be entirely objective (de la Garza Toledo, 2006; Denscombe, 2002: 157), or that in the qualitative research or naturalistic paradigm objectivity is an illusion (Rice-Lively, 1997: 185). However, the natural sciences cannot be entirely excluded from the subjectivity factor either. For instance a physicist (von Baeyer, 2003) argues that subjectivity is always present in order to make choices of what types of phenomena conduct research about, or which experiments to conduct from those phenomena, and with which instruments to make measurements, which in turn would become objective.

This controversy of the 'pure' objectivity in the quantitative research approaches versus the 'pure' subjectivity in the qualitative research approaches has been known as "the paradigm wars" (Bryman, 2006), or the "wars of science" (Sokal and Bricmont, 1999). However, some commentators note that these epistemological "wars" are fictitious (Sokal and Bricmont, 1999), and that instead there exist 'peace' (Bryman, 2006), or "methodological reconciliation" (Lawal, 2009). That is, quantitative and qualitative research paradigms both contain the subjective factor, and both can attain objectivity, because both are conducted by human beings, and human sciences (broadly speaking) encompass all kinds of sciences, either classified as natural, hard, social, soft, etc.

As for the social sciences where this project fits in, another commentator notes that "researchers need to be open-minded and self-reflective" (Denscombe, 2002: 158) for them to attain objectivity as it is best known in the quantitative or positivist paradigm. He explores the questions if research can really be impartial and unbiased, and if the findings are not inevitably biased by the researcher's prior attitudes and conceptions, and he answers them in this way:

> "The research has been designed, conducted, and reported in genuine spirit of exploration and the research explicitly acknowledges, as far as possible, the ways in which any vested interests, social values, and aspects of the researcher's self-identity have had a bearing on the nature of the research" (Denscombe, 2002: 157).

Likewise, the researcher has adhered to this spirit of Denscombe (2002) by having attained the most rigorous objectivity in order to conduct this doctoral research thesis through all of its different stages.

For instance, an important aspect related to neutrality is the ideological and political position of researchers with regards to their research projects. Hence, the researcher played only a mediatory role between the data generated (respondents' perceptions and interpretations, documents and observation), his own interpretation as a researcher noted it (Delanty, 2005: 171). In addition (as explained in section 2.3.3.2 within this chapter), the author conducted his research project acting as the outsider non-participant observer that he is to the Broomhall people without taking any ideological or political position towards any respondent or data source. And this approach was the one that best worked for this project. Otherwise, access to the neighbourhood or to all the participants in this research project would have been more difficult, or would have not worked at all. If it was not completely easy, it was not completely difficult either, a fine balance in approaching all sorts of groups (some of them highly conflicting amongst themselves) played well for everyone, especially for the researcher who could access other groups where conflicting groups could not. If the author had taken partisan sides with some individuals or groups then he would not have gained access to individuals of different or conflicting political and ideological views.

Furthermore, this position of being an outsider non-participant observer adopted by the author is worth mentioning here, because he lived within the Broomhall neighbourhood for 1 year and 10 months in two different time periods (nine months from October 2003 to July 2004, and one year and one month from July 2006 to August 2007). However, as mentioned in the section of the *Background to this study* in the Introduction (see Chapter 1) the author is a Mexican national student who only came to Sheffield to study a doctoral program in Information Studies at the University of Sheffield. That is, he was only a transient student resident of Broomhall who before 29

September 2003 had never lived in any locale within the UK. And the two occasions that he lived in Broomhall happened randomly because in those two times the only places for rent available were located within Broomhall.

Certainly, the author mingled as much as he could with neighbours in the two occasions he lived in Broomhall or in other different places in Sheffield, but simply like any other citizen would do living in a different place (e.g. saying hello to neighbours around his house, or when he saw them in corner shops, or pubs). But he never became a member of any community of the Broomhall neighbourhood. In that sense his research project could not be assessed as the views of an insider participant observer, because he never became a long-standing resident who has lived all of his life or for many years in the neighbourhood like a commentator suggests to be the case for an insider participant observer within a given neighbourhood (Smith, 2002). The author neither belonged to any organisation within Broomhall in order to become an insider participant observer within an organisation as suggested by another commentator (Labaree, 2002).

Therefore, that being said, the researcher never participated at all with people, or events from the Broomhall neighbourhood as far as the non-participant observation method is concerned (see the explanation of this method above in section 2.3.3.2 within this chapter). Thus, the reader can be assured that the researcher, by not having conducted his research project as an insider observer by taking political or ideological sides with the people, and their events within the Broomhall neighbourhood, guaranteed the most ethical, unbiased, and objective approach to the employment of the method of non-participant observation.

Nevertheless, after this thesis had been made public (see Chapter 7 to assess the different forms this thesis is going to be communicated), and its readers (e.g. Broomhall people) would like to consider any of its contributions as a documental information source to carry out either political or ideological actions, or further research, or other, then those would be the readers' sole responsibility or action, and their own interpretation of the author's own original interpretation as written within the thesis. The author is responsible for what he has analysed, discussed, and reported here, but he cannot bear any further responsibility of how Broomhall readers, or any other readers interpret this thesis.

Furthermore, by not having conducted the observation method as a participant observer (e.g. taking political or ideological sides with people of the Broomhall neighbourhood), that does not mean that the researcher is devoid of his own world view, subjectivity, and ideologies. As explained above within this chapter relating to the limitations of the method of interviews (see section 2.3.3.3.2, and after Lenin, [1908], 1964 and Ilyenkov, 1960; 1977), no human being is devoid of his or her own world view, subjectivity, and ideologies. However, as explained above in this section, in order to attain objectivity and neutrality, the author put his world view, subjectivity, and ideologies aside and let the data configure the overall interpretation of the thesis following the spirit of Denscombe (2002: 157) mentioned above. Or like Sagan and Druyan would put it: "We humans are biased observers, with a vested interest in the answer. The cure for this disease is more data" (1992: 400). Thus, the reader could value the objectivity of this thesis according to the data generated, analysed, discussed, and reported.

Another aspect related to neutrality is to give equal treatment to all data sources by presenting views in favour as well as competing views of an argument. Hence, an equal treatment has been given to all data sources analysed, discussed, and presented in this thesis by intertwining in a balanced manner the different perceptions (e.g. from interviewees, or from the literature, or the author's own analysis from observation, interviews, and literature review). In addition, the analyses, discussions, and findings have been presented "disinterestedly" as a physicist would put it (Feynman, 2001: 108), and only for the sake of knowledge (Hawking, 1988: 13). That is, only for the sake of having shed sufficient sources of light to illuminate the phenomena under research and to make a sound but humble contribution to the wealth of human knowledge where conclusions and recommendations can be drawn for the benefit of the different actors related to this research (e.g. Broomhall residents and information providers, library and information science practitioners, policy makers).

Another important aspect of the neutrality process is "to acknowledge any vested interests in the research or sources of sponsorship that could potentially compromise the objectivity of the findings" (Denscombe, 2002: 171). Accordingly, the author declares that he has not had any vested interests of any kind in this research; he has had only a genuine pursuit of knowledge for its own sake. Neither the author nor his sponsor CONACYT has any vested interest in the research.

The next section explains the generalization or transferability of this thesis.

2.6.4 Generalization or transferability

Some researchers (Silverman, 2005; Mason, 2002) note that qualitative research cannot be assessed with the same degrees of generalizability as in positivist paradigms. However, provided that someone conducted research in a similar scenario and context such as Broomhall, then some of the findings of this thesis might be generalized or transferrable to different scenarios with similar characteristics. Nevertheless, those possible generalizations of findings could not be made in the same way like in positivistic research, since qualitative research is rooted within the context under study. In this case, this project was comprehensively rooted and shaped by the historical and territorial features of Broomhall, which are very unlikely to be repeated in any other neighbourhood within or outside UK with different historical and territorial features.

In this sense, when researchers and practitioners conduct research based on this thesis, they could relate the eight major findings (and information needs) that emerge from this study to their studies. Not by making a literal translation, but by pointing out that these findings might also emerge in future studies, provided that the various concepts, methodologies and methods used, and the factors analysed here were similar to theirs.

2.7 Summary

This chapter has shown the reader all the methodological steps taken into consideration to conduct this doctoral research through its different stages (from methodological design through data generation and analysis, and reporting of the findings, discussions, conclusions and recommendations), and it has also explained how the measures of validity, replicability, neutrality, and generalization were achieved.

The chapter was divided into five major sections: a) theoretical framework, b) rationale for choosing a qualitative research methodology, c) design of the data generation, d) design of the data analysis, and e) the processes of to obtain validity, replicability, neutrality, and generalization or transferability of the research project.

As for the theoretical framework, it highlighted the ideas that support employing a theoretical framework within the qualitative research methodology. Instead of employing a theoretical framework solely based on *deductive reasoning* (where theory is used at the beginning of the research process), or *inductive reasoning* (where theory emerges at the end), this project, building on the ideas of Mason (2002: 180-181), employed an *abductive or retroductive reasoning*. This is a flexible and open mixture of the other two notions, but it allowed the author to employ concepts deductively, but with an inductive flexibility, and adapt them going back and forth from the early to the later stages of the research project in order to adapt on a continuum the theoretical framework to the findings, and vice versa in order to obtain theoretical consistency throughout the thesis.

The conceptual scheme of the theoretical framework included these concepts: a) the concept of the materialist conception of history, b) the social class struggles concept (the classes employed in this study were: working, middle and capitalist or bourgeois), and c) the concept of configuration as an open structure of theory. In Table 2.1 (see above) the concepts are defined as employed in this thesis and the interrelationships with other concepts (including a reference to the chapters where they are found in the thesis) are explained. A rationale for choosing each concept, and some of their views in favour and competing views are analysed.

As for the views in favour of the Marxist materialist conception of history, it was found as an adequate concept to analyse the material conditions of living of the people of Broomhall and the material conditions of the neighbourhood through the methods of non-participant observation, and interviews, since this project was geographically delimited. The competing views of this concept were found more politically or ideologically inspired in idealist philosophical conceptions against Marxism than on sound epistemological grounds.

As for the views in favour of the *social class struggles* concept, it emerged in the pilot study that Broomhall had some conflicts caused by social class divide. The author re-conceptualised the Marxist philosophical concept of *social class struggle* and added to it the concept of the *dominance hierarchy* from the natural sciences in order to understand why society is divided in social classes, and why contradictions, conflicts, and struggles emerge those social classes. The competing views of this concept were found related to the postmodernist notions of *social capital* and *community cohesion*. However these notions, besides the fact of not having been accepted as sound concepts within social science epistemology, failed to address the contradictions, conflicts, and struggles as they emerged in this study.

As for the methodology employed in this thesis, the qualitative research methodology, and particularly interpretivism or interpretivist approach, proved to be the most adequate approach for the purposes of this study. The qualitative research methods employed through the process of *triangulation of methods* were analysis of documents, non-participant observation, and interviews (individually and through focus groups).

As for the design of data generation, the study employed purposing sampling through snowball or chain sampling. A database was created by the author (*Directory of Broomhall respondents),* where he used throughout the process of data generation to assure a balanced sample reflecting the different communities within Broomhall. This balance could only be attained for respondents of the working and middle classes from sections A, B, and C of Broomhall, as no member of the capitalist or bourgeois class could be interviewed. However, perceptions of the latter from the literature could be triangulated with the perceptions of the actual interviewees to overcome that limitation. Hence, only 32 individuals were interviewed: 24 residents, and 8 information providers. From the pilot study an interview schedule was designed to conduct two focus groups with Broomhall residents with five questions to appraise the major features of Broomhall and where residents find information. In the main study the questions of interview schedule of the pilot study were maintained, improved, and two more questions were added to differentiate the three types of respondents: focus group residents, individual residents, and information providers.

As for the design of data generation, the theoretical analysis of data was made literally (when excerpts from interviews transcripts or literature were cited literally) and interpretatively (as the author analysed and discussed data). As for the structure of the analysis of data, the eight major findings analysed in Chapter 5 were presented from the more negative to the more positive, since Broomhall emerged as having more negative issues than positive features. As for the methodological analysis of data, it was conducted through the generation, analysis, and writing of data blended into one another (Linley and Usherwood, 1998: 15), by following the pattern of the five themes that emerged in the pilot study that became transformed into the eight major findings of the main study.

Finally, the study followed rigorous procedures to obtain validity, replicability, neutrality, and generalization or transferability throughout the different stages and processes of data generation and analysis and the presentation of the findings, conclusions, recommendations, and further research that emerged in the project. Validity was obtained through the operationalization of the three working concepts of the theoretical framework, and through the triangulation of methods. Replicability is related to verification, and this was obtained through the presentation of a detailed audit trail that explained the research processes and decisions taken by the author. Neutrality was obtained through: a) a disclaim of any vested interests of the author with any sponsor, b) a mediatory role played by the author as an outsider non-participant observer between the respondents' perceptions and actions, instead of any standpoint, or partisan, or insider role, and c) through an equal treatment and presentation of views in favour and competing views of the data analysed and discussed. Generalization or transferability is suggested methodologically where the findings of this thesis might be transferable to some extent to other contexts by considering similar concepts, methodologies, and methods employed here, and that other contexts might be similar to Broomhall.

The next chapter is devoted to a comprehensive review of the literature related to the main elements of this thesis: community profiling tool, information needs, and information provision.

3. REVIEW OF THE LITERATURE

"80. Caution when getting informed. We live more of what we hear than what we see. We live of someone else's faith. Hearing is the second door of truth and the main for lie. Ordinarily truth is seen, and exceptionally is heard." — Baltasar Gracián, Huesca, Spain, 1647 (Gracián, [1647] 1993: 47) (Translation Muela-Meza, ZM).

"If information could be passed on merely by word of mouth, how little we should know of our past, how slow would be our progress! Everything would depend on what ancient findings we had accidentally been told about, and how accurate the account was. Past information might be revered, but in successive retellings it would become progressively more muddled and eventually lost. Books permit us to voyage through time, to tap the wisdom of our ancestors." –Carl Sagan, *Cosmos* (Sagan, 2001: 282)

3.1 Introduction

This chapter presents a literature review about the three key elements of this project: the community profiling tool, and the concepts of information needs, and information providers. It explains the different definitions and approaches found in the literature that served as a theoretical background for this study. Hence, the reader can assess their scope, limitations, and interrelationships with other concepts, approaches, terms, and keywords from the rest of the thesis.

The chapter is grouped into three major sections:

The first major section explains the community profiling tool and its integral parts. These are grouped as follows: a) the concept of *community,* b) the community profiling tool (this includes: 1) merging of community analysis into the community profiling tool, 2) community profiling as a tool, 3) implementation and definition of the community profiling tool, 4) community profiling based on territoriality, and 5) effectiveness of community profiling in LIS.

The second major section addresses the concept of information needs and its integral parts. These are grouped as follows: a) the concept of need (which includes: 1) a relatively broad materialist conception of need, 2) a narrower conception of need and "bottom up" research approaches), b) the concept of information (which includes the concept of documental information needs).

The third major section addresses the concept of information providers and its integral parts. These are grouped as follows: a) the working definition of information providers, and b) type of provision: information, advice, or help.

The next major section is the community profiling tool.

3.2 The community profiling tool

These sections will explain the community profiling tool and its integral parts. The next section explains the *community* concept.

3.2.1   The community concept

It can be stated that there are definitions of *community* as there are definitions about anything; as there are people talking and writing about it or about anything. To illustrate this, the *Chambers Dictionary* (2003) in its ninth edition records 56 derivations of the term *community*. A LIS commentator in 1992 mentioned that there were at least 90 variations of the term *community* (Usherwood, 1992: 19). The variations of *community* show the remarkable fact that this term has meant so much for humankind as does the term *society* since its inception in history. Hence, as much as it has been written about in human history, the term *community* has always been one of those perennial topics. In addition, *community* has not only been written as tangentially related to any of its many senses, but it has specifically been the topic of many books relating to it at a theoretical and epistemological level, like the book *Community* recently written by the British sociologist Gerard Delanty (2003), whose ideas provide more clarity to help underpin the concepts linked to *community* in this project.

In this project, there is awareness that there might be many variations of *community*, however, in order to bring clarity to what is going to be understood as a *community*, the definition from the *Chambers (2003)* English language dictionary is going to be the basic starting definition to be employed here. However, this is just a starting definition as the project has configured another definition more adequate to its findings (see below in this chapter).

Community noun (*communities*) 1 a the group of people living in a particular place; b the place in which they live. 2 a group of people bonded together by a common religion, nationality or occupation [e.g.] *the Asian community*. 3 a religious or spiritual fellowship of people living together. 4 the quality or fact of being shared or common [e.g.] *community of interests*. 5 a group of states with common interests. 6 the public; society in general. 7 [*in biology*] a naturally occurring group of different plant or animal species that occupy the same habitat and interact with each other. ETYMOLOGY: 14c: from Latin *communitas* fellowship, from *communis* common.

This definition above is succinct, sufficient and clear, especially from its Latin etymologies of *communitas* meaning "fellowship," or from *communis* meaning "common." Therefore, the essence of the term *community* is derived precisely from its etymologies in its early inception in Latin in the 14th century meaning a *fellowship* of several people and meaning they had something in *common*. Hence, by looking at the above definition in more detail these are the senses in which this study is employing the term *community* as a starting point:

Sense 1: A. The group of people living in a particular place.

This could be the group of people who live in the boundaries of the Broomhall neighbourhood. The community profiling tool was employed here to profile the features of these groups of people living in the neighbourhood of Broomhall.

Sense 1. B. The place in which they live.

The place in which people live, which could be the Broomhall neighbourhood. The community profiling tool was employed here to profile the geographical features of this neighbourhood of Broomhall.

Sense 2. A group of people bonded together by a common religion, nationality or occupation, e.g. *the Asian community*.

In the Broomhall neighbourhood there are several groups of people bonded together by common features, like religions (there are Christians, Moslems, Catholics, and so on), nationalities (although all the people there tend to be of British nationality by naturalisation, some people are bonded there by their original nationality backgrounds such as Somalis, Pakistanis, Yemenis, Jamaican), and others. The community profiling tool was employed here to profile the features of these groups of people living in the neighbourhood of Broomhall bonded by these common ties.

Sense 3. A religious or spiritual fellowship of people living together.

In the Broomhall neighbourhood there are different religious or spiritual fellowships of people living together like those mentioned above. The community profiling tool was employed here to profile the features of these groups of people living in the neighbourhood of Broomhall and their religious or spiritual fellowships and others alike.

Sense 4. The quality or fact of being shared or common, e.g. *community of interests*.

In the Broomhall neighbourhood like in any geographical area in the world where people live, there are different groups of people bonded by different shared or common features: language, nationalities, religions, and so on. The community profiling tool was employed here to profile these features.

Going beyond this basic definition from the language dictionary, this project also holds the idea that people bonded by different symbolic ties such as nationalities, religions, languages, geography and others, they do so by belonging to each other as a group or looking or longing to belong to each other. Delanty explains this concept of belonging like this:

> "Community offers people what neither society nor the state can offer, namely a sense of belonging in an insecure world. However, community also destroys this by demonstrating the impossibility of finality. The new kinds of community are themselves, like the wider society, too fragmented and pluralized to offer enduring forms of belonging" (Delanty, 2003: 192).

The author agrees with Delanty's sense of belonging that people seek through community. In addition, another assertion this project agrees with Delanty's notions about *community* is the way that he defines community as an essentially communicative world.

> "It is in this essentially communicative world that community is revived. In going beyond the symbolic approach of community, I am arguing for a more pronounced constructive approach. The notion of community as a "symbolic construction" suggests a too affirmative sense of community, neglecting its capacity for cultural transformation. It is in this stronger constructivist sense that I argue that community is communicative – communicative of new cultural codes of belonging.... Whether in the form of the numerous nationalisms, ethnicities, multicultural, and communitarian politics, the new and essentially post traditional assertions of community allow little room for a shared public culture, although they presuppose the possibility of shared values... The forms of community are multiple and are expressed in communicative structures that are essentially abstract or imagined –they do not correspond to something clearly visible or to an underlying identity" (Delanty, 2003: 191).

Therefore, *community* is considered in this project, after Delanty (2003), as a communicative mechanism people pursue in order to obtain a sense of belonging with other people. However, in this project, as explained below in this chapter, the geographical boundaries of Broomhall (see also further explanation in Chapter 4) were also employed in order to obtain a spatial area where the community profiling tool could be applied. In addition, as explained below in this chapter, the way that the *community profiling tool* was found effective for library and information science is interrelated to territoriality.

The next section explains the *community profiling tool*.

3.2.2   The community profiling tool

These sections explain the *community profiling tool* employed in this thesis. These are grouped as follows: 1) merging of the community analysis into the community profiling tool, 2) community profiling based on territoriality, 3) community profiling in library and information science (LIS), 4) historical issues in defining LIS geographical boundaries, and 5) effectiveness of community profiling in LIS.

The next section explains the merging of the *community analysis* into the *community profiling tool*.

3.2.2.1   MERGING OF COMMUNITY PROFILING AND COMMUNITY ANALYSIS

This section explains the merging of the *community analysis* into the *community profiling tool*.

Community profiling and *community analysis* have been considered the same in this study under the name of *community profiling tool*. However, through the literature review they have been found as different terminologies. For instance, *community analysis* was found as a standardized thesaurus descriptor from some scientific peer-reviewed bibliographic databases such as Library and Information Science Abstracts (LISA), Social Science Citation Index, and Sociological Abstracts (see Chapter 2 above for a comprehensive review of all the databases used in this project). On the other hand, *community profiling* was not found in the literature reviewed as an internationally standardised thesaurus descriptor.

There is mixed use of the terms community profiling and community analysis in the literature, some authors preferring the former (e.g. Beal, 1985; Chagari, 2005; Roddy, 2005; Budnick, 2006; and Long, 2006), others the latter (e.g. Satyanarayana, 1997; Sarling and Van Tassel, 1999; Westbrook, 2000; 2001; and Worcester and Westbrook, 2004). However, the one single author from the social work field who has conducted more research on community profiling than any other LIS author is Green (e.g. 1996a; 1996b; 1996c; 1997; 2000a; 2000b; 2000c; 2005).

Hence, the rationale behind the merging of *community analysis* into the *community profiling tool* was due to this fact that most of the sources reviewed for this study employed *community profiling*.

The next section explains the community profiling as a tool.

3.2.2.2   COMMUNITY PROFILING AS A TOOL

This section explains the community profiling as a tool.

The author has made sure that the reader when reading this thesis will find a clear connection of the terminology of *community profiling* with a *tool;* that is, *community profiling* being a *tool*. This clarification is relevant, because other commentators do not find this connection. For instance, Kalyane, and Devarai (1994: 91) who analysed the community profiling tool in relation to public libraries noted that a community profiling is not a tool, but a method to predict needs and wants of a given community. Another author (Calva González, 2004: 228) notes that *community studies* is the equivalent to what has been considered here as *community profiling*. However, this terminology of *community studies* has not been epistemologically accepted in the literature reviewed (e.g. Green, 2005; 2000a; 2000b; 2000c; 1997; 1996a; 1996b; 1996c; Hawtin, Hughes, and Percy-Smith, 1994; Beal, 1985; Jordan and Walley,1977). In addition, *community studies,* however being found equivalent to the *community profiling tool* as employed here, still poses a major methodological problem. This commentator (Calva González, 2004: 228), along with those mentioned above (Kalyane, and Devarai, 1994: 91), confuses a tool (his *community studies)* with a method. However, a tool cannot be a method, because a tool is an instrument employed to analyse or measure research problems, and a method is a procedure of how to employ tools, or other instruments to generate, and analyse data relating those research problems.

However, these commentators (Kalyane, and Devarai, 1994: 91; Calva González, 2004: 228) are not alone in their methodological confusion, the author (Muela-Meza, 2003a) during his first months of his PhD program also showed a methodological confusion of the *community profiling* tool by classifying it, as a general qualitative research methodology. In the case of the author, he wrote this paper (2003a) on 17 September 2003 as part of a literature review on qualitative research methodology which eventually got published in 2006 when a journal editor saw it as a pre-print in the author's self-archiving at E-LIS (Muela-Meza, 2006b). Hence, he could not make the proper corrections and the 2006 journal version is the same as the 2003 pre-print. However, from 2004 onwards, the author realised the nature of the methodological confusion, and the self-critique he is now exercising is evidence that he has self-corrected his mistake. Hence, he solved his confusion, based on the further empirical research he conducted from 2004 onwards and the reporting of the findings, discussions, conclusions and recommendations of this thesis.

In the case of the journal article by Kalyane and Devarai (1994), they have not conducted any empirical research for that paper and they have not published anything else related to information needs, or community profiling, or at least anything that the author is aware of. They mainly focused on empathy of the service in public libraries. Hence, the author is reporting the confusion of these authors to show evidence that he has assessed thoroughly the literature at great depth of detail on a global scope (these authors are from India), both in English and Spanish languages. However, he has not found any major epistemological consequences that would be relevant to this study.

Nevertheless, in the case of Calva González (2004) this methodological confusion might have some methodological consequences for the international epistemological community of LIS. This is due to the fact that he has been researching the phenomena of *information needs at* least since 1991 (Calva González, 1991). Calva González (1991; 2004), and has made a master's dissertation on the same topic (1991) and a doctoral thesis (2004) entitled: *Information Needs: Theoretical Foundations and Methods.*

However, the main issue concerning this author's (Calva González, 1991; 2004) work is that he has devised his 'theoretical foundations and methods' without having conducted any empirical research, neither in his master's dissertation (Calva González, 1991), nor in his PhD thesis (Calva González, 2004). Both studies (Calva González, 1991; 2004) are simply comprehensive literature reviews, and his research papers too. What might have some adverse methodological consequences for the Spanish speaking LIS practitioners who might read his book, is precisely his confusion of a *tool* with a *method.*

Some researchers from the social sciences out of the LIS field (Hawtin, Hughes, and Percy-Smith, 1994: 12-13), observe that needs assessments, social audits, community consultations, and community profiles, while they share certain features, can be distinguished from each other in terms of the agencies that are typically involved, the purpose of the exercise, the extent of community involvement and the scope of the exercise. They note that a community profiling is probably the broadest of these terms.

The next section explains how the *community profiling tool* was implemented in this study.

3.2.2.3   IMPLEMENTATION AND DEFINITION OF THE COMMUNITY PROFILING TOOL

This section explains how the *community profiling tool* was implemented in this study.

Most of the authors in the LIS literature reviewed have addressed the issue that *community profiles* should be considered as the first step for planning in a particular library to know about its community to be served. For instance in public libraries (e.g. Jordan and Walley, 1977; Ewart, 2004; Roddy, 2005; Louie, 1976; Sarling and Van Tassel, 1999; Satyanarayana, 1997; Amorós i Fontanals, 2000; Galluzzi, 2001; Kaniki, 2001). Others have used it in academic libraries (e.g. Westbrook, 2000; 2001; Worcester and Westbrook, 2004).

However, the present research project can be distinguished fundamentally from those authors mentioned above by not having applied the *community profiling* tool for any specific documental information institution (DII) (e.g. libraries), or documental information professionals (DIPs) (e.g. librarians), but only for the sake of knowledge and discovery. Only for the sake of conducting empirical research regardless of any practical applications, but to learn tools (e.g. community profiling), methodologies (e.g. qualitative research interpretivism), and methods (e.g. analysis of documents, interviews, observation). Thus, this project has been conducted more as a critical exercise of a theoretical type rather than practical.

Hence, this thesis has implemented the community profiling tool as rigorous empirical research project, instead of a loose and short report of any on-the-desk pragmatic literature review (comprising mainly outdated census statistics) like has been the tradition of most LIS and non-LIS community profiles. For instance this tradition can be appraised through time, e.g. from the 1970s (e.g. Bedfordshire County Library, 1975), or the 1980s (Harrison, 1982; Backhouse, 1986; Borough of Sunderland Department of Recreation and Libraries, 1986), or the 1990s (e.g. Manzi, 1993; Warwickshire County Library, 1991), or even in the 2000s (e.g. Sheffield City Council, 2006b; Whitehead and Rowan, 2005; North West Museums Service, 2002).

This is the working definition of the *community profiling* tool employed in this study.

"[The community profiling tool is] A comprehensive description of the needs of a population that is defined, or defines itself, as a community, and the resources that exist within that community, carried out with the purpose of developing an action plan or other means of improving the quality of life of the community" (Hawtin, Hughes, and Percy-Smith, 1994: 12-

13).

The next section analyses the *community profiling tool* based on territoriality and history.

3.2.2.4   COMMUNITY PROFILING BASED ON TERRITORIALITY AND HISTORY

This section analyses the *community profiling tool* based on territoriality and history.

In order to analyse the communities' information needs from a given geographically limited neighbourhood, and the levels of information provision according to these needs, LIS practitioners need to use a tool, methodologies, and methods to conduct such research. The community profiling tool, the qualitative research methodology of interpretivism, and the qualitative research methods (analysis of documents, interviews and observation) have been considered the most adequate to conduct this doctoral research.

All human created or mediated geographical boundaries as with all human creations necessarily have to do with the non-human and human historical facts that precede them. LIS as well as all the disciplines are not the exception to that fact. Hence, this section explores the historical issues in defining LIS geographical boundaries.

From the literature reviewed, a multi-cited LIS community profiling expert (Beal, 1985) found three major forms of how librarians and other *documental information professionals* (DIPs) could identify the geographical boundaries where their library users live, study, or work. By: a) the library users' catchment area where a library serves; b) the conceptions of community by residents where a library serves; and c) the census and local government boundaries (Beal, 1985; 28).

This project conducted research to investigate the information needs and issues of the people who live in the Broomhall *territorial* neighbourhood and how documental information professionals (DIPs) satisfied their needs or addressed their issues through their information provision. However, by considering Broomhall as a geographical area in a broader citywide sense, that is like a neighbourhood (e.g. Greig, Parry and Rimmington, 2003: 258; Smith, 2002: 37), rather than as a given particular library's catchment area of library users, and by considering DIPs in the broader sense as members of any documental information institutions (DIIs) and not just libraries. Hence, the observation of defining the geographical boundaries of Broomhall as "a library catchment area" by Beal (1985) is not employed here.

As for Beal's (1985) second observation on community boundaries as defined by the residents' perceptions of a given community, she noted that: "The boundaries of such areas are now often extremely vague, it would take considerable field research in the locality to be able to tease out local perceptions of community boundaries and it is uncertain whether, for our purposes [of librarians carrying out community profiling for library services provision], such exercise would be either valid or worthwhile" (Beal, 1985: 32).

Then, she moved on to explain her third observation by noting in her manual that librarians or any other DIPs, in order to make a valid and worthwhile community profiling exercise, they have to employ local government and census data: "the main administrative units to be considered here [in her manual of *Community Profiling for Librarians*] for use to community studies are local government and census areas" (Beal, 1985: 34). And despite the fact that she addressed few disadvantages of employing any of these three ways to define the community, particularly because they are mutually excluding, she was evidently more in favour of the use of census and local government data to define community boundaries and hence to conduct the community profiling or analysis.

Beal's (1985) local government and census geographical boundaries were not considered here as completely valid or free from contrasting arguments as it is explained below in this chapter (see Chapter 4 for further analysis of the working boundaries of Broomhall). This is due to the nature of the qualitative research methodology employed here. Furthermore, Beal's (1985) analysis, which has been more focused on the quantitative research paradigm instead of the qualitative as explained in Chapter 2, presents an analytical gap, because she has missed some important elements relating to the historical and political elements involved in the definition of communities' boundaries. For instance, she (Beal, 1985) did not consider the roles that history and politics played behind the configuration of community geographical boundaries by census and local authority perceptions.

Hence, she (Beal, 1985) found the idea of people's perceptions of community boundaries as subjective, and vague, and instead she considered census and local authority boundaries as objective. However, in reality, those forms of boundaries have been since their inception and through their historical development, being shaped by humans; hence, human subjectivity is implicit in every human creation or forms of expression. Moreover, since they have been created by humans over historic time, then those people who created them have introduced in different ways their or someone else's political conceptions, or ideologies, which issue Beal (1985) has not been sufficiently addressed.

Beal's (1985) gap has been filled by two community profiling experts in LIS, Jordan and Walley (1977), on whose work Beal (1985) built hers. Unlike Beal (1985), they (Jordan and Walley, 1977) identified that "history of the community is an important element in any understanding and something of the history should be included" (Jordan and Walley, 1977:29-30). It should be clarified nevertheless, that Beal (1985) did not reject all notions of history from her manual, she did in fact consider some kind of history, but related only with the history of the economic structure of a given community (Beal, 1985: 54), but she did not consider history in itself as it is considered by Jordan and Walley (1977), and the author of this thesis.

On the other hand, Jordan and Walley (1977), unlike Beal (1985), did indeed put strong emphasis on the people's perceptions of their own neighbourhoods: "we think the best guide, as often is the case, lies with the perceptions of the community members, the psychological feelings of belonging and shared interest in a geographical area ... others have defined communities in different ways or simply drawn lines on maps [where] there is a difficulty in collecting statistics on the area e.g. ward boundaries may differ from our definitions" (Jordan and Walley, 1977: 29). Hence, "communities, especially where they are self-defined, do not normally fit ward boundaries, postcode areas, police subdivisions, health districts or local authorities service boundaries" (Hawtin, Hughes and Percy-Smith, 1994: 64).

After all being said, the findings of this doctoral study have given an updated corroboration of Jordan and Walley's (1977) suggestions on defining geographical boundaries according to people's perceptions on a given time when a research project takes place. Hence, the geographical boundaries of Broomhall are defined primarily by its residents' perceptions following the "bottom-up" approach by Green (2000a: 22), where residents identified and analysed "their problems and needs within the wider context of their lives," but also underpinned on human historic facts of the communities within their neighbourhood.

The next section explains the effectiveness of *community profiling* in library and information science (LIS).

3.2.2.5 EFFECTIVENESS OF COMMUNITY PROFILING IN LIBRARY AND INFORMATION SCIENCE (LIS)

This section explains the effectiveness of *community profiling* in library and information science (LIS).

First, the working definition of effectiveness is explained.

"It is the human action of: having power to effect (to produce, or to accomplish, or to bring about); causing something; being successful in producing a result or effect; being powerful; of being serviceable; of being actual; of being in force" (*Chambers Dictionary, 2003*).

Thus, the community profiling tool has been found still effective for LIS as long as it is related to the concept of territoriality and to the notions of social needs rooted in the materialist conception of history (see above Table 2.1 in Chapter 2 for further explanation).

For the community profiling to be effective, practitioners should distinguish between community and neighbourhood (or any other group of people geographically or spatially circumscribed). Community as in Delanty (2005) is a group of people united by intangible bonds, but neighbourhood, in line with the materialist conception of history (see Table 2.1 for a definition in Chapter 2) is a materially grounded spatial place where communities might live in, or work.

Thus, all the notions of community profiling as portraying communities as intangible without any relation to territoriality might be limited and might not assess well any given territorial location. This is because, for instance, if a library is being planned to be built in any given geographical location, if people only think of the human communities (users) who might use the library without any relation to the materially conditioned physical and environmental conditions related to the territorial location, then that planning would be limited and inadequate. Hence, that implementation of community profiling would be ineffective. Likewise, if any implementation of community profiling only focuses on territoriality and forgets about human communities, then it would also be ineffective.

Therefore, an effective model for an implementation of community profiling would be that which combines human communities and natural material territoriality. Human communities do not live (or work, enjoy, suffer, etc.) in the vacuum, or in the void, or in the ether, or on any virtual communicational and informational human-made machine (e.g. Internet). They need by *sine qua non* condition to live (and do anything else, work, enjoy, suffer, etc.) in any given material territory where the provision of goods for the satisfaction of their needs (e.g. information recorded in documents) can be obtained (including information recorded in documents, help, advice, and so on).

Hence, those research models, which claim to approach community profiling without any relation to territoriality, should be assessed sceptically. Because as far as the physical natural laws of the cosmos are concerned, any science and technology (either theoretically or experimentally developed) needs a territorial cosmic matter to be based on.

Furthermore, a community profiling can be more effective when the datasets employed are empirically generated by first hand as primary data generated by the researchers, because although there might be other territoriality-based studies such as Creaser (1999) or Bath et.al. (2005) which may resemble a territorial community profiling study, their limitations lie in their use of secondary datasets, which are generated mainly by government census and statistics, and by the time they employ them they might be already outdated. Moreover, as explained above (see Chapter 4), studies which employ census datasets (e.g. Creaser, 1999; Bath, et. al, 2005) such as enumeration districts (EDs) or super output areas (SOAs) fail to make precise territorial matches, as they were conducted here by physical observation on the ground, and people's perceptions. That is, focusing on territoriality for effective community profiling is not enough, it is also necessary that one makes use of qualitative research methods such as observation and interviews.

The next major section explains the concept of information needs and its integral parts.

3.3 The concept of Information needs

This section explains the concept of information needs and its integral parts. The next section explains the concept of need.

3.3.1 The concept of need

The analysis of information needs begins with the analysis of the concept of need. The next section explains a relatively broad materialist conception of need.

3.3.1.1 A RELATIVELY BROAD MATERIALIST CONCEPTION OF NEED

This is a definition of need from *Chambers Dictionary* (2003):

> "Need. n. Lack of something which cannot well do without; necessity; a state that requires relief, such as extreme poverty or distress; lack of means of living. V.t. To have occasion for; to want; to require; to require or to be required to do something."

As explained in Chapter 2, this project underpins its theoretical foundations from several concepts (see also Table 2.1 for a definition of concepts). A fundamental concept is the *materialist conception of history* which namely gives primacy to the materiality of the cosmos (Earth, flora, fauna, life, and so on), over its idealist spirituality.

Therefore, this conceptualization of need based on the *materialist conception of history* was found to be of paramount importance for this thesis, because it has given clarity to the project. This materialistic concept of need has given a sound background to this project, which has imbricated nicely with the data generated or configured throughout the study.

Nevertheless, the author is cognizant of some other theories that reject the materialist view of needs. For example, there is a psychologist (Maslow, 2005) who has been an important reference for the conceptualisation of needs, and he disagrees with the materialist views of needs. He (Maslow, 2005: 247) criticises that there are other superior human needs which are not material, such as: protection, dependence, security, friendship, affection, respect, love, acceptance, dignity, self-respect, and freedom that are as basic as the material needs (e.g. food, shelter, clothing, etc.), and very important for the self-realization of humans.

However, even though Maslow's (2005) view of needs disagrees with materialism, still his assertions can be integrated to the materialist conception of needs of this thesis. Because, for humans, in order to need, give, and receive love, affection, friendship, and so on, as explained by Maslow (2005), they need before everything else to be alive, and they need to have covered all the material needs. Hence, the author does not see much contradiction in Maslow's (2005) conceptualisation with the materialist approach employed here.

The next section explains a narrower conception of need and "bottom up" research approaches.

3.3.1.2 A NARROWER CONCEPTION OF NEED AND "BOTTOM UP" RESEARCH APPROACHES

This section explains a narrower conception of need and "bottom up" research approaches.

Green, a social work scientist who has been conducting research for some years into the poor, the marginalised, and the oppressed (e.g. 2000a; 2000c), has built a conceptualization of *needs* which fits with the broader *materialist conception of need* explained above, in line with the *materialist conception of history* (as explained in Chapter 2). Green has made a strong case against what he calls the "top down" paradigm of *needs,* or research on needs, or needs assessment or community needs profiling.

He argues that "top down" research approaches to the needs of people in their communities by excluding the needs of the poor, marginalised, and oppressed groups of society: "The needs and daily experiences of ordinary people particularly those in marginalised and oppressed groups such as clients, users, and receivers of services are ignored." (Green, 2000c: 21).

He argues that most of the researchers of the "top down" paradigm appraise needs as normative needs, in the way that city council, statutory, and voluntary sector professionals, politicians and powerful and dominant groups, or agencies, in society ascribe them. However, these normative needs focus only on expressed needs and avoid felt needs: "The expressed needs elicited by the research were 'felt' needs grounded in their personal, family, and collective experiences of living on a much stigmatised and impoverished social housing state" (Green, 2000c: 17).

In addition, a philosopher theorist (Heller, 1996) of the needs concept elaborates further Green's "bottom up" approaches of needs. She notes that within democratic societies the ascription of these normative needs by powerful and dominant groups and agencies fall into fundamentalism, substitutionalism, and paternalism, and hence affect people's freedom of choice, autonomy, and happiness relating to their needs. By fundamentalism, she notes that those groups and agencies act as if they are the guarantors who should tell people what and how they must need. By substitutionalism they substitute people's actual needs by what they think they should need. In addition, by paternalism they act like people's parents relating to people needs (Heller, 1996: 107-108). Furthermore, she argues that in non democratic regimes (e.g. of Soviet type), where the central power of state attributes people's needs, they create a dictatorship of attribution of needs, hence, the people's freedom, autonomy, and happiness is more restricted (Heller, 1996: 93).

Heller's elaboration of Green's "bottom up" approach of needs gives more relevance to Green's approach. Hence, this is how Green defines his conceptualization of community needs profiling.

"Community needs profiling using the 'bottom up' approach sought to get participants to... identify and analyse their problems and needs within the wider context of their lives. The research process therefore became the start of this awareness-raising process which allowed individuals to gain some insight into their situation whether it be their poverty, their mental health needs, schooling, quality of life, or housing conditions" (Green, 2000c: 22).

Thus, this study has considered Green's (2000c) "bottom up" approach to needs, as people perceive them or interpret them, in line with the *materialist conception of need*. In addition, these "bottom up" perceptions of needs are rooted in people's material conditions of life, work, enjoyment, leisure, and suffering in line with the *materialist conception of history,* and also in line with the *concept of configuration as an open structure of theory* as explained in Chapter 2 above (see also Table 2.1 in that chapter for both definitions).

Hence, this is the explanation of the first part of the concept *information needs*. The second part, at the heart of LIS, is *information*. The next section explains the concept of *information*.

3.3.2   The concept of information

This section explains the concept of *information.*

In LIS literature, there are views that consider it important to define the concept of *information,* and *information needs,* while others consider it to be unproductive. For instance, a LIS commentator who wrote a master degree dissertation about the information needs of trade unionionists and unemployed workers found that it was unproductive to define *information* and *information needs,* by observing that: "Definitions of 'information' and 'information needs' have produced much debate amongst librarians and information scientists. I do not feel it would be productive to go over intricacies of this debate" (McManus, 1987: 7). Other LIS commentator notes that "people [in LIS] talk about information need without ever bothering to define it" (Nicholas, 2000: 19).

Hence, in this thesis definitions of *information,* and *information needs* are given in this and the following sections. This is done without the intention of debating, but simply with the idea to give the readers the working definitions employed in the study in order that they may clearly assess its theoretical and methodological scope, and any possible limitations.

The configuration of the definition of *information* runs along the theoretical lines of two philosophers: Rendón Rojas (2005), a Mexican philosopher of LIS and Floridi (2002; 2004), an Italian philosopher of information. The author is cognizant that there might be some LIS researchers who might have done research in LIS than these two authors, e.g. in clarifying the concept of information (e.g. Capurro, 1996; Madden, 2000). However, the author has found the former more adequate for this study. For instance, the former place LIS' object of research within documents or information recorded in documents (Floridi, 2002: 46; Rendón Rojas, 2005: 180).

Hence, documents are core elements of library and information science (LIS), particularly *documental information, or information recorded in documents*. Now that information appeals to all professions as a kind of omniscience (von Baeyer, 2003), it is very important to distinguish what is the pertinent type of information which should matter to LIS or at least for the working definition of this thesis.

For example, information matters for different professions other than LIS, e.g. journalists. However, the type of information which matters for those professions, and that make their professions unique is not the type of information that matters to LIS, and that makes LIS unique. Certainly all of them use the term information as their common device, e.g. taking a picture by a journalist at a moment that captures any event. Nevertheless, the meaning of information for those professions is different for the library and information science. Hence, when information matters for LIS is when the information employed by other professions becomes recorded in documents and communicated to the public (e.g. a journalist's picture published in a newspaper).

In addition, it is when they become documents that these socially meaningful symbols begin to be of the interest of the LIS community. Therefore, documents, or information recorded in documents, or "recorded data" (Floridi, 2002: 46), or "information sources" (Floridi, 2002: 41) are the kind of information which matters to LIS and which makes LIS unique. "LIS does not cover all PI's (philosophy of information) ground, but is concerned more specifically with documents' life cycles" (Floridi, 2002: 46).

Hence, this is how Rendón Rojas defines a document relating to LIS.

"The document is taken as a social and cultural product, that is the result of the objectivation of the human thought and spirit, and it has as a function to preserve the social memory. From the different types of documents, library, and information science focus its attention in those that were created expressly with the purpose to communicate "intentions of the soul" [sic] and that they have a structural and articulated logic and that they have passed through the hands of the professional of documental information. From this it is understood that those objects that can generate information but that they do not include an expressed syntactical and semantic structure, they will not be taken into account for the library and information science" (Rendón Rojas, 2005: 180).

Moreover, what is the concept of information that matters for this project? It has to do with a combination of the concepts of *document* and *information*. Hence, documental information or the information recorded in documents. This is how Rendón Rojas defines it.

"... Information is a secondary quality of the objects that are made by the subjects from the structuring of properties present in those objects. The utilized structures by the subject to interpret those objective properties are found conditioned by the psychogenetic development of the individual and by his or her socio-historic-cultural context. [...] A document does not contain information like a bag of oranges; the subject does not have to face the oranges to see them and take them out of the bag; but in the document is not like that, information comes up only when the subject through that document arrives to the world of information; that step from the symbol to information is an activity that is conducted and that repeats every time that a structuring of data is being conducted by different subjects or by the same subject. If the rules of this structuring are not known so that those symbols guide us to the world of information, the document can be there in front of us and not saying anything. It is man who connects himself to that world too through those objects of the senses, but library and information science is interested in certain specific objects, created specially to connect to the world of information: the articulated linguistic signs [the documents, Muela-Meza,Z.M.]" (Rendón Rojas, 2005: 158-9).

In addition, this is how Rendón Rojas concludes his definition of documental information or information recorded in documents.

"According to this information comes from a synthesis of what is objective and subjective, from the data and some structures of the subject which allow to process those data, to interpret them, to organize them and convert them into something that may have a use value; they allow us to act and to take decisions. Man receives stimuli in the organs of his senses (sound waves, light rays of certain frequency and amplitude, etcetera) but those stimuli are not the information, they need to be given an organization, a form. It is important to remember on this point the etymology of the word "information": in-form, "to give form" (Rendón Rojas, 2005: 94-95).

After the working definition of the concepts of *need* and *information* for this project have been configured, then in the next section the combined concept of *information need* or *information needs* is examined: needs of information recorded in documents.

3.3.2.1   THE CONCEPT OF DOCUMENTAL INFORMATION NEEDS

This section explains the concept of documental information needs or needs of information recorded in documents.

As mentioned above, this study has employed Rendón Rojas' (2005) concepts of *information* and *documental information* or *information recorded in documents*. Still following him, this is how he defines the concept of *documental information needs or needs of information recorded in documents* as employed in this study.

"Man looks for information to do something, not to act. Some of these duties are scientific research, to learn, to conduct a practical theoretic activity, recreational aesthetic, and to make a decision in the political, or economic, or managerial, sphere, or even in the daily life. But with the difference of other information needs, those of interest to library science or librarianship are the documental information needs, that is, those which look for information in material formats [documents] which were made specifically to transmit [documental] information." (Rendón Rojas, 2005: 114).

Hence, Rendón Rojas' concept clarifies that the information needs of interest for library and information science are the *documental information needs or needs of information recorded in documents*. In addition, those who need information are *users of documental information* or users of information recorded in documents (Rendón Rojas, 2005: 115).

The author has found in the literature conceptualizations of information needs. For instance, there are some commentators who note that for library and information science the concept of *information behaviour* or *information-seeking behaviour* is more relevant than the concept of *information needs* to conduct research about information needs (e.g. Wilson, 1981; 1994; Calva González, 2004; Kaniki, 1989; 1995; 2001). A commentator elaborates this idea by noting that: "the correct term would be an investigation of the information behaviour or the manifestation of information needs" (Calva González, 2004: 103). On similar lines, another commentator, building on Wilson's (1981: 3) positivist information behaviour paradigm notes that: "because information needs cannot be measured or understood in abstract, the term "information needs" [sic] should be removed from the library and information science vocabulary and instead be perceived as information seeking for the satisfaction of needs" (Kaniki, 1989: 71).

This concept of information behaviour has been found more related to the study of the behaviour of users of information, or study of user behaviour (Wilson, 1981; 1994). However, this study was not focused on the behaviour of users of information, but on the information needs residents of the Broomhall neighbourhood perceived according to an interrelationship of several factors explained above, such as community bonds, and territorial bonds. Furthermore, the application of community profiling to information needs is more focused on trying to analyse information needs of communities, in a collective fashion, instead of the behaviour of individuals in an individual fashion. Hence, however valid the positivist information behaviour paradigm might be to the study of user behaviour, it was not found adequate for this study.

The next section explains the concept of information providers.

3.4 The concept of information providers

This section explains the concept of information providers and its integral parts as employed in this thesis. The next section explains the working definition of information providers.

3.4.1   The working definition of information providers

Building on the concepts of Rendón Rojas (2005), the definition of *information provider* considers any institution, whose reason for being is the collection, organisation, and dissemination of *documental information, or information recorded in documents*. This is how Rendón Rojas defines a *documental information institution*:

> "[Documental Information Institution (DII). This concept, notes Rendón Rojas], "saves us from falling into ambiguities since the generic being of the information institution can be specified in different types of information institutions: journalism, television, radio, etcetera, which do not fall into the field that we are analysing; but it does fall indeed if the information institution is restricted to the documental scope..." [...] The DII is also "an organism created by society and if fulfils a social function (P), that is why we have chosen the term institution and not to follow the general consensus to call it unit of information. The fact of being a social institution means that its existence is due to a social need and like all other political institutes (State, and others which historically have appeared: parties, ministries or secretaries of State, presidency, congress [parliament, Muela-Meza, Z.M.], in the case of representative democracies) or juridical (police, public ministry, judges, Supreme Court of Justice)—, it is placed within the structure of society for its better functioning, independently of the persons who occupy a position in such institution." (Rendón Rojas, 2005: 136-7).

In addition, following Rendón Rojas (2005) conceptualizations, the person who works in a library or any other *Documental Information Institutions (DII) or Institutions of Information Recorded in Documents (IIRD)*, can be defined as a *Documental Information Professional (DIP)* or a *Professional of the Information Recorded in Documents (PIRD)*:

> "[The Documental Information Professional (DIP)] is an active agent inside the social communication circuit. Precisely it is the information professional that through his activity makes possible the conditions in order to de-objectify the internal word converted into symbol; that is, it is he who opens the doors of the world of information: if he ceases doing that, he ceases being an information professional. [... the DIP] can allow or hamper and deform the social communication depending if he fulfils his function of providing the necessary conditions to ensure that his user [of information recorded in documents] gets introduced into the world of information and dialogues with the texts and his authors" (Rendón Rojas, 2005: 145). Furthermore, Rendón Rojas argues that [...] "the information professional is neither a merchant of information, nor an educator. He may become both, but that is not a *sine qua non* characteristic to become an information professional." (Rendón Rojas, 2005: 146).

As it can be read in the definition above, the keywords for this concept are *documental, information,* and *institution,* and the idea of *institution* is key to denote the *institution of information recorded in documents*. Thus, *documental information institutions (DIIs)* can be libraries, information centres, documentation centres, advice centres and other similar institutions. A LIS researcher (Sander Villarino, 1992: 40) also agrees with Rendón Rojas in calling for example a library as an institution.

Nevertheless, terming these organizations as institutions is rare amongst *document information professionals (DIP)* as termed by Rendón Rojas (2005: 145-146) or in LIS theory. The most common way of calling them is as *units of information* (e.g. Calva González, 2004). However, a radio station, and a newspaper can be units of information, but they are not *documental information institutions (DIIs)*. They may include a library within their organizations, and in such a case, a *documental information institution* might be hosted inside those organisations, but they *per se* are not *documental information institutions*.

Other commentators try to term them in different ways. For instance, a recent study (Usherwood, Wilson, and Bryson, 2005) has lumped libraries, archives and museums together under the umbrella term of *repositories of public knowledge*. Perhaps that new term has to do with the compliance of the study with the Museums, Libraries, and Archives Council of the British government. However, as in the example of radio stations and newspapers, although the museums are well-established institutions in society, they are not *documental information institutions (DIIs)* as defined above. If they host libraries or documentation centres within their walls then these would be DIIs inside other institutions. Furthermore, museums have little to do with LIS, except for the case if they hosted libraries or information or documentation centres inside; the discipline of museology is the science that studies museums, not library, and information science (LIS).

As it can be seen, defining an *information provider* is not an easy task. However, by defining them as *units of information (UI)*, or *repositories of public knowledge (RPK)* does not help either to obtain more clarity. A UI or a RPK could be virtually any kind of organization that deals with information, but the organizations that matter for this study are those related to *documental information, or information recorded in documents.* This will prevent LIS practitioners or researchers from getting lost every time that governments create new nomenclatures, like Museums, Libraries, and Archives in the UK, in order to name documental information institutions, or whenever any societal change takes place as nowadays that *information* seems to permeate all layers of society and academic and political discourse (von Baeyer, 2003).

Nevertheless, even after the exposition explained above, the difficulties are not removed completely with the definition of *information provider* this thesis has configured. The idea of *documental information institutions (DIIs)* comes alongside with the idea of a LIS researcher (Leach, 1999: 74) who observes that broadly speaking *information provision* "is used to encompass issues such as sources, sites and mediums [of information provision]." That is, this thesis covers the broad spectrum of information provision in the community of Broomhall. However, the definition of this term, including all the features of this thesis, is flexible to the configurations emerged from the data generated in this project. In like manner, Leach (1999: 74) also talks about *information provision* in a narrower sense.

For his study, and following other authors, *information provision* in a narrower sense could be transacted in the way information is transacted: a) put across, b) transmitted, c) disseminated, d) transferred, e) diffused, and f) communicated (Leach, 1999: 74). In order to group those terms of information communication as *information provision in a narrower sense,* Leach (1999: 74) talks about an information channel; a medium used to convey information, and mechanism of transmission. Thus, mechanisms, channels, and mediums of information encapsulate his analysis of *information provision* in a narrower sense. In this sense, this project has also considered some of Leach's (1999: 74) elements of *provision of information* in a narrower sense.

The final section of this chapter makes an approximate differentiation between the provision of information, and advice, and help.

3.4.2   Type of provision: information, advice, or help

This sections addresses the differences amongst the provision of information, advice, or help.

The concept of *documental information institution (DII)* configured by Rendón Rojas (2005), might be suitable for libraries and similar DIIs. However, that concept is limited when applied to identify other types of documental information providers who do not serve their users in the same way as e.g. libraries, even when they also employ documental information to provide their services. An example of those providers is the Citizens Advice Bureau (CAB). The CAB might be considered a DII because it collects, organises, and disseminates documental information. However, the institution collects and organises its information only to feed its home-made nationwide information system; its dissemination is seldom in the form of printed document, e.g. like libraries. The delivery of the service –through their previously organised documental information–takes the form of advice (Johnson, 1995).

This is how the *Concise Oxford English Dictionary* (Oxford University Press, 2004) defines *advice* and *help:*

> Advice: guidance or recommendations offered with regard to future action.

> To help: make it easier for (someone) to do something. ☐improve (a situation or problem); be of benefit to. ☐support (someone) to allow them to move in a specified direction: I helped her up.

Thus, *advice and help providers* have a clear aim of providing social welfare services, or services related to state agency as some suggest (Delanty, 2005). That is, advice and help providers do not need to stock documents or information recorded in documents with the purpose of serving users through them, either through their direct help, or through their indirect help of previously having organised them in stacks or providing them diverse technologies to access them (e.g. computers, Internet, DVDs, CDs).

3.5 Summary

This chapter has presented a literature review relating to the three major integral parts that comprise this study: the community profiling tool, and the concepts of information needs, and information provision. These are the key points of these integral parts.

1)   Key points of the community profiling tool.

As for the community profiling tool, this was analysed as being interrelated with different concepts such as *community,* and *territoriality. Community* was configured in this study, following Delanty's (2003) conceptualizations, as a communicative mechanism that people pursue in order to obtain a sense of belonging with other people. *Territoriality* was related to the geographical boundaries of Broomhall as a spatial area where the community profiling tool was applied.

The community profiling tool emerged in the literature as having a synonym terminology called *community analysis*. The latter was found as a thesaurus descriptor from scientific peer-reviewed bibliographic databases (e.g. Library and Information Science Abstracts); however, the former was found to be more useful for most of the documental sources reviewed. Hence, the author merged the *community analysis* into the community profiling tool without complications.

The author of this study made the methodological clarification that the terminology called *community profiling* is a tool that serves to analyse social needs (e.g. information needs) of any human community. Hence, the author criticised and rejected the notions of some commentators who confused the *community profiling tool* with methods. The author also made a self critique, and hence rejected as well his earlier confusion of this tool with a qualitative research methodology (Muela-Meza, 2003a; 2006b). Hence, those studies that pretend to serve as theoretical and methodological foundations of information needs, but that confuse *tools* with *methods* (e.g. Calva González, 1991; 2004) should be criticised and rejected, because instead of giving a sound epistemological foundation for LIS they bring confusion. Hence, LIS like any other science needs sound epistemological foundations, not confusion, in order to improve its development as science to better equip its practitioners to understand and solve LIS research problems.

The community profiling tool implemented in this study, in contrast with the different studies reviewed had been conducted only for the sake of knowledge and discovery. Whilst the studies reviewed have implemented this tool as part of their planning processes within their libraries, and most of them had been conducted on-the-desk as very short reports supported mainly with outdated census data, this study has been fundamentally distinct from the former in the sense that it was conducted only as a rigorous empirical research for the sake of pushing the theoretical and epistemological boundaries, and without any pressure to obtain practical applications, or to comply with the policies of any library, or any other institution from the statutory or voluntary sector.

Nevertheless, the working definition of the community profiling tool, after some social scientists who have made a manual on the subject (Hawtin, Hughes, and Percy-Smith, 1994: 12-13), acknowledges that this tool can be employed for practical applications by a given community or communities within their neighbourhoods, or by researchers who conduct research on their behalf, to obtain an action plan that describes their social needs and the resources that would satisfy their needs in order to improve the quality of life of the members of those communities. Hence, the author subscribed to this definition because he theoretically considers that LIS researchers should conduct research bearing in mind the social responsibility of trying to improve the quality of life of the populations of their studies (e.g. Muela-Meza, 2007). In addition, this reasoning was made at a theoretical level, because as mentioned above the author did not pursue any practical application. However, as explained above in the Methodology chapter (Chapter 2), the author is responsible for his own analyses, discussions, and interpretations of the data, and presentation of the findings of this study, and will renew that responsibility once this study had been made public (see Chapter 7 below for the ways it is going to be made public). However, as a consequence, if the readers within the different communities of the Broomhall neighbourhood should ever build a practical action plan, then that would be their own responsibility.

Another key element of community profiling is its interrelationship with territoriality. This study found it to be of paramount importance that this tool should be employed within a material territorial space, or geographical boundaries, and that these should be configured by the perceptions of the members of the communities of those geographical boundaries. This assertion goes in contrast with those commentators who support the idea that the geographical boundaries should be assigned by the statutory sector through census (e.g. Beal, 1985). In addition, this interrelationship of community profiling and territoriality goes in line with two of the three major concepts employed in this study as a theoretical framework (see Table 2.1 in Chapter 2 for definitions). Territoriality is related to the *materialist conception of history* because a community profiling needs a material territory geographically delimited where communities live or work to be applied upon. Territoriality is also related to the *concept of configuration as an open structure of theory* in the sense of being the geographical boundaries being delimited (e.g. configured) by the members of the communities of a given territorial area (e.g. Broomhall).

Therefore, the model of effectiveness of the community profiling tool for library and information science that emerged in this study should combine, through mutually conditioning interrelationships, human communities, and natural material territoriality. In addition, the configuration of any given territorial area should be made through primary source datasets obtained from the perceptions of the members of the different communities that live in that territorial area, and through the use of qualitative research methods such as observation and interviews, instead of relying on secondary sources datasets of statutory sector census or private sector statistics, which might be outdated, or politically and commercially biased.

    2)   Key points of the concept of information needs.

A relatively broad materialist conception of need has been explained in line with the *materialist conception of history* (see Table 2.1 for definition in Chapter 2 above), which gives primacy to the materiality of cosmos over its idealist spirituality. That is, people first need to be alive in order to satisfy survival (e.g. water, food, shelter, clothing, housing) or cultural (e.g. information recorded in documents) needs.

Along the lines of the *materialist conception of history,* and the *concept of configuration as an open structure of theory* (see definitions above in Table 2.1 of Chapter 2), this study has employed the conceptualizations of Green's (2000c) "bottom up" approach to needs, as people perceive them or interpret them, instead of how powerful and dominant groups and agencies ascribe them.

This study, building on the concepts of LIS philosopher Rendón Rojas (2005) has employed the *concept of information recorded in documents* of paramount importance to LIS, because epistemologically the only information that matters for LIS is that that has been recorded in documents.

3) Key points of the concept of information providers

Building on the concepts of Rendón Rojas (2005), this study underpinned his concept of information provider in the form of *Documental Information Institution (DIIs)*, or *Institution of Information Recorded in Documents*. DIIs include libraries, documentation centres, or any other institutions whose social function is to preserve humankind social, historic and cultural memory and heritage for the purpose of introducing users to the world of information recorded in documents according to their needs.

However, as for the Broomhall neighbourhood, these DII information providers were limited in their operationalization, because there were found other centres that offered advice and help mostly in oral form; hence they did not need stack documents as in libraries (e.g. Citizens Advice Bureau)

Finally, Chapter 4 will present a historical and demographical background of the Broomhall neighbourhood.

4 HISTORICAL AND DEMOGRAPHIC BACKGROUND OF THE BROOMHALL NEIGHBOURHOOD

> "Why concentrate on the past? Why upset ourselves with painful analogies between human and beasts? Why not simply to the future? These questions have an answer. If we do not know what we're capable of —and not just a few celebrity saints and notorious war criminals—then we do not know what to watch out for, which human propensities to encourage, and which to guard against. Then we haven't a clue about which proposed courses of human action are realistic, and which are impractical and dangerous sentimentality." – Carl Sagan and Ann Druyan, *Shadows of Forgotten Ancestors: A Search for Who We Are* (Sagan and Druyan, 1992: 7).

4.1 Introduction

This chapter presents a general historical, territorial, and demographical background of the Broomhall neighbourhood, going as far as the 16th century until the year 2006, when the generation of data for this project ended.

The chapter is divided into three major sections: 1) historical background of Broomhall, 2) territorial background of the Broomhall neighbourhood, and 3) demographic background of Broomhall.

Section 1 comprises these historical aspects: a) Broomhall related to wider Sheffield historical facts, and b) Broomhall's earliest urban housing developments (from 18th century).

Section 2 comprises these territorial aspects: a) overview of the territorial background of Broomhall and its interrelationships with social class, b) division of the Broomhall neighbourhood in four sections, c) analysis of sections A, B, C, and D of Broomhall, d) historic boundaries of Broomhall, e) boundaries of Broomhall from the 1940s onwards (this includes: 1) the Broomhall Forum's geographical boundaries of Broomhall, (Section D), 2) the Sheffield NHS (National Health Services) Broomhall boundaries, 3) the Broomhall boundaries according to the Broomhall Park Association, 4) Broomhall boundaries according to the Broomhall Community Group (BCG), and 5) the Nazi Blitz that substantially altered the Broomhall (and Sheffield) landscape), and f) expansion of Hallam and Sheffield universities (University Student Villages).

Section 3 comprises demographic aspects from census statistics of Broomhall relating to: a) the Broomhall Index and Domain Scores from 2001 census (which includes: 1) economic activity, 2) education, 3) housing, 4) environment, 5) access to services, 6) health and social care, and 7) community safety), b) Broomhall 2001 Census Key Statistics compared with Sheffield (which includes: 1) total population, 2) area (km²), 3) density of population per (km²), 4) population under 16, 5) population over 65, 6) Black and Minority Ethnic residents, 7) households with dependent children, and 8) households in social housing), c) an Heptagram of Broomhall Index and Domain Scores from 2001 census, and d) Broomhall Neighbourhood Locator Map within Sheffield from 2001 census

The next major section explains the historical background of the Broomhall neighbourhood of Sheffield, UK.

4.2 Historical background of Broomhall

The next sections present an overview of the historical background of the Broomhall neighbourhood of Sheffield, UK.

4.2.1 Broomhall related to wider Sheffield historical facts

Broomhall is a neighbourhood, which originally was bonded to one of the most affluent large landed estates all across England since five centuries ago. This was the Broom Hall estate located in the west side of Sheffield (Batho, 1968). Much of the land in this estate in the 18th century was owned by the Reverend James Wilkinson, Vicar and Magistrate, whose name is commemorated in Wilkinson Street (Hey, 1998: 95).

As emerged from historical documents, the Reverend James Wilkinson was surrounded by controversial political facts. In the late 18th century, the poor and working classes made many revolts against Wilkinson because he passed many laws, which enclosed poor people's common land, and as a result, Sheffield was under strong military control by a military division named the Dragoons from Nottingham.

Hence, it emerged from literature that those political issues where Wilkinson was involved had an impact on the neighbourhood studied here. In 1791 a massive revolt went up the Wilkinson's Broom Hall with the purpose to kill him because many people lost their lands and many others were put in prison under Wilkinson's ruling: "[In 1791] The shout then went up: 'To Broom Hall', the home of Vicar Wilkinson, the town's only magistrate. The mob broke all his windows, smashed part of his furniture, damaged and burnt his library, and set his haystacks on fire, before the Dragoons dispersed them"(Hey, 1998: 136).

This historical fact was also recorded in a popular song, which was also coincidentally related to librarianship to some extent. J. Senior (cited on Bambery, 1983: 7-8) in his book *Owd Shevvild and its celebrities* related the incident in a rhyme in local dialect spoken by the working and poor class people of those days:

"When Wilkinson, the Magistrate, / (A man ta larning gen) / Wer t' lord o't' owd Broomhall estate, / Far! Far! i't' country then. / E t' room hard by t' owd dial true, / He's scowded many a knave, / An gen ta honest men ther due / An eulogys'd the brave. / Abant this time the ancients say / "A mob i' lawless ire, / Destroy'd hiz books an' scar'd hiz rooks, / An set hiz stacks afire" (cited on Bambery, 1983: 7-8).

Next section will explain the earliest Broomhall's housing developments since 18th century.

4.2.2 Broomhall's earliest urban housing developments (since 18th century)

The owners of the Broom Hall in the 18th century began to divide the land to build the first earliest massive signs of urban housing developments for renting. The houses built on the Broom Hall estate in the 19th century had nice gardens and were too expensive for middle or working classes to afford them (Hey, 1998: 96). One of the earliest owners of houses in the Broom Hall estate was Mark Firth, a steel manufacturer who lived at the top of Wilkinson Street in 1863 before he built a large house at Ranmoor, which he named Oakbrook. (Hey, 1998: 149). However, he was not the only one, that was the trend of the wealthiest and earliest capitalist classes, to move towards the nice west side of Sheffield included Broomhall:

[In the 1820s] "The middle classes had first moved towards Broomhill, but Sheffield's expanding industries moved in that direction too. The new West Street and Portobello Street soon accommodated steelworks and cutlery businesses as well as houses. Industry did not get as far as Glossop Road, however. Professional people and successful businessmen set up homes and consulting rooms thereabouts, away from the smoke and the grime. In time, the Mappin Art Gallery and the University helped to give the district a genteel air." (Hey, 1998: 185). "From the 1830s onwards, the more prosperous of Sheffield's inhabitants moved further west to build villas on south and the south-facing slopes of Broomhill, Broomhall, Ranmoor, Fulwood, Ecclesall, Nether Edge and Abbeydale. The Mount of Broomhill was unusual being designed by William Flockton as a row of eight houses linked by a monumental classical facade. ... During the 1840s, the growing professional and managerial classes favoured Collegiate Crescent and neighbouring parts of the well-wooded Broomhall Park estate, where no commercial development was allowed. Lodges still stand at the former gated entrances to the private roads there." (Hey, 1998: 186).

From the literature, it was found that since the 1820s Broomhall was a very pleasant

residential area for wealthy families, sharply contrasting with the poor living conditions of
the working classes who lived in other cramped and unsanitary conditions elsewhere in
Sheffield. [2] For example, inadequate or non-existing sewers exacerbated the cholera
epidemic, which killed 402 people in 1832, and the smoke menace increased with the
number of industrial chimneys. (Olive, 2002; Engels, ([1845], 2000). By 1892 the estate
had been almost fully developed, the suburb seems to have become fashionable amongst
the professional and manufacturing classes, the capitalist classes, and many prominent
Sheffielders had houses in Broomhall since then and by the early 20th century (Bambery,
1983: 1). As a result of the Nazi German blitz many houses in Broomhall were demolished
or listed for clearance in the 1940s, and in the 1960s the notorious Broomhall Flats were
built, but for less than 20 years, for in the 1980s they were demolished again (Jenkins,
1990: 80). Housing and territorial issues have the most negative and controversial issues
for most Broomhall residents, particularly for current poor working classes.

From mid 19th century can be traced that the Broom Hall estate became Broomhall, then
Broomhall Park. When the owners of the estate divided it, the western part (what it is now
actually the Broomhall Park, or section D of Broomhall of this thesis) was the protected
area away from commercial development, but the same owners of the estate leased the
land for all types of commercial developments in the eastern side. For example, "a century
after, by 1939 German steel industries were settled at Broomhall Street. Sipelia Works and
Paul and Stephan Richartz employed 400 workers there (Hey, 1998: 217).

However, the German Nazis began the WWII in 1939 and Sipelia had to shut its business
in those years, although there were many little mesters –small steel or cutlery
manufacturing shops– all around Sheffield, which was worldwide considered a power in
steel manufacturing until the 1970s. As a result of the WWII, the German Nazis bombed
UK in different cities and Sheffield was also targeted in 1940 because most of the steel
industry was devoted for the war. Thus, many sites of the city were blitzed, including
houses on the current eastern side of Broomhall Street, in the current Havelock Street, and
Glossop Road, which belonged to the Broomhall geographical boundaries of this project
(Hey, 1998: 227).

However, in the 19th century not only the wealthiest, and capitalist classes moved
westbound Sheffield, in 1805, the University of Sheffield was built in its current location of
Firth Court, on Western Bank, being Firth its first chancellor. Thus to the north of
Broomhall the University of Sheffield was built, to the north-east the Royal Hallamshire
Hospital, the Children's Hospital and the Weston Hospital and to the east the Hallam
Sheffield University. A historian recollects the facts:

> Local residents, especially in and around Broomhill, have seen the character of their area
> altered in ways that they have often thought undesirable. For example, the side streets have
> become one vast car park. But as an employer of 5, 393 people and an annual income of £159.6
> million, Sheffield University makes a large contribution to the local economy. The collective
> purchasing power of students is also of great benefit to local traders. The university's
> significance lies not only in its international standing for its research and teaching, but in its
> role in the local community, providing expertise to local industry and public services and,
> through its Medical School, enhancing skills and facilities offered by the Hallamshire and
> Northern General Hospitals" (Hey, 1998: 251).

Nevertheless, as the reader will assess, this optimistic view of history of the University of
Sheffield contribution to the community is not shared by the middle and working classes
who live in Broomhall. It is also important to highlight the fact that the earlier owners of

---

[2] Now the cramped and unsanitary conditions are located in section A in the Hanover Flats, just off
the road of the most affluent part of Broomhall: section D, the Park. This thesis has divided
Broomhall in four sections: A, B, C, and D. The reader will be referred to these sections in most
parts of the thesis. For a geographical division of these sections see maps on Figures 4.1 and 4.2.
For an explanation of the density of dwellings per ground area in square meters of the four sections
see Tables 4.1 through 4.4.

the Broom Hall estate were the first in leasing their lands for upper market housing development for the most affluent and capitalist classes to live and to exploit such a profitable business. This did not emerge from data, but perhaps these were the origins of the earliest massive housing development in Sheffield. This fact is interesting, because the owners of the many surviving properties of what used to be the original Broom Hall area, now the Broomhall Park, are now opponents of any type of developments in the area. The earlier owners of the Broom Hall estate built schools in the area for the most affluent kids of the time, such as the King Edward VIII. They put the names to the Broomhall Park streets that show very distinctive features of the area since early 19th century such as: Collegiate Crescent, Broomhall Street, Ecclesall Road, and Victoria Road.

Thus, a historic review is important at each stage of this thesis because history will show the reader how historic and contemporary times tensions and how historic personages created many prosperous industries and businesses such as housing developing industries and educational industries (Sheffield and Hallam universities).

The next section will assess the background of the territorial or uses of the land of the Broomhall neighbourhood.

4.3 Territorial background of the Broomhall neighbourhood

These sections will give a comprehensive overview of the evolution of *the territoriality or uses of the land* of Broomhall since its earliest times until nowadays.

4.3.1 Overview of the territorial background of Broomhall and its interrelationships with social class

The features on *territoriality or uses of the land* emerged in this thesis as having the most adverse effects for most of the people in the Broomhall neighbourhood, regardless of their social class differences. *Territoriality or uses of the land* emerged, thus, as the major issue of Broomhall and at the same time the major information need as perceived by residents.

For instance, poor working class residents felt them as having the most adverse effects for the reason that most of them do not own their social housing and this housing and the environment around are in deplorable conditions (e.g. rats, vermin, lack of adequate winter double-glazing, anti-arson fire protection, security, etc.).

On the other hand, the most affluent capitalist and middle class residents felt them as having the most adverse effects, because due to the expansion of Hallam and Sheffield universities, and the upper market high-rise housing development, it has been a constant threat for their large Victorian, Georgian, or Manor residences (e.g. Broom Hall). Due to the destructive effects of the Nazi German blitz since the 1940s onwards, those mansions were short-listed for demolition and to be developed for Housing in Multiple Occupation (HMO). In spite of the fact that they enjoy some legal protection derived from the Broomhall Park Conservation Area (Sheffield City Council, 2007a; 2007b; Jenkins, 1990; City of Sheffield, 1989; Hall, 1981; Sheffield Corporation, 1974; Connell, 1968; Batho, 1968).

Moreover, *territoriality or uses of the land* also emerged as having the most all-embracing interrelationships with most of other features found in this project. In one way or the other, all Broomhall issues and features are interrelated with *territoriality or the uses of the land*. Thus, most of the community information needs and their corresponding provision and, or, implications for policy makers are related largely to *territoriality* issues as well. In addition, the way that each individual and groups of individuals −e.g. families— cope with those needs, depend fundamentally on *territoriality or uses of the land*. Therefore, the territorial location where individuals or groups of individuals live in Broomhall would be the most determinant material condition of most other living conditions, namely: health, jobs, education, leisure, et cetera. Territoriality goes in line with the *materialist conception of history* (see definition in Table 2.1 in Chapter 2) which states that the material conditions of living are determinant of other conditions (e.g. social, historic, cultural).

However, it has also emerged from this study that the *concept of the social class struggles* (see Table 2.1 in Chapter 2 for further explanation) has also been determinant of people's material living conditions. Hence, when interrelated with *territoriality the concept of social class struggles* helps the reader to understand better the connexion between social class and territoriality. The way individuals and groups would cope with community information needs would also depend on the social class each individual or group belongs to and the struggles each face within each class or amongst different classes, or within each territorial area or amongst different areas within the neighbourhood. Therefore, it was found that the better the territorial conditions [3] and the upper a class [4] individuals belong to, the better chances they have to cope better with information needs, and basically with everything else in life, and vice versa.

After all being said, the readers will find a strong presence of the features of *territoriality or uses of the land* throughout this thesis.

4.3.2 Division of the Broomhall neighbourhood in four sections

In Figure 4.1 (see map below) Broomhall is divided into four sections, A, B, C, and D. These sections drawn in red are precisely an integral part of the findings, discussions, and conclusions of this thesis, where the author deliberately sub-divided Broomhall in four sections correlating territorial size with population, but only after the analysis of data.

How were these subdivisions made. They came both, from the literature and from the perception of residents and information providers. When the author conducted the interviews, he took a large plane map of Sheffield (see Geographers' A-Z Map Company, Ltd., 2002) and asked the interviewees to draw the boundaries of Broomhall according to their views. Most of the residents perceived Broomhall circumscribed only within sections A, B, and C, but not D, the Park, and from literature the residents from the Park also perceived the Park a distinctively separated area from sections A, B, and C. Therefore, that is the reason why the author divided the Broomhall territory in four sections.

Thus, it is important that the readers have a road map so they can appreciate better how were the territorial analysis conducted and the many interrelationships to other features that emerged from it. Hence, the two working maps being used for Broomhall and to which the readers will be constantly referred throughout the thesis are these (see below figures 4.1 and 4.2).

---

[3] Housing, green open space, play areas, etc.
[4] Measured by how much property individuals own; how much knowledge they have; and how much physical labour they do for their living, as Edgell (1993: 52) has summarized the *social class struggles* concept (see Chapter 2 for further analysis).

Figure 4.1 shows a street map snapshot of Broomhall from a paper printed map of Sheffield the author has used since 2003.

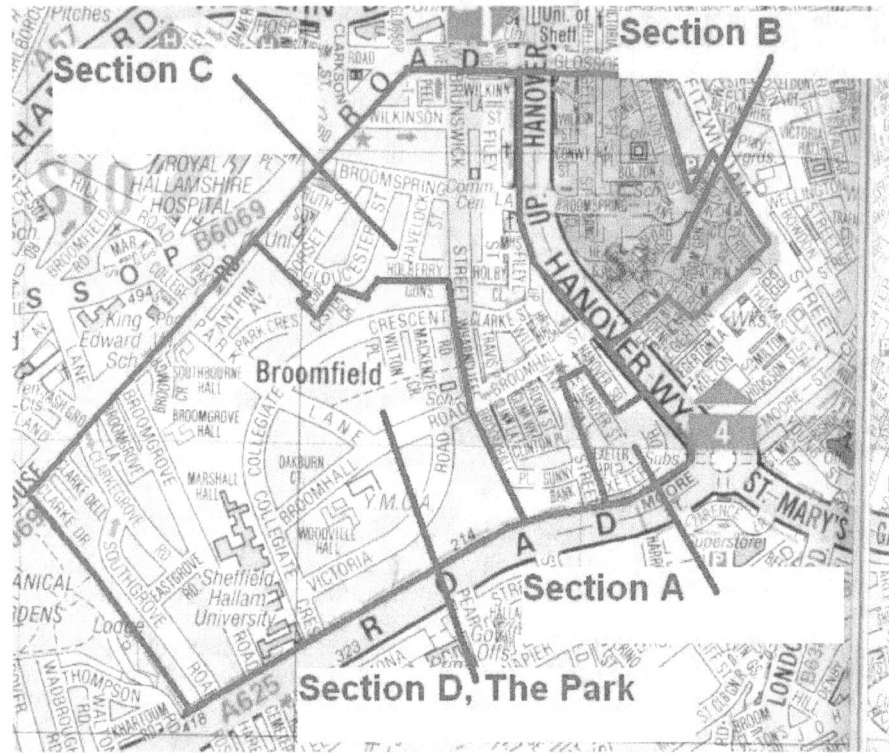

Figure 4.1 Broomhall street map. Source: (Geographers' A-Z Map Company, Ltd., 2002)

Figure 4.2 shows a map of Broomhall showing its actual geographical relief as taken from a Google Earth's satellite snapshot circa 2004-2005. Here, the reader can assess the high density of green areas (e.g. section D), or the lack of them (e.g. section A); the high density of houses in some areas (e.g. section A) and the lowest density of houses in others (e.g. the small amount of large houses and mansions from section D), and so on. See map below.

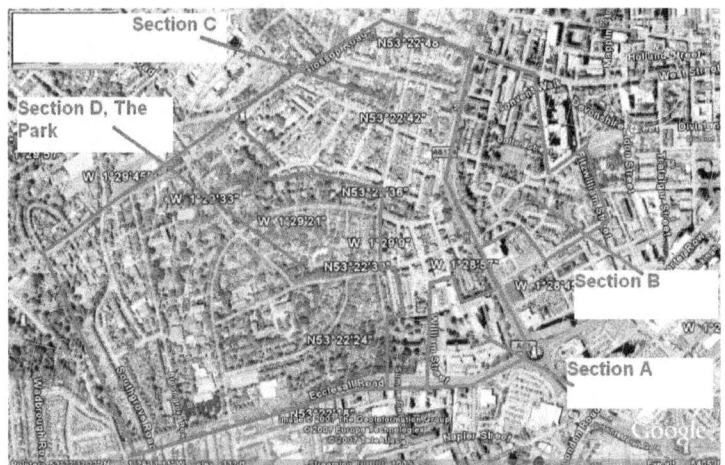

Figure 4.2 Actual satellite map of Broomhall circa 2004-2005 as emerged from the data of this thesis. Source: (Google Earth, 2007).

4.3.3 Analysis of sections A, B, C, and D of Broomhall

This section analyses at detail the four sections in which the Broomhall neighbourhood was
divided: sections A, B, C, and D.

Section A is the smallest territory with the highest density of dwellings per ground area and thus
population. There are 494 flats in the distinctive Hanover Estates and thousands of people live
there overcrowded; it has the least amount of green space by square meter in high contrast with the
other sections such as section D. See Table 4.1 below to learn more.

Table 4.1 Density of dwellings per ground area in square meters of Section A (the Hanover Estates) [5]	
Type and amount of flats	**Ground area**
Hanover Twin Tower Flats (156 flats distributed in 15 storeys)	1, 155 m2 (55m of front per 21m of bottom)
Hanover maisonettes flats (40 flats on average distributed in 4 storeys on average, 32 of them double bedrooms and 8 single bedroom)	420 m2 (30m of front per 14 of bottom)

In section B, see Table 4.2 below, there are approximately 450 dwellings where only the
Broomspring Estate amounts about 280, the territorial space is larger and greener than section A,
the dwellings are mostly low-rise modern block of spacious flats.

Table 4.2 Density of dwellings per ground area in square meters of the Broomspring Estate of Section B	
Type and number of flats	**Ground area**
Maisonettes flats (9 three bedroom flats on average distributed in 3 storeys on average)	420 m2 (30m of front per 14 of bottom)

In section C, see Table 4.3 below, there are about 480 dwellings, it is larger than sections A and B,
but smaller than D, the Park; it's greener than A and B, but less green than the Park; unlike sections
A and B, most of C's dwellings are semi detached terraced houses with very few low rise block of
flats of Housing for Multiple Occupancy (HMO).

---

[5] These measurements were carried out physically by the author with a domestic tape most of the
times under much pressure due to a constant scrutiny or questioning by residents of some areas,
thus they could only be consider approximate and not 100% accurate. However the margin of error
of the measurements is very slight and they can be considered as valid if compared with official City
Council measurements. The reason for not using City Council measurements was due to a lack of
information or to its access in the corresponding Council departments. Also, the author trusted
more his own observation as he recorded on the ground because he obtained his data according to
the research questions of this project and the council's might have been not adequate for this
project. Furthermore, in Figures 4.1, 4.2 and 4.5 the readers can assess at a glimpse the density of
households per ground area according to each section, and in Muela-Meza (2003-2007) they can
access pictures to assess at a detail this density comparing the pictures from each section and
therefore corroborate the validity of these ground area measurements.

Table 4.3 Density of dwellings per ground area in square meters of Section C	
Type and number of dwellings	**Ground area**
Detached houses (6 bedrooms on average distributed on 2 storeys on average plus cellar and attic)	750 m2 (25m of front per 30 m of bottom)
Semi-detached houses (3 bedrooms on average distributed on 2 storeys on average plus cellar and attic)	512.5 m2 (on average, some of them measure 400m2 (20m x 20m) and some 625m2 (25m x 25m))

Finally, in section D, the Park, see Table 4.4 below, there are approximately 300 dwellings, but the Park is the largest territory of all the four sections; the houses there are very large and many are mansions; they have big gardens, and it is the greenest area, etc.

Table 4.4 Density of dwellings per ground area in square meters of Section D	
Type and amount of dwellings	**Ground area**
1 average small size detached house (6 to 9 bedrooms on average distributed on 2 storeys on average plus cellar and attic)	1, 068 m2 on average (28.5m of front per 37.5 of bottom)
1 average medium size detached house (between 9 and 18 bedrooms on average distributed on 2 storeys on average plus cellar and attic)	3, 132 m2 (54 m of front per 58 m of bottom)
1 average mansion (more than 18 bedrooms on average)	16, 024.87 m2 (measure obtained by averaging the actual Broom Hall mansion and the ex YMCA when it was located on Broomhall Road)
The ex YMCA property when it was located on Broomhall Road	10, 956 m2 (132 m of front per 83 m of bottom)
The current Broom Hall mansion (still the largest property of all of the Broomhall 4 sections counting as one single dwelling)	21, 093.75 m2 (187.5 m2 of front per 112.5 m of bottom) [6]

The reader will notice that those figures just mentioned came from either physical observation, or residents' perceptions, or analysis of maps, but not from the official census statistics. The author did not use any census statistics because he found them or either inadequate for this qualitative study. Hall (1981) found in his master's research project that "there was primarily a lack of statistical information on Broomhall —it was not a ward, and its actual boundaries were subject to some dispute. Furthermore it seemed initially that little had been written on the area —or its history – outside of the odd press piece" (Hall, 1981: 24). The author of this project agrees with Hall (1981) that there is a problem with statistics and that the boundaries of Broomhall were and still are subject of disputes.

Despite the fact that Hall (1981) pointed out that there was a lack of statistics of Broomhall, he failed in analysing why there was a problem with statistics. Hence, the main cause for this problem was already analysed by Jordan and Walley (1977) in their still valid and sound guide of *community profiling* for public libraries, namely that the government census statistics do not match with people's perceptions. Jordan and Walley did not base their guide on Broomhall, but it can be applied to this neighbourhood or to any other as well. Furthermore, LIS practitioners in order to know the communities their institutions of documental information (IDD) are to serve and satisfy their information needs, they need to know physically their neighbourhood, that is, they need "to walk around the neighbourhood, preferably with a known member and with open eyes and mind, to be aware of it, the read the local newspaper, to participate in their matters and progress and to know the persons who run the city, as well as the leaders of minority groups, *instead of studying*

---

[6] These measurements correspond to the current Broom Hall property.

many statistics [emphasis, the author]" (Wheeler and Goldhor, [1962], 1970: 36).

Therefore, the major problem with census statistics related to Broomhall is that the government, after the Broomhall Forum (BF) drew its 2005 map (see Figure 4.5 below) almost with the same boundaries as the NHS (National Health Services) 2006 map (see Figure 4.6 below), lumped together all the four ABCD sections analysed here in Part I in one single neighbourhood. But as shown in Table 4.5 below, the Super Output Areas (SOA) geographical levels of the census as created by the central government every ten years in order to provide socio-demographic information at a neighbourhood level, when contrasted with the sections ABCD of Broomhall as emerged from the qualitative research data of this study, they present deep incompatibilities. Thus, none of the census statistics matched the ABCD section division criteria employed in this thesis.

Table 4.5 Incompatibilities amongst census Super Output Areas (SOA) or Enumeral Districts (EDs) levels and sections, A, B, C & D of Broomhall	
Section of Broomhall (as emerged from qualitative research data)	Representation at SOA level
A (Hanover social housing Estate)	Partially by 031C and partially by 031B
B (Broomspring up market & mixed upper social housing Estate)	Mainly by 031C and partially by 031B
C (Holberry)	Mainly by 031D and partially 030A, 036B, and 036D
D (The Park)	Mainly 036E, and partially 031D, 036B, and 036 D
Source: (Office for National Statistics, 2006).	

Therefore, what emerged from these data is that the census lacks of a reliable monitoring system that groups people according to homogeneous geographical areas and at a deeper level than its SOAs. Moreover, the census is carried out every ten years, and although some statutory sector institutions like the NHS (National Health Services) have annual census updates (NHS Sheffield PCT, 2006) mainly related to health services, the core of the census remains unchanged and outdated. In addition, it has emerged that the Sheffield Neighbourhood Information System (SNIS) (Sheffield City Council, 2005) has even more incompatibilities than the census with the geographical ABCD sections of Broomhall employed here, because whereas the census collects statistics at a national level, the SNIS employs the census statistics as the council and other elected members see fit, but this applicability, at least for Broomhall does not match. Only the NHS Sheffield PCT (2006) made a slight distinction by clarifying that in section A lived the most deprived population with the highest rates of health problems all across Sheffield (particularly mental health problems), unlike the people of the other three sections.

As it has been explained above, Broomhall is a neighbourhood remarkably divided on its territorial or uses of the land features. These territorial features in Broomhall emerged as having also a remarkable relationship to social class divides. It emerged that the people living in section A are the poorest residents, belonging mainly to lower working class. Those from section B are a mixture of lower working class and middle class, but working class prevails. Those from section C are mainly from middle class, but with some working class too. And those from section C (the Broomhall Park area) are mainly from upper middle class mixed largely with capitalist class.

Hence, the social classes that describe the residents of Broomhall live in a very close proximity, within each section, or in any of the four sections, which as shown in the maps above are just divided by a road. However, these remarkably contrasting poorer and wealthier social classes of the residents, living together, or nearby in sharply divided poorer and wealthier territories have not emerged in this thesis free from social conflicts.

For instance, some researchers and surveyors in urban planning and development at the Sheffield

Hallam University, when analysing the Broomspring mixed housing estate of section B of Broomhall, the West End upper market estate, located just across the road off the limits of the eastbound limits of section B, and the Nether Edge gated upper market estate, argued that when poorer neighbourhoods coexist next to wealthier ones can lead to conflicts:

> "Rather than promoting mutual support and understanding and improving relations between different social classes, these mini-ghettos of public housing alongside wealthier neighbours can lead to tensions, resentment, and distrust. Private owners fear vandalism and crime from social tenants, where planners restrict private and social housing to different roads and blocks" (Blandy and Parsons, 2004).

The next section explains the historical boundaries of Broomhall.

4.3.4 Historic boundaries of Broomhall

This thesis relies primarily on the people's perceptions of how they define Broomhall and from documents. As for historical documents, Beal (1985), a LIS researcher and promoter of *community profiling* in the UK who is multi cited in this project, had identified that maps were "one of the most useful tools in community profiling" (Beal, 1985: 381) for librarians and any other documental information professionals (DIPs) to be able to understand the geographical boundaries of a given community. Nevertheless, the techniques for profiling geographical areas do not date from Beal's (1985) times in the 1970s or 1980s, but from Eratosthenes in the year 246 BC (Hacyan, 1986: 28; Muela-Meza, 2008; 2007: 434; Reale and Antiseri, 2004a: 264; Sagan, 2001).

Hence, as for Broomhall, the author of a LIS master's dissertation, which is the only direct and preceding work covering a large area of Broomhall, found in the summer of 1981 that the actual Broomhall boundaries "were subject to some dispute" (Hall, 1981: 24), however he neither explained what types of disputes he found, nor he made a thorough historical account about those boundaries. Nonetheless, it is interesting to note that the author of this thesis found not only a similar situation of disputes, but also major contradictions on how different organisations have tried to draw the boundaries of Broomhall according with their particular views.

These disputing and contradictory views of the Broomhall boundaries date back when the Broom Hall large landed estate was built and its boundaries delineated. For instance, one historian (Bambery, 1983) stated that Broom Hall was first built in the 14th century. However another historian has disagreed with that fact: Vickers (1990: 7) argued that "the earlier portion of Broom Hall was built in the time of Henry VIII, that is from 1509 to 1547," that is, in the 16th century. And to make it even more difficult to establish the true historical origins of the Broom Hall large rural landed estate, others argued that it was actually built circa 1498 (Harman and Minnis, 2004), hence in the 15th century. These four historians appeared in the literature review as having published more than one book on history of Sheffield, thus due to the dearth of more historical documents on Broomhall their historical accounts have not been dismissed.

Thus, what seemed to be the cause of this apparent historical mismatch of these three sources might have been that whilst Vickers (1990) and Harman and Minnis (2004) talked specifically about the origins and architectural features of the house called Broom Hall, on the other hand Bambery (1983) talked about the whole of the large rural landed estate which belonged to the owners of the Broom Hall house. This is the most likely reason of why there is a difference of three centuries to establish the Broom Hall historical origins. Then, provided that Bambery's (1983) account is accurate, this study could reach the provisional conclusion that the Broom Hall large rural landed estate was established in the 14th century, but that its historical Manor architecture house was built circa the late 15th century and early 16th century.

Therefore, if establishing the accurate historical record of the date of the origins of the Broom Hall large rural landed estate, or its house, has been found to be problematic and open to contradictory interpretations, then the reader could only expect that historical or contemporary boundaries of both the house and the large rural landed estate attached to Broomhall to be also problematic and contradictory.

As for the historical boundaries of the Broomhall large rural landed estate *per se,* from the many documents reviewed in this thesis it was found particularly one which could serve as the basis to define the historical boundaries of Broomhall as suggested by Bambery (1983), a historian of Sheffield. She established these historic boundaries of Broomhall:

> "In Wilkinson's times the estate [the Broom Hall large rural landed estate] consisted of bushes, fields and meadows, with a large pond in the North and watered by the Porter Brook in the South... It was extensive, stretching from what is now Glossop Road in the North to the River Porter in the South. In the West the boundary ran Northwards from Sharrow Mills on the Porter, while in the East the boundary ran along what is now Upper Hanover Street. The turnpike road to Chapel-en-le-Frith (now Ecclesall Road) was not driven through the estate until after 1811. Before this, the turnpike road had left Sheffield by a different route, running from Sheffield Moor to Banner Cross via Highfield, Sharrow Lane and Psalter Lane" (Bambery, 1983: 1).

Bambery's (1983) boundaries are in general loosely explained and since she did not provide any map or bibliographic references to substantiate her assertions, she leaves the boundaries to be set by the reader's imagination. As it can be read she left open to the reader's imagination the Broomhall borders on the east, south and west borders, particularly these last ones. Notwithstanding, that did not prevent the author to consider them as important elements to investigate about the configuration of the actual historic boundaries of Broomhall and thus the current ones too. But the reader has to bear in mind that arriving to that conclusion of giving some relevant importance to Bambery's (1983) assertions, considering she did not include bibliographic references or maps, it took the author more than three years of analysis of more than one thousand documents [7] in order to consider her boundaries with some validity.

Thus, Bambery's (1983) assertions are taken partly as evidence of boundaries of Broomhall since no more documents were found to prove otherwise. However, the author found a historic map of Derbyshire and Yorkshire from 1849-1899 (see Figure 4.3) that shows clearly that the east borders of Broomhall, through its namesake street, stretched until the junction of West Street and Eldon Street. However, he could not find a map of 1805 as to work out Bambery's (1983) arguments for setting the boundaries where she did.

Therefore, the author has merged both data and configured a new historic map of Broomhall from Bambery's (1983) arguments of boundaries as of 1805 and the Ordnance Survey (1849-1899) historic map (see Figure 4.3 below). This working configuration of this map is of course far from being conclusive due to the dearth of more historic documents, but it is considered here as the historic working map of Broomhall which the reader will be guided to as a reference throughout this thesis. The boundaries of this compounded historic map —marked in red— stretch until Eldon Street to the east, then they run south along Eldon Street and the nearby streets until Cemetery Road, then they run westwards until the Sharrow Mills, then they border the mills and then run northwards along the borders of the Botanical Gardens until the intersection of Clarkehouse Road on the north, then they run eastwards on Clarkehouse Road until they intersect with Glossop Road and finally the continue on that road until Eldon Street. It was not possible to find a map of the 18th century to represent Bambery's (1983) boundaries, but it was found a map produced between 1849 and 1899 (see Figure 4.3 below).

---

[7] See Muela-Meza (2003-2007) where the author shows more than 800 pictures and maps, and not to mention all the documents included in the main bibliography of the thesis.

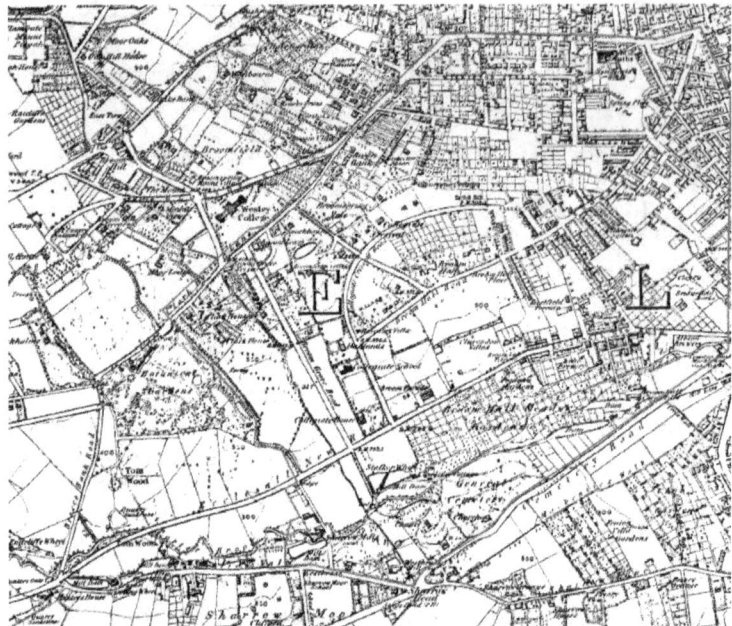

Figure 4.3 Map of Broomhall circa 1849 and 1899 according to the *Map of Derbyshire and Yorkshire, 1st ed. 1849-1899*. Source: (Ordnance Survey, 1849-1899).

According to the maps available analysed here, Broomhall geography remained basically unchanged since that map analysed of 1849-1899 (see Figure 4.3 above). However, that situation changed dramatically during WWII, thus the next section explains the major changes of Broomhall boundaries from the 1940s onwards.

4.3.5 Boundaries of Broomhall from the 1940s onwards

This and the following sections will focus on analysing the major changes of Broomhall from the 1940s onwards. It was during this decade and onwards where the major changes of Broomhall were found, in features such as territories, geography, landscape, population influxes, and basically in every aspect derived from the territorial major changes.

The next section will analyse how the Broomhall Forum, a major political organisation acting in the name of Broomhall have drawn Broomhall's boundaries.

4.3.5.1   THE BROOMHALL FORUM'S GEOGRAPHICAL BOUNDARIES OF BROOMHALL, (SECTION D).

The Broomhall Forum (BF) is one of the recent organisations from the voluntary sector acting within Broomhall. It was created in October 1998 (Broomhall Forum, 1999) and it is located at 7 Broomgrove Road, Sheffield, S10 2LW, UK at the YMCA premises in the section D, the Park (see Figure 4.3 above).

Thus, in 1999 the BF drew the limits of what they considered to be Broomhall at that time (see Figure 4.4 below) in a major research they carried out in that year (Broomhall Forum, 1999). The limits were no rigorously drawn following any scale from any map from the Ordnance Survey of the UK HMSO, and they were set rather in a sketchy manner.

However the reader could have some kind of idea clear enough to know that they perceived Broomhall within this geographical perimeter: beginning on Glossop Road on the west-north side and running eastbound, perhaps until the intersection with Fitzwilliam Street to the east side, then maybe westbound through Egerton Street until the junction with Hanover Way, then down south until Ecclesall Road, then westbound on that road until Broomhall Place, then up northbound

through that street which changes its name to Warncliffe Road until the intersection of Holberry
Gardens and somehow going westbound until intersecting with Glossop Road.

As just mentioned, the roads assumed from this map could not be well established because around
the sections number 6, 1, and 4 of their map they did not include all the names of streets, roads, and
so on.

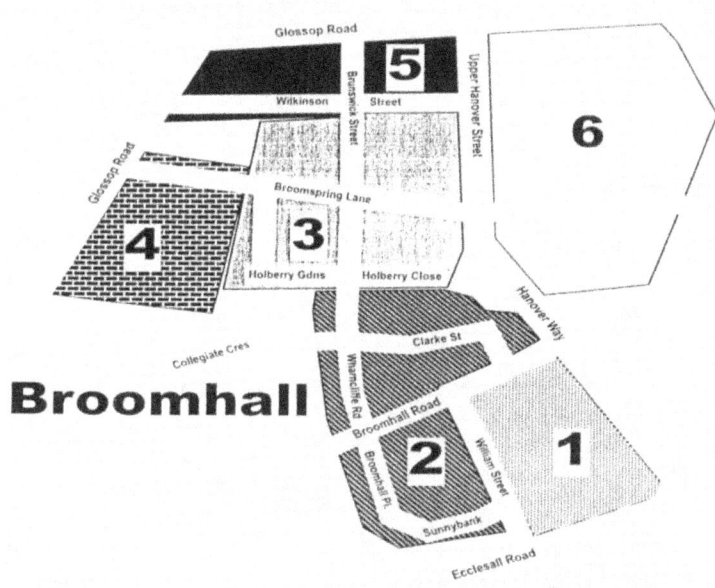

Figure 4.4 Map of Broomhall geographical limits according to the Broomhall Forum in 1999.
Source: (Broomhall Forum, 1999: 6)

Six years later, in September 2005, the Broomhall Forum (BF) designed a bigger and more detailed
map of how they perceived the new boundaries of Broomhall (see Figure 4.5).

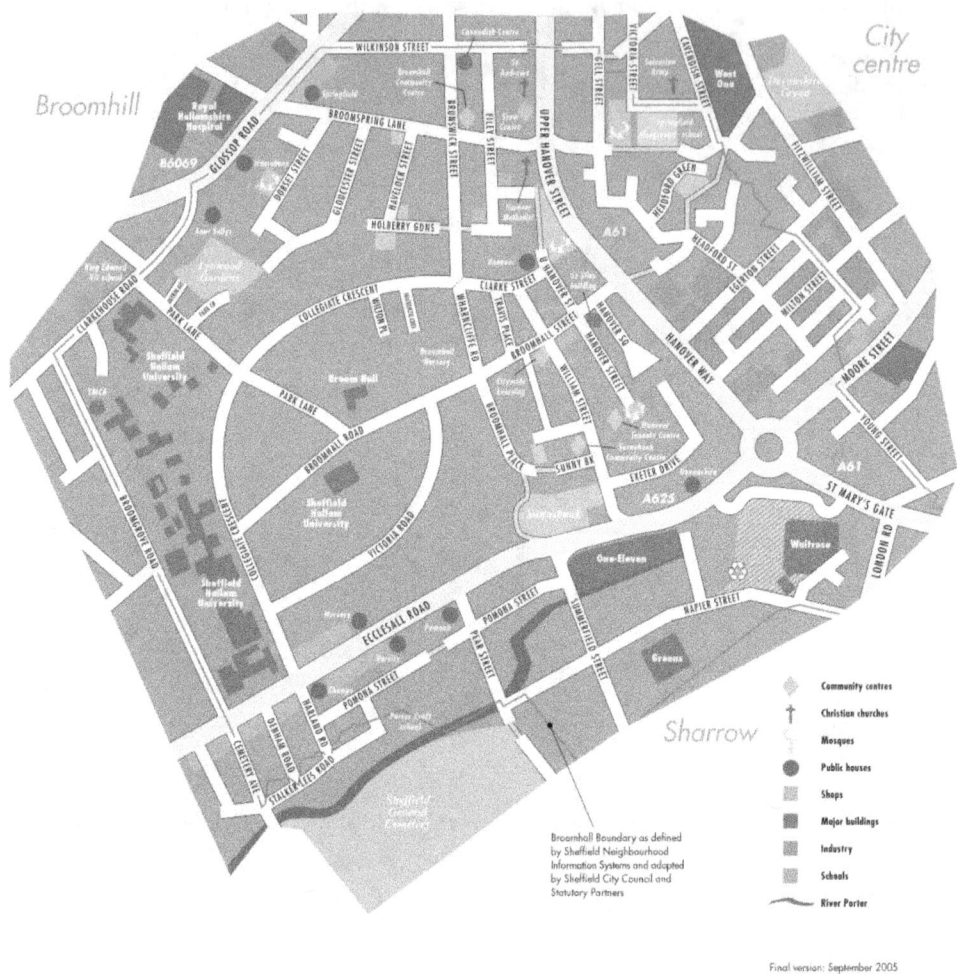

Figure 4.5 Map of Broomhall geographical boundaries according to the Broomhall Forum in 2005. Source: (*Broomhall News*, 2006: 4).

However, the BF is not the only organisation acting on the name of Broomhall that has drawn boundaries.

There are also others from the statutory sector that have drawn Broomhall boundaries, such as the Sheffield NHS (National Health Services) explained in the next section.

4.3.5.2   THE SHEFFIELD NHS BROOMHALL BOUNDARIES.

It is interesting to note that a year later of the Broomhall Forum' map, in 2006, the Sheffield National Health Service (NHS) also crafted a map (see Figure 4.6 below) very similar to that of Broomhall Forum shown in Figure 4.5 above.

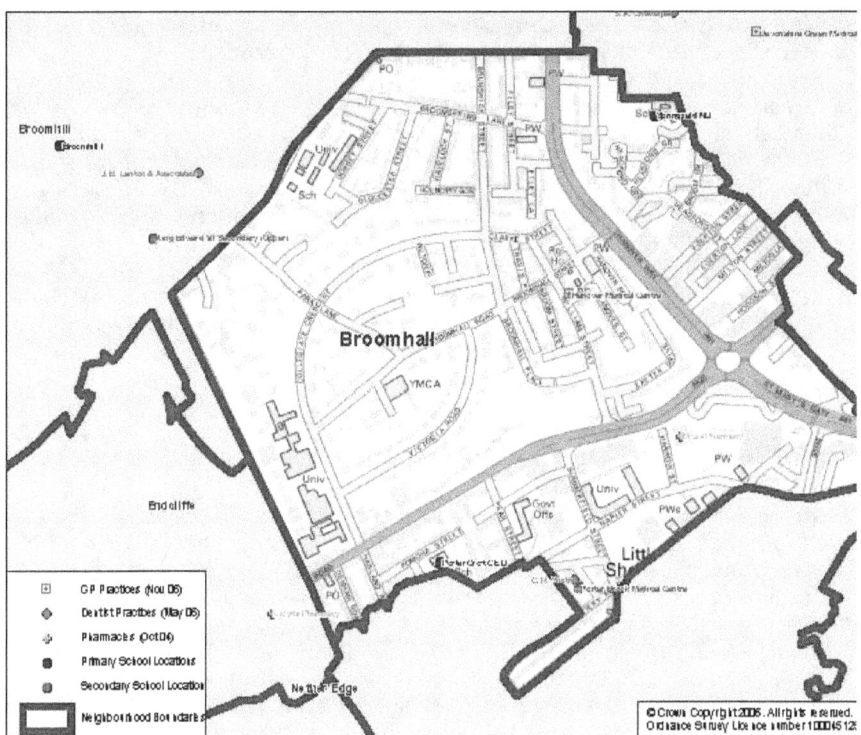

Figure 4.6 Map of Broomhall according to the Sheffield NHS (National Health Services), 2006.
Source: (NHS Sheffield PCT, 2006).

Notice that the maps of both the Broomhall Forum (BF) of 2005 (see Figure 4.5 above) and NHS
(National Health Services) (Figure 4.6 above) keep a close resemblance not only with each other but
also with the original historic map according to Bambery's (1983) boundaries of Broomhall circa
1805 (see Figure 4.3 above). However, as for these two maps neither the BF (Broomhall Forum,
1999: 6), nor the NHS (National Health Services) (NHS Sheffield PCT, 2006) made a clear
distinction of what are the actual Broomhall boundaries. As seen above, in 1999 (see Figure 4.4
above), the BF (Broomhall Forum, 1999: 6), after one year of its creation, had a kind of clear idea of
what the boundaries of Broomhall were. That is, in 1999 they clearly excluded the Broomhall Park
side, section D of Broomhall.

However, it has been found as a contradictory change that whilst the Broomhall Forum (BF) clearly
excluded the Broomhall Park from the Broomhall boundaries in 1999, six years later, in 2005, they
included it on their map (see Figure 4.5). Furthermore, what it has been found even more
contradictory is that the BF (Broomhall News, 2006: 4; Figure 4.5) claimed that their 2005 map
(see Figure 4.5) was drawn according to the Sheffield Neighbourhood Information Systems (SNIS)
(Sheffield City Council, 2005). However, the author consulted the same source and he did not find
any evidence that indicated that such boundaries were defined by the SNIS. In that source it was
found only a very small blue coloured boundary within a slightly bigger citywide Sheffield map as
the reader can verify it, but not clear boundaries as stated by the BF.

Thus, either the BF has cited a different SNIS unknown to the researcher, or they cited it wrongly,
or they have created their own map from the scratch before the SNIS and simply cited the SNIS to
give it authority. Hence, not having more documents than these, the evidence suggests that the
Broomhall Forum in 1998 when they officially launched their organisation they thought that the
Broomhall boundaries were as shown in Figure 4.4, that is excluding section D, the Park, but then
in 2005 (Figure 4.5) either they were influenced by the Broomhall Park Association, which is more
likely, and then they changed their map and extended it as shown on Figure 4.5. Therefore, this
evidence indicates that it is the BF that rather designed their map and later suggested the SNIS
(Sheffield City Council, 2005) to employ their map, not the other way around as they claim.

The BF's claims appear also contradictory because some information providers argued that the BF drew the boundaries of Broomhall according to the residents' perceptions:

"If you would like to make boundaries you would have to obtain the people's perceptions of what their community boundaries so as to get the actual boundaries. For example... So I tend to work with the people's perceptions on their community boundaries, instead of transport or local authorities perceptions, or parking boundaries, or the ward boundaries, because they change, depending on how they shift their mood." [an information provider from section D] [I.P.06]

However the perception of the information provider I.P.06 above could not be considered as evidence, because most of the residents interviewed do not include the Park, section D, as part of Broomhall. See for example some opinions by residents of sections A, B, and C, which contradict the I.P.06's views.

A respondent even argues that the Broomhall Park (section D) does not even receive the *Broomhall News* newsletter because they are not part of Broomhall:

I am leaving Broomhall Park out of the equation because I consider Broomhall Park so distinctively middle class that I don't consider it part of Broomhall, and I am not the only person who thinks that way. For example the Broomhall News newsletter that goes out 10 times a year it doesn't circulate to Broomhall Park unless they have a spare copies in that month. Because it is not seen part of the Broomhall neighbourhood [a middle class resident from section C] [R.I. 01]

A working class resident from the overcrowded Hanover Flats of section A explains better the idea of why the Broomhall Park (section D) does not belong to Broomhall and points out several contrasting features between the residents of the Park and rest of Broomhall:

[Broomhall] is a divided community. There are many small communities. Just looking at the map [the map the author showed to the respondent] you've got Victoria Road, Broomhall Road, Broomgrove Road, and Clarkgrove Road, these areas are not really part of Broomhall. I'm just saying, it is a silly point but you've got Victoria Road, Broomhall Road, Park Lane, Ecclessall Road, Collegiate Crescent, and they own all the big houses, posh houses, they've got gardens, and they are predominantly white. ... I can only think of one person who has a black person there and it's in Victoria Road and he is a dentist. And they consider themselves as part of Broomhall because they have their own association, Broom Park, is it called Broom Park? Yes Broomhall Park that's what is called and their concerns are for instance on a local level, they united together for instance because they want to get rid of the prostitutes they say were hanging around in their streets, and basically affecting the values of their properties, and if they could not come and go freely they'll feel threatened or whatever. However, if it hasn't been brought on their doorstep [prostitution], if it would happen here they wouldn't come together and founded an association. But they [Broomhall Park Association, section D of Broomhall] didn't work with us [residents in sections A, B, and C of Broomhall], they just work for themselves, that's what I'm saying, they are a different section, they don't consider themselves part of Broomhall, because they "are better than us" [respondent makes the sign of quotes "" with her fingers]. Because they are home owners, they have a job, and they have several cars, and they drive their kids to school in cars, and they won't drink in the local pubs, they won't shop in the local shops, they will get on their cars and go shopping to the big Tescos, you know... I know them because... [a working class resident from section A] [R.I. 07]

A working class resident from section B perceived the Broomhall Park as a self-ghettoized, that is self-divided from the rest of Broomhall with an imaginary wall, he called it the "Broomhall Wall":

"it's very interesting, I would say... there is like, it's not a physical wall but there is what I call the Broomhall Wall which runs from [pointing on a map the boundaries of section D of Broomhall as shown in Figure 4.1]... you know, where there are the Broomhall Park Association, Broomhall Forum... middle upper class associations run by rich people who own big houses in the Broomhall Wall, the rich side of Broomhall" [a working class resident from

section B of Broomhall] [R.I. 10]

Moreover, it has also been found as an unclear and odd coincidence that the NHS (National Health
Services) map (see Figure 4.4 above), one year after that of the Broomhall Forum (see Figure 4.3),
included also the Broomhall Park as part of the whole Broomhall territorial boundaries. There has
not been found much evidence as to understand why the Broomhall Forum changed the Broomhall
boundaries other than the contradicting views of the BF and the residents from sections A, B, and
C, or why they also match almost exactly with those of the NHS (National Health Services).

However, the NHS (National Health Services) (NHS Sheffield PCT, 2006) reported that they are
working in partnership with the Broomhall Forum in order to provide better health services for
Broomhall, hence, that connection could explain why both organizations' maps are almost exactly
the same.

Nevertheless, Bambery (1983), Broomhall Forum (Broomhall Forum, 1999: 6; *Broomhall News*,
2006: 4), and the NHS (National Health Services) (NHS Sheffield PCT, 2006) are not the only
organisations drawing boundaries of Broomhall, also the residents of the Broomhall Park area,
section D, where stands the Broom Hall house, have also drawn their limits.

4.3.5.3   THE BROOMHALL BOUNDARIES ACCORDING TO THE BROOMHALL PARK ASSOCIATION (SECTION D)

Despite the fact that there is not much evidence of why the Broomhall Forum excluded (in 1999)
the Broomhall Park (BP) out of the Broomhall boundaries, and then included it (in 2005) within
those boundaries, there is on the contrary plenty of evidence that the Broomhall Park residents
have in contemporary times drawn clear boundaries distinguishing and distancing the Broomhall
Park area, section D, from Broomhall, or rest of Broomhall, or Broomhall except the Park area, or
sections A, B, and C of Broomhall.

The Broomhall Park (BP) has historically been home of the most affluent capitalist and upper
middle class residents (Batho, 1968; Hey, 1998). In 1967 they created their *ad hoc* association, the
Broomhall Park Residents Association (BPRA). A commentator mentioned in a two pages popular
magazine article that the BPRA looked after only for the interests of the BP territorial area, section
D (Batho, 1968).

A LIS researcher not only did confirm that fact, but he (Hall, 1981), in his LIS master's research
dissertation of 131 pages long, found that the BPRA's interests had had conflicts with those of the
rest of Broomhall, e.g. the Broomhall Community Group (BCG) of the Havelock area, section C (see
Figure 4.3 above).

And the major interests the BPRA look after were their own territorial interests, the Park's
territorial interests. In 1968 the BPRA made a proposal to the Sheffield City Council to create a
conservation area for "Broomhall" (see Connell, 1968 and Figure 4.7 below).

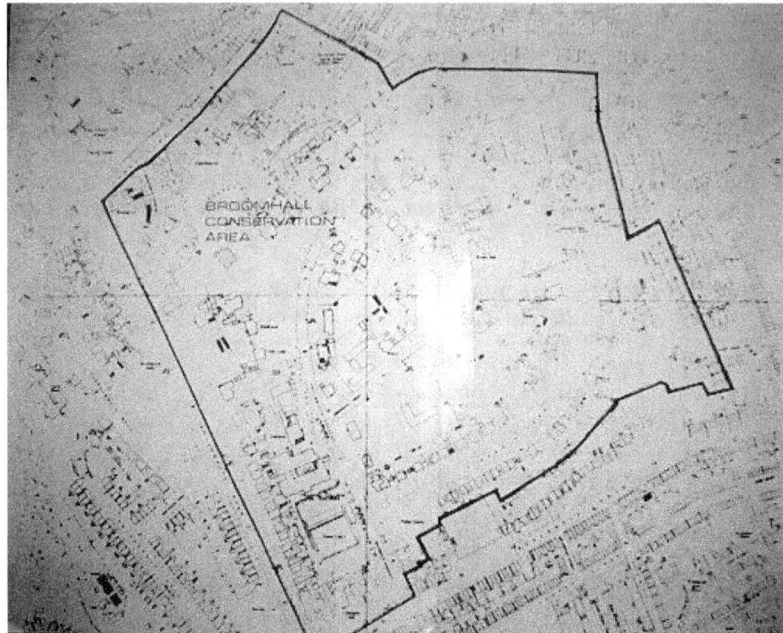

Figure 4.7 Map of the original proposal of the Broomhall Park Conservation Area, 1967. Source: (Connell, 1968).

Such petition shown in Figure 4.7 the residents of the BPRA signed it as *Broomhall Residents Association* and not as Broomhall Park Residents Association, BPRA. And they entitled it: *Interim Report on the Proposal to Designate the Broomhall Area as a Conservation Area Submitted to the Sheffield City Council* (Connell, 1968). That is, the BPRA residents submitted their petition with a map showing a rather small piece of land in the name of the whole "Broomhall."

The "Broomhall's" boundaries of their conservation area were delimited within the following roads:

> Broomgrove Road to the east, Clarkehouse Road to the north, then they drew a southern line where there was no road at the end of Clarkehouse Road at the junction with Glossop Road in the limit of the Aunt Sally pub, further down on the eastern border of the Lynwood Gardens, then bordering the north-eastern backyard of the College Crescent mansions, then down through Warncliffe Street, then on the corner with Broomhall Road they turned east until Clinton Road to include all the mansions of Broomhall Place from their backyards, and then down until the Sunnybank Wild Reserve park, but not until Ecclesall Road, but only until the backyards of all the mansions of Victoria Road and then they continued westbound until the intersection of Broomgrove Road by getting to it somehow through Ecclesall Road by enclosing completely all the current Hallam University Buildings (see Figure 4.7 above).

Therefore, this is a clear evidence of contradictions of the residents of the Broomhall Par Residents Association (BPRA) who used the name of "Broomhall" as a catchword in order to persuade the Sheffield City Council that they were looking after the interests of the whole of the people living within the territory comprised within the Broomhall boundaries (Connell, 1968), that is all sections A, B, C, and D that emerged in this thesis, and shown in Figure 4.3 above.

However, in reality they only meant their particular type of "Broomhall": the Broomhall Park area, comprised within the boundaries of section D. It is also evident that they concealed their real name, BPRA, and changed it for BRA. By withholding "Park" from their real organisation's name they also appealed before the council and the public as an association which at least in name represented all the interests of all the people living in the Broomhall territorial boundaries, but as explained, that was not the case (see Figures 4.8 and 4.9 for further evidence).

The response of the Sheffield City Council. The council approved on the 2nd of September 1970 the

BPRA's petition and officially named it Broomhall Conservation Area, but it excluded basically all
the buildings which now belong to the Sheffield Hallam University (SHU) limiting the new map
until Collegiate Crescent and included 14 more mansions on Broomgrove Lane which were not
originally proposed by the BPRA (see Figure 4.8 below).

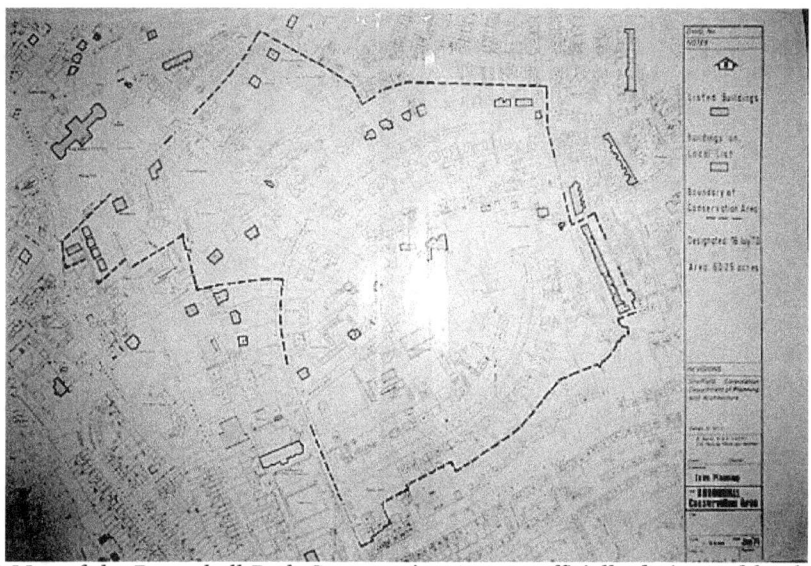

Figure 4.8 Map of the Broomhall Park Conservation Area as officially designated by the Sheffield
City Council, 16 July 1970. Source: (Sheffield Corporation, 1974).

However, in 1989 the Broomhall Park Residents Association (BPRA) lobby achieved to have the
council enlarging the Broomhall Park Conservation Area (BPCA) conservation boundaries
stretching to their desired original plans of 1967, that is, engulfing the Sheffield Hallam University
(SHU), plus those 14 mansions on Broomgrove Lane (see Figure 4.9 below and compare it with
Figure 4.8 above).

Figure 4.9 Map of the Broomhall Park Conservation Area as officially enlarged by the Sheffield City Council, 5 July 1989. Sources: (City of Sheffield, 1989; Sheffield City Council, 2007a: 23).

Hence, being the Broomhall Park (BP), section D, the largest area of the Broomhall territories, legally protected as a Broomhall Conservation Area under the *English Planning (Listed Buildings and Conservation Areas) Act*, that meant that the owners of the properties or developers could not be free any longer to develop any property which affect the architectural, or historic features from those buildings and the land where they were built (HMSO, 1990).

Nevertheless, from the data generated in this project could not be established on which basis the Council appraised the BPRA's petition for a conservation area. The author tried hard to find more information to fill this gap but it was not possible due to the outdated of the documents and that they were not available at the Sheffield Central Library or anywhere else.

However, from the information available, the author could establish that the BPRA does not seek culturally genuine interests, because for example the Sheffield City Council through the department of Libraries, Archives and Information (LAI) since 1974 is under the ownership of the Bishop House Museum which along with the Broom Hall house is the major Manor architectural entire house truly in conservation in Sheffield (Vickers, 1990: 15). That is, the Bishop House is a large Manor house converted into museum and well maintained by the SCC's LAI department and most of all open and free for all the public to learn about the history of Sheffield from Manor days.

On the other hand, the Broom Hall has only few Manor logs and masonry and it is not a cultural building open for the public, but a private organisation office and nursery, hence the Broomhall Park Residents Association promised in 1967 the council and the Sheffield people that they would transform the Broom Hall into a library and museum (Connell, 1968). It is four decades now since that promise, but the BPRA never fulfilled it; not even close, the managers of the estate almost prohibited the author to take pictures, and they keep the Manor side of the estate locked with steel gates.

Nevertheless, the author found more contradictions of the BPRA, which put into question the real intentions of their aims as conservation area. For instance, in 1967 the YMCA

Sheffield was established in the Broomhall Park (BP), section D, within the premises of a huge Victorian house built in early 19th century (Hey, 1998: 253). It was located on the numbers 11-15 of Broomhall Road, Sheffield, S10 2DQ, on a massive area of land of 10, 956 m2 (132m of front per 83m of bottom). However in 2001 the YMCA sold its massive land to the Sheffield Hallam University (SHU) including its "old building, along with its conference centre and sports facilities" (Star (Sheffield), 2002b).

See below Table 4.6. to assess the comparative ground areas in square metres of the ex YMCA property on Broomhall Road and the Hanover Flats (section A):

Table 4.6. Comparative ground areas in square metres of the ex YMCA property on Broomhall Road and the Hanover Flats (section A)	
Area of ex YMCA property in Broomhall Road (one single property owned and inhabited by a single owner and few YMCA staff)	Area of the Hanover Flats (comprising 156 flats where thousands of people live)
10, 956 m2 (132 m of front per 83 m of bottom)	1, 155 m2 (55m of front per 21m of bottom)

The negative consequences for the poor residents outside the section D of the Park from such sale have been explained further in Chapter 5. However, the Sheffield Hallam University (SHU) did indeed demolished completely the old nineteenth-century building down to its foundations, and it also transformed, and developed the whole of the land. That is, they affected the architectural and historic character of the land and the building, hence the author considered this a type of circumventing of the Conservation Area Act. Certainly that building was not a listed building like the Broom Hall house, but nonetheless, from these data it is not clear why the BPRA, and the Sheffield City Council allowed the SHU to affect the historic character of the ex YMCA building.

This is only one example that contradicts the original aims of the BPRA, but there are others. If readers would review the hundreds of pictures and maps employed by the author (Muela-Meza, 2003-2007) they could find many other historic or Victorian buildings within the BP, section D, with "sale" signs by developers, or in other areas of Broomhall outside BP, there are also many historic building which deserved to be under a conservation law, but the BPRA excluded them.

Nevertheless, it is part of human nature for humans to adhere to certain territory. Hence, all the cases assessed above are not unique, in other areas of Broomhall outside the BP, section D, people have also got together to draw their own Broomhall boundaries.

That is also the case of the Broomhall Community Group (BCG), which is analysed in the next section.

4.3.5.4   BROOMHALL BOUNDARIES ACCORDING TO THE BROOMHALL COMMUNITY GROUP (BCG)

Hall (1981) mentioned that there were some tensions amongst the residents of the Broomhall Park (BP), section D, with those of Havelock, section C. However, from his study (Hall, 1981) and other studies (Crook, et. al., 1976; Crook, 1983; Gibson, and Dorfman, 1981) exclusively related to Havelock area, section C, could not be established either the relationships or the tensions between the residents from Section D and C. Instead, from the data emerged that both sections D and C only looked after their own territorial interests excluding those of the other three sections. For instance, the Broomhall Community Group (BCG) of Havelock, section C, they also did a grassroots lobby similar to the BP's in order to preserve their large Victorian terraced houses because the council wanted to 'bulldoze' many derelict or semi derelict.

In addition, in 1978 they achieved from the council to be recognised as a Housing Action, but only for Havelock, Havelock Housing Action (HHA), see Figure 4.10 below. The HHA meant that the government would not demolish their properties and instead they would give residents grants to refurbish them (Hall, 1981; Crook, et. al., 1976; Crook, 1983; Gibson and Dorfman, 1981).

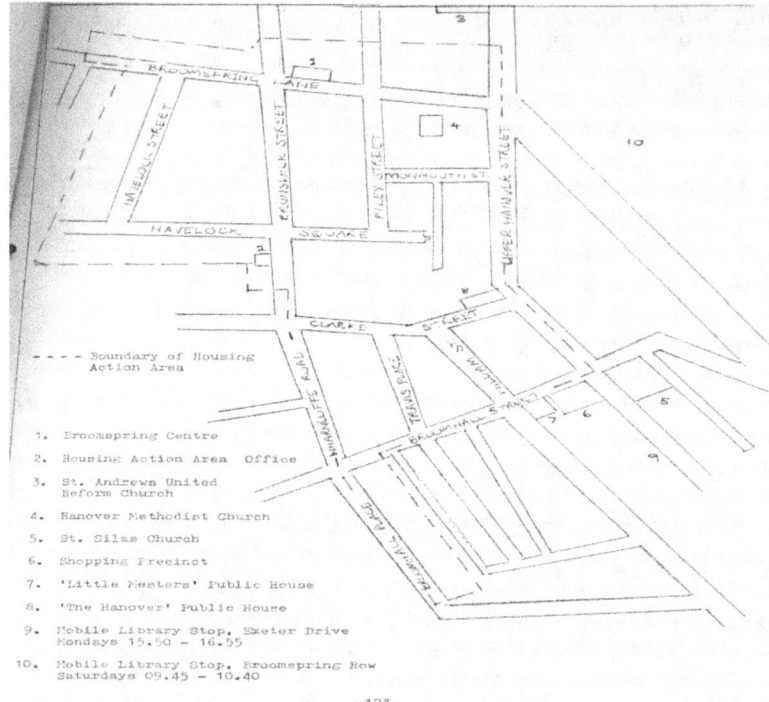

-123-

Figure 4.10 Map of Broomhall featuring the Havelock Housing Action boundaries. Source: (Hall, 1981: 123).

However, not everyone in Havelock was happy, not everyone received grants to refurbish their properties. The HHA established by the council did not include all the properties comprised in section C as shown above in Figure 4.3. They also excluded the properties from sections A and B, and of course from section D.

Therefore, from this, evidence could not be established that there is an homogeneous division of the Broomhall Park as being the better off territory, and sections ABC the worse off, because even section C is better off than B, and B better off than A, and the sections DCB altogether are better off than A. And even within each sections there are many subtle intricacies of social class divides on territoriality, for instance, those people living in maisonettes are better off than those living in the twin tower overcrowded high rise flats within section A.

Still, all that has been already explained in the previous sections does not clarify comprehensively why there have been many tensions and conflicts over territoriality or uses of the land.

Hence, in the next section the reader will assess the single one most remarkable historic fact that changed for good most of the territorial features, not only of the Broomhall neighbourhood, but also of Sheffield on a citywide scale and some other British largest cities. The single one most remarkable historic fact was the Nazi Blitz of World War II.

4.3.5.5   THE NAZI BLITZ THAT SUBSTANTIALLY ALTERED THE BROOMHALL (AND SHEFFIELD) LANDSCAPE

The WWII Nazi Blitz bombs dropped in Sheffield on the 12th December 1940 and they altered substantially and dramatically the Sheffield landscape forever because of the large damage caused to the city, buildings, houses, land, and mostly people's lives, and Broomhall was also severely hit (see Figure 4.11 below). This can be accounted by a Sheffield historian (Lofthouse, 2001) who was born in the Broomhall Park, section D, on the number 69 of Southgrove Road,[8] and who was also a survivor of the Blitz. Three other survivors (Czerwinski, 2005; Hall, 2006; McElvenney, 2005) of the Nazi Blitz, who were born in Broomhall, in section C, Havelock, also corroborate Lofthouse's (2001) accounts.

As mentioned above, the Broomhall Park (BP) has historically been home of the most affluent capitalist and upper middle class residents (Batho, 1968; Hey, 1998). However, not only BP had those characteristics, but the whole of the Broomhall territory. The reader can recall above that originally Broomhall was a large landed estate that stretched far as the limits drawn here on the map of Figure 4.3, that is, beyond the limits of sections ABCD of the working map employed here (see Figure 4.1 above). Therefore, it could be fairly said that before WWII Broomhall had unaltered geographical features.

But all of that changed fatally and dramatically overnight. As it can be seen in Figure 4.11 below in red dots, twenty highly explosive bombs were dropped by the Nazis in Broomhall: ten bombs were dropped in section D; the Park, eight in section C; one near section B (what is now the big Devonshire Green park); and one in section A. These twenty bombs dropped on the territories of Broomhall according to the contemporary map as analysed and employed in this thesis (see Figure 4.1). [9]

Thus it was that, Britain being at war against Nazi Germany, and above all, the Nazi Blitz over Sheffield, and Broomhall, this event can be considered here as the single most remarkable historic fact which in itself explains many other issues and features related to Broomhall. However, it is interesting noting that none of the authors reviewed who have done research specifically related to Broomhall (Hall, 1981; Crook, et. al., 1976; Crook, 1983; Gibson and Dorfman, 1981) and none of the respondents of interviews made a connection of the Second World War (WWII) with post-war changes of Broomhall. Only Hall (1981) and Crook (1976) did mention that the city council after WWII wanted to clear derelict or semi derelict properties, but they failed to make a comprehensive analysis as it is being made here.

---

[8] The major road that the Broomhall Forum and the NHS omitted from their respective maps.

[9] If the reader compares the maps of Figure 4.3 and 4.11, the amount of bombs dropped in the historic Broomhall map would increase from 20 up to 34, 14 more than the registered here on the working map (Figure 4.3). That is, it is not clear from the evidence collected when the historic limits shown in Figure 4.3 were reduced to the limits of the working map employed here in Figure 4.3, but even if the historic limits shown in Figure 4.3, were the currently valid limits, instead of the ones employed here in Figure 4.3, still Broomhall territories would have been severely damaged, actually more than how it is assessed here. That is, in either case Broomhall territories resulted damaged and altered.

Where The Bombs Dropped

Figure 4.11 Map of Broomhall, c 1944, where the highly explosive bombs of the WWII Nazi Blitz were dropped on the 12th December 1940. Source: (Lofthouse, 2001: 73).

Nevertheless the reader can only attempt a re-imagining of the effects on Broomhall as major parts of Sheffield were bombed, and thousands of people became homeless overnight, not to mention that 589 were killed; 750 were missing; 500 seriously injured; more than 3, 000 shops and houses damaged beyond repair; 82, 000 other properties with severe damage; the tram lines destroyed (and 2 lines used to run along Broomhall); water and gas pipes destroyed; and many other post-war damages and issues affecting thousands of families (Lofthouse, 2001: 4), hence the building of fast "pre-fab" houses, and the Broomhall Flats and many others alike which still stand like the Park Hill flats, was within this context a sound solution.

Nonetheless, other factors have affected the territorial character of Broomhall. As Sheffield has become a city with highly developed universities, and thus attracting through times more and more students, then it is logical that universities should increase in facilities and services to cope with the ever-increasing demand of students. In this context two major universities, Sheffield Hallam

University and the University of Sheffield, were found remarkably related to the Broomhall neighbourhood.

The next section explains how the territorial expansionism of these universities has been affecting Broomhall through time.

4.3.6 Expansion of Hallam and Sheffield universities (University Student Villages)

This territorial expansionism has been more particularly increasing and steady from Hallam Sheffield University, HSU, which basically owns one third of the land of section D, but at least since the 1960s as far as documental evidence derived from this project is concerned they have planned to take over much of the land of what has been configured here in this project belonging to the Broomhall neighbourhood (Warman, 1969; see also Figure 4.12 below).

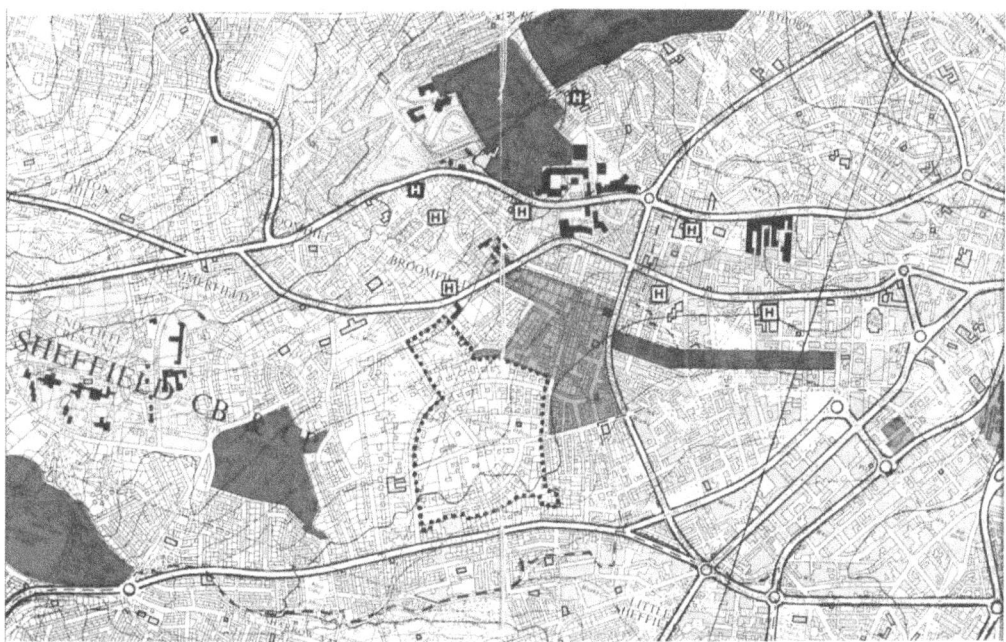

Figure 4.12 Map of the plans for territorial expansion of Sheffield Hallam University within the Broomhall neighbourhood, c 1969 (Source: Warman, 1969: 72-73).

In Figure 4.12, colour blue indicates the expansionist plans by SHU where residents, mostly from section C, actually lived; yellow indicated existing University of Sheffield territories; and green indicated existing and proposed green areas, such as the proposed corridor aligned with Broomspring Lane, but where residents actually lived. Whilst it is true that the German Nazi Blitz altered substantially some parts of Broomhall, by 1969, almost 40 years after the Blitz, people from section C had already showed a great deal of resilience to recover from the extremely severe effects of the war and also of determination to preserve their homes (Hall, 1981; Crook, et. al., 1976; Crook, 1983; Gibson, and Dorfman, 1981).

However, the Sheffield Hallam University (SHU) plans to simply 'bulldoze' virtually all the section C of this project, and their proposed "green corridor" from Hanover Street until the city centre without considering the residents' opinions, or feelings, show in itself evidence of the clashes amongst residents and SHU. That may explain why there is a radical watchdog group named Rage Against Sheffield Hallam University watching and denouncing over and over every SHU expansionist plan to take over citizens' land.

On the other hand, with more tact, the University of Sheffield (UofS) indeed makes an effort at public consultations with residents (Student Residences Strategy Team, 2004; Department of Marketing and Communications, 2005), but still it should not be seen as a great consolation. It would be interesting someone conducted a research such as this and ask the residents who live in and around Endcliffe and Ranmoor, where the new fancy UofS student village is being, what they think of the UofS expansionist plans in that area.

But the big issue for the residents of Broomhall is Sheffield Hallam University. SHU themselves show in large physical campus maps all the territories they own in Broomhall in order to guide their students, staff, etc., see Figure 4.13 below.

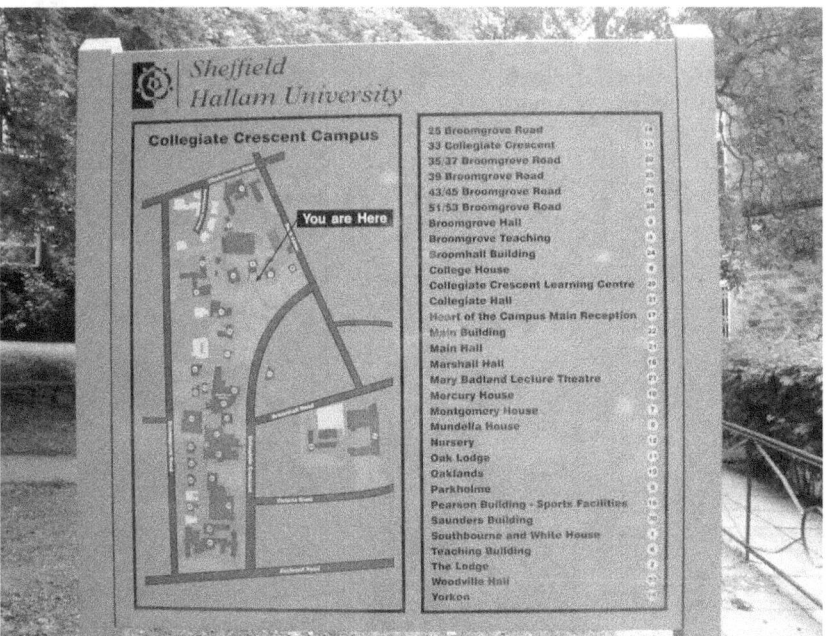

Figure 4.13 Map of Sheffield Hallam University Broomhall Park campus, section D, picture taken on 19 May 2007 (Source: the author, Muela-Meza, 2003-2007).

The next section will show a demographic background of Broomhall from official statistical sources.

4.4 Demographic background of Broomhall

As mentioned before, the author of this project has not relied on government statistics because he found them outdated in most cases, and inaccurate in others. However, for the reader to have a snapshot profile of the statistical data of Broomhall, a series of statistical tables and figures are shown below where the reader can assess how the government describes Broomhall and compares it with a citywide index. Nonetheless, the reader should bear in mind that these tables and figures are shown here only in a descriptive manner without further analysis, and should not be considered as the major findings analysed throughout this thesis. For a comprehensive analysis and discussion of findings the reader should refer to the rest of the thesis, and particularly to Chapter 5, which is entirely devoted to the major findings.

In the next pages the reader will find different statistical figures in tables and figures that show how the Sheffield City Council profiles the Broomhall neighbourhood.

In Table 4.7, see below, it is described the Broomhall Index and Domain Scores from 2001 census. In this table the Sheffield City Council compares the Broomhall scores with the Sheffield citywide scores on the following categories: 1) Economic activity; 2) Education; 3) Housing; 4) Environment; 5) Access to services; 6) Health and social care; and 7) Community safety.

Table 4.7 Broomhall Index and Domain Scores from 2001 census				
SNIS		Broomha	Sheffiel	Gap

Neighbourhood		ll	d	
1 Economic Activity	Score	22.8	38.4	-15.6
	Rank	23	37	-14
2 Education	Score	39.9	44.1	-4.2
	Rank	43	49	-6
3 Housing	Score	44.0	49.4	-5.4
	Rank	33	46	-13
4 Environment	Score	20.2	47.1	-26.9
	Rank	8	43	-35
5 Access to Services	Score	60.8	53.1	7.7
	Rank	53.1	56	14
6 Health and Social Care	Score	38.6	43.5	-4.9
	Rank	34	43	-9
7 Community Safety	Score	20.2	35.6	-15.3
	Rank	13	32	-19
Total Index	Score	33.4	43.5	-10.1
	Rank	20	42	-22
Source: Sheffield Neighbourhoods Information System (2005).				

Table 4.8 shown below shows the Broomhall 2001 Census Key Statistics compared with Sheffield. It describes these elements: 1) Total population; 2) Area (km²); 3) Density of population per (km²); 4) Population under 16; 5) Population over 65; 6) Black and Minority Ethnic residents; 7) Households with dependent children; and 8) Households in social housing.

Table 4.8 Broomhall 2001 Census Key Statistics compared with Sheffield		
Census Key Statistics	**Broomhall**	**Sheffield**
Population (total)	5,277	513,234
	1.0%	100.0%
Area (km²)	0.96	366.76
	0.3%	100.0%
Density (pop^n/km²)	5,491	1,399
	392.4%	100.0%
Population under 16	708	98,031
	13.4%	19.1%
Population over 65	496	84,121
	9.4%	16.4%
Black and Minority Ethnic Residents	1,778	55,536
	33.8%	10.8%
Households with Dependent Children	382	59,424
	18.8%	27.3%
Households in Social Housing	823	65,940
	40.5%	30.3%
Source: Sheffield Neighbourhoods Information System (2005).		

Figure 4.14 below, related to Table 4.7 above, shows graphically the domain scores of Broomhall compared with Sheffield at large.

Figure 4.14 Heptagram of Broomhall Index and Domain Scores from 2001 census

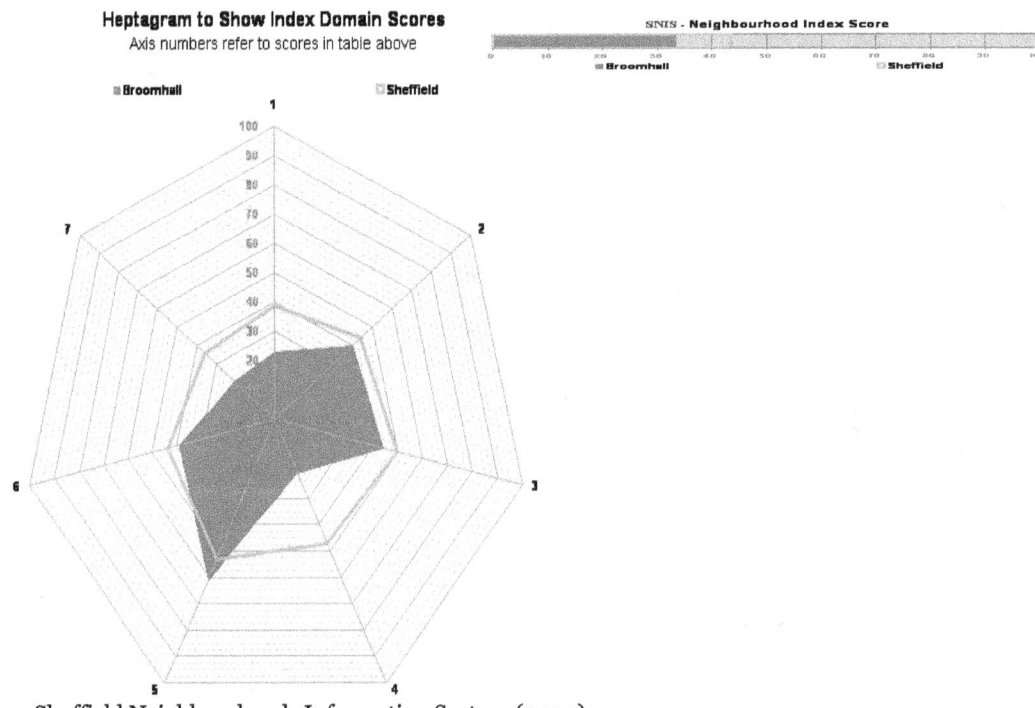

Source: Sheffield Neighbourhoods Information System (2005).

Figure 4.15 below shows the approximate geographical boundaries of the Broomhall neighbourhood within an actual map of the city of Sheffield.

Figure 4.15 Broomhall Neighbourhood Locator Map within Sheffield from 2001 census

Neighbourhood Locator Map

Source: Sheffield Neighbourhoods Information System (2005).

2.5 Summary

This chapter has presented a general historical, territorial, and demographical background of the Broomhall neighbourhood. These are the key points.

4)   Key points of the historical background of Broomhall.

A remarkable historic fact found was that the Broomhall neighbourhood of Sheffield, UK, five centuries ago was related to one of the most affluent large landed estates of England: the Broom Hall estate located in the west side of Sheffield. In the 18th century the Broom Hall estate was owned by the Reverend James Wilkinson, Vicar and Magistrate of Sheffield. Another remarkable fact was that Wilkinson passed many laws, which enclosed poor people's common land. In response these people made many revolts against him. In one of these his property was attacked and his library was set on fire. Hence, during those controversial times Sheffield was under strong military control.

One of the major findings and information needs that emerged in this study is related to the issues of territoriality or uses of the land (see Chapter 5 for analysis and discussion of findings). This finding can be traced from the history of Broomhall. In the 18th century the owners of the Broom Hall estate began dividing to divide the land to build the first earliest massive signs of urban housing developments for renting. In the 19th century these housing developments were too expensive for middle or working classes to afford them. By 1892 the estate had been almost fully developed, and became fashionable amongst professionals and members of the capitalist class who built steel factories (e.g. Sipelia Works). The pleasant residential character of Broomhall for wealthy families remained unchanged until 12th December 1940 when due to the WWII Nazi Blitz several bombs fell in Broomhall, and many houses were destroyed (see above in this chapter Figure 4.11).

5)   Key points of the territorial background of Broomhall.

The most outstanding finding and information need of this study is related to *territoriality and uses of the land*. This finding has also been closely interrelated with the *social class struggles concept* and the *materialist conception of history* (see Table 2.1 in Chapter 2 for definition). Hence, people from the three social classes of this study (working, middle, and capitalist or bourgeois) interact by living or working in Broomhall. Most poor working class residents live in section A (Hanover Flats) rent social Housing in Multiple Occupation (HMO). A mix of working and middle class residents, but prevailing the former, live in social and private HMO (Housing in Multiple Occupation) in section B (Broomspring Estate). Most middle class residents live in detached and semi-detached houses and few live in social and private HMO (Housing in Multiple Occupation) in section C (Havelock). A mix of middle and capitalist or bourgeois class live in semi-detached houses, and detached houses and mansions in section D (The Park). This class division (as analysed in chapters 2, and 5) has emerged in the study as determining the section where residents live. Hence, the materially determined territorial conditions of living amongst the four sections have been found remarkably different and contrasting (see above Figures 4.1 and 4.2 Broomhall maps to assess at a glance the density of houses and green open spaces, and Tables 4.1 through 4.4 to assess the density of dwellings per ground area in square meters). Thus, the better the territorial conditions of living and the upper a class individuals belong to, the better chances they have to cope better with information needs (e.g. they have inline telephones; they buy information; they go to libraries; they have Internet connection), and basically with everything else in life, and vice versa.

As mentioned earlier, *territoriality and uses of the land* issues emerged as an all encompassing finding and information need in this study. For the territorial background of Broomhall, one of the most problematic issue that emerged from the literature was the delimitation of the historic and contemporary boundaries. For instance, it was not possible to establish the exact foundation date of the Broom Hall large rural landed estate in order to trace the historic boundaries. A historian noted that Broom Hall was built in the 14th century (Bambery, 1983). Another noted that it was built from 1509 to 1547 (Vickers, 1990: 7). In addition, a third historian noted that it was built circa 1498 (Harman and Minnis, 2004). The author reached the provisional conclusion that the Broom Hall large rural landed estate was built in the 14th century (Bambery, 1983), and that its historical Broom Hall house with Manor architecture features was built circa the late 15th century (Harman and Minnis, 2004), and early 16th century (Vickers, 1990). However, this mismatch of three centuries to establish this date only shows the difficulties found to establish the historic boundaries of Broomhall, whose name was taken from the Broom Hall landed estate and Manor house. Hence, building on Bambery's (1983) accounts of the earliest boundaries of Broom Hall and a *Map of Derbyshire and Yorkshire circa 1849-1899* (Ordnance Survey, 1849-1899), the author configured an approximation of the historic boundaries of Broom Hall (see Figure 4.3).

If establishing the historic boundaries of Broom Hall was problematic, establishing the contemporary boundaries of Broomhall was no less problematic. The analysis of the contemporary boundaries began from the 1940s onwards due to the WWII Nazi Blitz that altered substantially the Broomhall and Sheffield landscape. The contemporary boundaries of Broomhall as emerged in this study, both from documents and interviewees' perceptions, are shown in the two working maps of this study in Figures 4.1 and 4.2 above in this chapter. These maps included the four sections in which Broomhall was divided in this study: A, the Hanover Flats, B, the Broomspring Estate, C, Havelock, and D, the Broomhall Park.

As shown above in this chapter, most interviewees did not consider section D as part of Broomhall, but the Broomhall Park Association, located in section D, did not consider sections A, B, and C as part of Broomhall either (see maps above in Figures 4.7 through 4.9). These findings show evidence of how divided is Broomhall geographically, but also of some lack of awareness of the history of Broomhall most interviewees and the Broomhall Park Association have shown. Regardless of these contrasting views, the author included the four working sections of Broomhall because historically they belong together. However, this geographical divide is interrelated with social class. That is, the author has maintained together in this study the contemporary geographical boundaries of Broomhall into the four sections as emerged from data, but he has also highlighted the social class contrasts, contradictions, and conflicts that emerged in the study derived precisely from the sharply marked social class composition of these four contrasting sections.

6)   Key points of the demographic background of Broomhall.

As for the demographical data, it is presented just a snapshot profile of what the Sheffield City Council, through its comprehensive statistical Sheffield Neighbourhoods Information System (2005), quantified as the main features that describe Broomhall. However, since this thesis is mainly a qualitative research study, readers should not consider the demographical background as the most relevant description of Broomhall, but they should instead focus on the historical background, and mainly on Chapter 5 where the major findings of this thesis have been analysed and discussed at length.

The next chapter presents the analysis and discussion of the major findings of this thesis, and the perceptions of residents and information providers about the Broomhall issues, features, information needs, and provision.

CHAPTER 5. ANALYSIS AND DISCUSSION OF FINDINGS. PERCEPTIONS OF THE ISSUES AND FEATURES OF BROOMHALL, INFORMATION NEEDS, AND PROVISION

> "What's the right way and the wrong way to report results [of research]? Disinterestedly, so that the other man is free to understand precisely what you are saying, and as nearly as possible not covering it with your desires." — Nobel laureate, Richard Phillips Feynman, *The Pleasure of Finding Things Out*, (Feynman, 2001: 108).

5.1 Introduction

This chapter presents the analysis, and discussions of the major findings of the thesis (which includes the merging of both: the pilot and the main study).

5.1.1 Overview

This chapter also analyses and discusses the interrelationships of those findings, with the needs of information recorded in documents from the residents of the Broomhall neighbourhood, and with the various ways that information providers tried to meet them.

5.1.2 How the issues and features of Broomhall became information needs

The same six major issues, and two major features, that emerged as the major variables and findings of this thesis, have been translated at the same time by the researcher as the eight major information needs (as explained in the following sections).

Broomhall, like any other neighbourhood where people live, work, play, enjoy, and suffer, has negative (or controversial, or adverse) or positive (or less controversial or adverse) features, which affect people. People perceive these as problems, or issues, but seldom as needs, and almost never as information needs. Thus, the researcher considered that these six major issues, and two major features that emerged in this thesis were precisely the eight major information needs perceived by the residents of Broomhall.

However, Broomhall has also positive (or less negative, or controversial, or adverse) features. However, the negative features, thus problems, and issues, are the more pervasive throughout the outcomes, discussions, conclusions, and recommendations of this project. This was due to the fact that the interviewees belonged only to the working and middle classes and the majority of the population belonged to the poor working class (mostly from section A, and partially from B) as emerged from observation and the literature.

As explained in Chapter 4 (see section 4.3.2), these findings evolved from the pilot study –*The Broomhall community profile*– that the researcher conducted from 30 September 2003, until 18 October 2004, and that he presented as part of the requirements towards his MPhil/PhD Transfer report in 2005 (Muela-Meza, 2005a).

The major issues of Broomhall in 2005 that emerged from two focus groups, literature and observation were:

1)   Housing issues.
2)   Unemployment issues.
3)   Health issues.
4)   Multiculturalism and social exclusion issues (including social class divides).
5)   Educational issues.

The findings of this thesis have been classified into two categories: issues and features. Whereas issues represent a more negative perception of the reality, features a more positive perception.

From the findings of the pilot study, the issues from 1 to 4 (housing, unemployment, health, and multiculturalism and social exclusion issues) remained as being issues, but number 5 (educational issues) evolved from being an issue into a feature, thus having a more positive perception. This means that the issues found in the pilot study not only remained as being perceived negatively, but also that they evolved in negativism throughout the four years of the PhD research span. However, on the contrary, in the case of the educational issues, the preliminary negative perceptions from the pilot study evolved into positive perceptions; educational features. Thus, this merging of the findings from the pilot and the main study shows not only a consistent evolution in the negative perceptions of residents, but also a prudent reconsideration of an issue becoming a positive feature.

Thus, the findings of the pilot study were used as a basis for the main study. Hence, this chapter presents the findings of the pilot study that evolved and merged into the findings of the main study; the whole of the findings of this thesis. Thus, the findings of the thesis were grouped into six major issues and two major features that emerged from the Broomhall neighbourhood.

These are the six major issues that emerged from the thesis, where the evolution from the pilot study is also represented:

1)Issues of territoriality or uses of the land (e.g. housing; expansion of Sheffield and Hallam universities becoming university student villages). These issues evolved from the *housing issues* of the pilot study.
2)   Issues of poverty, social and economic inequalities (e.g. unemployment, debt, crime). These issues evolved from the *unemployment issues* of the pilot study.
3)   Health issues (e.g. drug addiction, lack of: green public open space, playgrounds, and sports and leisure facilities). These issues evolved from the *health issues* of the pilot study.
4)   Political issues;
5)   Cultural issues (e.g. multicultural, ethnic, religious, and national issues). These issues evolved from the *multiculturalism and social exclusion* from the pilot study.
6)   Communication issues.

These are the two major features that emerged from the thesis, where the evolution from the pilot study is also represented:

1)Transport features.
2)   Educational features. These features evolved from the *educational issues* from the pilot study.

5.1.2.1   NEGATIVE ISSUES, AND INFORMATION NEEDS PERCEIVED BY THE RESIDENTS OF BROOMHALL —AN OVERVIEW

In Table 5.1 below the reader can assess at a glimpse the most negative issues of the Broomhall neighbourhood as perceived by residents and some information providers, hence, the most negative information needs. Not all the perceptions form a consensus, but some single expressions are included in order to report more comprehensively the most significant features, or issues, or problems as perceived by respondents, which shed light on the aim and objectives of this project.

The table is divided in three columns: the first shows the major findings, the second presents evidence either by respondents or documents, and the third is the translation of the findings into the eight major information needs of the thesis (as emerged from the major six issues and two features).

Table 5.1 Negative issues of Broomhall		
Major findings	**Evidence by respondents and documents**	**Translation of findings into major issues, or features, or**

		information needs
British government politically oppressive and excluding people from their political rights	[a middle class resident from section C] [R.I. 08]	Political issues; communication issues
Christian charities with vested religious or commercial interests other than the social aims they pursue	[a working class resident from section A] [R.I.07]; [a working class resident from section B] [R.I.10]	Cultural issues; political issues
Closure of Broomhall Nursery at Mushroom Lane branch	(Star (Sheffield), 2004e)	Educational features; issues of territoriality or uses of the land; political issues
Communication features and issues	A general consensus	Communication issues
Crime (e.g. robberies; thugs; violent attacks against the person; muggings; car and property break-ins; drug dealing crime; intentional and unintentional shooting crimes; arsons)	A general consensus; (BBC News (Sheffield), 2003; 2004; 2005a; 2007; Star (Sheffield), 2004a; 2005a; 2005d; 2006a; 2006e)	Issues of poverty, social, and economic inequalities; political issues
Cultural forms of socializing with mild toxic substances (e.g. smoking tobacco [10] and drinking alcohol in British pubs and clubs; Khat chewing by Somali, etc.)	A general consensus	Cultural issues; health issues; political issues
Debt issues	[a working class resident from section A] [F.G.03.A]; (Muela-Meza, 2005b)	Issues of poverty, social, and economic inequalities; political issues
Deprivation in the provision of social services for the homeless, refugees, asylum seekers, and the destitute	A general consensus	Issues of poverty, social, and economic inequalities; political issues; cultural issues
Deprivation of green public open spaces (e.g. parks, playgrounds) for poor and working classes	A general consensus	Health issues; issues of poverty, social, and economic inequalities; political issues
Deprivation of health services provision	[a middle class resident from section C] [R.I. 01]; [a middle class resident from section C] [R.I. 08]; [a middle class respondent from section C] [F.G.01.C]; [a working class respondent from section C] [F.G.01.A]; (Star (Sheffield), 2005d; 2005e; 2006b)	Health issues; political issues
Deprived living conditions of poor and working classes	A general consensus	Issues of poverty, social, and economic inequalities; political issues
Developers and landlords	A general consensus; (Star (Sheffield), 2002a; 2004b; 2007a; Broomhall News, 2004a)	Issues of territoriality or uses of the land; political issues
Drug addiction	A general consensus	Health issues; cultural issues

---

[10] Smoking inside pubs was legal at the time of data collection.

Drug dealing	A general consensus; (*Star (Sheffield)*, 2004c; *BBC News (Sheffield)*, 2003; 2005b; 2006)	Issues of poverty, social, and economic inequalities; health issues
Education	(*Star (Sheffield)*, 2004g)	Educational features
Hallam and Sheffield universities territorial expansionism in the neighbourhood and becoming student villages	A general consensus; (*Star (Sheffield)*, 2007a)	Issues of territoriality or uses of the land; political issues
Housing for poor and working classes	A general consensus	Issues of territoriality or uses of the land; political issues
Intercultural misunderstandings (e.g. misunderstandings of Christians vs. Muslims, or vice versa)	A general consensus	Cultural issues; political issues
Intolerance of some neighbours to diversity (e.g. neighbours intolerant to pub life, student life, BME (Black Minority Ethnic) life)	(*Star (Sheffield)*, 2006f)	Cultural issues; political issues
Media vs. BMEs (Black Minority Ethnic) (mostly from African, Middle East and Arabic countries)	[a working class resident from section B] [F.G.02.A]	Communication issues; cultural issues; political issues
Poverty, social and economic inequalities	A general consensus	Issues of poverty, social, and economic inequalities; political issues
Racism of the police against BMEs (Black Minority Ethnic) (namely vs. Somalis)	[a working class resident from section A] [R.I. 07]; [a working class resident from section B of Broomhall] [R.I. 10]; [a working class resident from section B] [F.G.02.A]; [an information provider from section C of Broomhall] [I.P.01]	Cultural issues; political issues; communication issues
Resurgence of fascism, white supremacists, the fascist British National Party, and British National Front in Broomhall, Sheffield, and UK wide	[a middle class resident from section C] [R.I. 08]; (*Star (Sheffield)*, 2003; 2005b; 2006d)	Political issues
The Broomhall Forum and the Broomhall Cosmopolitan Centre, Ltd.	A general consensus	Political issues
The Sheffield YMCA having sold its premises on Broomhall Road (and depriving people from their gym, pitches and all sport and health providing services)	A general consensus (except for the positive perceptions self-granted by the YMCA, e.g. (*Star (Sheffield)*, 2002b)	Health issues; political issues; issues of territoriality or uses of the land;
Transport	*Star (Sheffield)*, (2007c)	Transport features
Tribalism of BMEs (Black Minority Ethnic) (namely from African, Middle East, and Arabic speaking countries)	[a working class resident from section B] [F.G.02.B]; [a working class	Political issues; cultural issues; communication issues

	resident from section B] [F.G.02.A]; [a working class resident from section B] [F.G.02.C]	
UK having made the war against the innocent people of Iraq and Afghanistan	[a working class resident from section B] [F.G.02.C]; [a working class resident from section A] [R.I. 07]; [a middle class resident from section C] [R.I. 08]	Political issues; cultural issues; communication issues
Unemployment	A general consensus	Issues of poverty, social, and economic inequalities

5.1.2.2   POSITIVE FEATURES, AND INFORMATION NEEDS PERCEIVED BY THE RESIDENTS OF BROOMHALL –
           AN OVERVIEW

On the other hand, in Table 5.2 below the reader can assess at a glimpse an illustrative range of positive features of Broomhall, hence, positive information needs, and be able to contrast them with their negative counterparts described above in Table 5.1.

At first sight, the reader may find the snapshot of Table 5.2 as a very positive profile. However, even though some respondents mentioned there that there are some positive features of Broomhall, the reader should bear in mind that those features did not emerge as purely positive.

Therefore, the author has addressed them as positive or less negative, controversial, and adverse features, because although they are positive they also include such negative aspects, which shadow their positive characteristics. Nevertheless, by triangulating the respondents' perceptions with data generated by observation and documents, it was possible to highlight some features as mainly positive, regardless of how negatively some respondents perceived them. The main positive features hence were: educational services provision, and transport services provision.

The table is divided in three columns: the first shows the major findings, the second presents evidence either by respondents or documents, and the third is the translation of the findings into the eight major information needs of the thesis (as emerged from the major six issues and two features).

Table 5.2 Positive (or less negative, controversial, and adverse) features of Broomhall		
Major findings	**Evidence by respondents and documents**	**Translation of findings into major issues, or features, or information needs**
A friendly community, not racist	[an information provider from section C of Broomhall] [I.P.04]	Cultural issues
A good place to live for people of different backgrounds	[an information provider from section C of Broomhall] [I.P.01]; [a middle class resident from section C] [R.I. 08]	Cultural issues
A peaceful area	[an information provider from section C of Broomhall] [I.P.01]	Issues of poverty, social, and economic inequalities
Being very near to the City Centre and to all council services, shops, Royal	A general consensus	Transport features

Hallamshire Hospital (RHH) and amenities (5 to 15 minutes walking, sections A and B are the closest to city centre and C and D to Royal Hallamshire Hospital)		
Broomhall Community Centre; Citywide Learning Centre	General consensus	Educational features
Diversity and mixture of cultures	[a working class respondent from section C] [F.G.01.A]	Cultural issues
Hanover Medical Centre	[a middle class resident from section C] [R.I. 01]	Health issues
People know each other in the Hanover Flats, section A; nice flats	[a working class resident from section A] [F.G.03.D]; [a working class resident from section A] [R.I. 07]	Communication issues; issues of territoriality or uses of the land
Sheffield City Council libraries providing books to children and their parents in partnership with central government Sure Start educational program (at Sharrow) through the Broomhall Nursery	[a working class resident from section A] [R.I. 09]; (Star (Sheffield), 2006c)	Educational features
The neighbourhood newspaper *Broomhall News*	[a middle class resident from section C] [R.I. 04]	Educational features
Transport	[a working class resident from section B] [F.G.02.A]; (Star (Sheffield), 2004f)	Transport features

5.1.3 Information provision

An information provider specifies this idea in relation to advice provision to Broomhall residents:

"I don't particularly think another library is what Broomhall needs, what they need is more advice services. There is Internet on the Stow Centre and the City Wide Learning [actually both closed doors for good by 2006, MUELA-MEZA, Z.M.], and in the libraries, libraries are not the places where you can find information and advice on your entitlements and benefits and stuff like that. I think it would be good if we would have better accommodation and outreach in Broomhall as a permanent basis, yes. And definitively it's much needed now." [an information provider from section C of Broomhall] [I.P.05].

And many residents confirm this need for *advice and help centres* rather than libraries. Their perceptions will be explained in the next sections, as appropriate in relation to the information needs analysed here.

5.1.3.1   INFORMATION PROVISION THROUGH LETTERBOXES OF BROOMHALL RESIDENTS' HOMES

The author collected, from 16 September 2006 until 16 March 2007, all the documents that arrived at his home through the letterbox when he lived on Broomspring Lane, section C of Broomhall.

Table 5.3 below shows a summary of the 72 documents or information recorded in documents non solicited by the author that arrived through his letterbox from individuals or organisations.

Table 5.3 Information provision through the letter boxes of Broomhall homes (at least in section C), from 16 September 2006 to 16 March 2007							
Type of document		Letters	Flyer	Newspaper	Booklet	Book	Total
Commercial sector							56
	Alcoholic drinks	1					
	Banking services (credit cards)	1					
	Domestic cleaning services	1					
	Fashion	1					
	Health & sports	1		1			
	Insurance (cars, homes)	3					
	Internet and cable TV	5					
	News & publicity		1				
	Organic community shop	1					
	Plumbing; boilers; gas	2					
	Restaurant	1					
	Social parties	1					
	Supermarket	15					
	Telephone & Internet	1					
	Takeaway fast food shop	19					
	Video entertainment	1					
Community & voluntary sector							11
	Educational	3					
	Farm animals						
	Health & sports	1					

	Home energy saving		1				
	Political		3				
	Poverty and Children		1				
	Religions & spirituality		2				
Statutory sector (Sheffield)							5
	Directory of council services					1	
	Environment		1				
	Home building public consultation	1					
	Public service accountability					2	
Total							72

As can be seen from Table 5.3 above, of the 72 documents received: a) 55 are related to commercial information (19 are related to fast food takeaway shops and 15 about supermarkets: CostCutter from Broomhall and Somerfield from Broomhill); b) 11 from the voluntary sector; and c) 5 from the statutory sector in Sheffield.

Given the nature of grey literature and elusive documents, the author could not establish which of these documents can be considered useful for the residents and which were 'rubbish unsolicited post,' because any of them could be perceived as either useful or useless by different residents. That is, it would be another research topic for future LIS practitioners if they wanted to find out what are the type of documents households receive in a given neighbourhood and in a given period.

However, this exercise was carried out because the author is trying to show the whole panorama of community information needs and their provision in the Broomhall neighbourhood, and living in Broomhall was a good idea to show another illustration of how needs might be prompted, or satisfied by 'unsolicited post'. This is only a small sample of documents collected during seven months and in itself does not shed the full spectrum of light of the information provision phenomenon in Broomhall, because whilst it may be true that some of that unsolicited post might be rubbish for some people, on the other hand it may be equally true that some of that unsolicited post might be of help or advice for some other people.

The following are examples that may help explain how the same piece of information recorded in a document and delivered through the post may be helpful for some people, and useless for others.

For instance, if a resident has the information need to know the telephone number of a pizza or kebab shop to order takeaway food to his doorstep, then those documents would meet effectively and efficiently his or her needs, provided he or she save them, organise them, and retrieve them for future use. On the other hand, if another resident prefers to cook at home, he or she follows nutritious food instead of non nutritious food, and he or she considers takeaway food as non nutritious food, then he or she would consider those leaflets useless.

Another example, two of the booklets provided came from the Sheffield City Council, and they are the most important documents from all the 74 collected and analysed, because they show in nearly 100 pages each the full range of services of the council. These sections on information, advice and help services, mainly from the library, amount in each more than 30 pages. That is, with this evidence no one can claim the council does not make an effort to inform in print in a colourful comprehensive booklet to each of its citizens, provided that that post be a citywide post.

However, in seven months, the council posted those two booklets and never again approached the author's home (and by inference, any other home), except for one letter related to some building extension applications. No other information from the Council came through the letterboxes. Hence, it might be inferred that the Council assumes that every citizen: a) keeps safe the semi-annual directory, b) reads English, and c) has a land telephone line and/or Internet. However, in this study that attitude of the council (and for that matter of its library, information, advice, and help services) is a patronising one, to say the least, because a recent major research project on families with disabled children found that written information in the form of leaflets and booklets, under some circumstances tends to alienate rather than inform families:

"It was apparent that written information was not enough by itself. Indeed, the assumption that as long as numerous leaflets and booklets are produced families will be able to inform themselves was dismissed as both simplistic and potentially dangerous" (Mitchell and Sloper, 2002: 78).

However, the documental information from the Council through the letterboxes is not the only form they provide to citizens. They also do it through more established organisations which may fit one way or the other into the Documental Information Institution (DII) form of information provider as defined in this thesis (see Rendón Rojas, 2005: 136-137, and Chapter 2).

The next section explains the information provision through displays at the premises of Broomhall organisations.

5.1.3.2   INFORMATION PROVISION DISPLAYED AT PREMISES OF BROOMHALL ORGANISATIONS (IN BOTH
           DOCUMENTAL INFORMATION INSTITUTIONS (DIIS) AND NON-DIIS)

During the time this project took place the author visited several organisations within Broomhall or nearby that collected documental information and displayed it in their premises for the public's free access. He collected a copy of each document displayed within their premises only once on a given date within the time span of four years this PhD research took place.

These are the information providers' premises assessed:

1) Broomhall Community Centre (BCC),
2)   Broomhall Forum (BF),
3)   Sharrow Citizens Advice Bureau (SCAB; this is located outside Broomhall but has a clinic at the Hanover Medical Centre in section C),
4)   Hanover Medical Centre (HMC),
5)   Mobile Library (from the council library and information services servicing in Broomhall),
6)   Sharrow Community Forum (SCF; off Broomhall but with clinics in section A),
7)   Stow Centre (SC) (now closed since mid 2006),
8)   Saint Mark's Church (SMC; this is located outside Broomhall but with other 2 churches within section C serves in coordination),
9)   and Waitrose (W; just metres off section A, just to show the high contrast of upper market supermarket off the road of the 10th most deprived estate in Sheffield: Hanover).

Only the CAB and the ML fit into the DII (Documental Information Institution) concept employed here, but the others were included as well just to show the reader what type of documental information other centres provide resembling a Documental Information Institution.

The Sheffield City Council Central Library at Surrey Street, city centre, was omitted for several reasons: because the mobile library already represented it; because residents considered it 'far away' from Broomhall (it is not far away, simply too big and depersonalised than smaller branches like Highfield); and for practical matters, because at the time the author tried to collect one sample of each document he found that this amounted to more than three thousand documents; thus it was beyond Broomhall neighbourhood range and beyond Broomhall-specific provision scope, since it had a Sheffield city-wide provision scope.

However, as a matter of fact, the Central Library in all documental information respects is the most complete Documental Information Institution (DII) from any other within or outside Broomhall. But paradoxically, it was the least used DII by Broomhall residents when advice or help services were needed. For advice or help services the Sharrow Citizens Advice Bureau (SCAB) was the most used by Broomhall residents, both at the Broomhall clinics at Hanover Medical Centre and at its main offices in Sharrow.

The next tables, then, show the different sources of information recorded in documents provided by the formal *Documental Information Institutions (DIIs)* such as the Sharrow Citizens' Advice Bureau (SCAB) and the Mobile Library of the Sheffield City Council Information Services, and other information centres similar to a *DII*.

Hence, in this section an analysis of those documents is presented in the following Tables from 5.11 to 5.15.

Table 5.4 below shows the *Community and voluntary sector documents collected at information providers' premises.*

Table 5.4 Community and voluntary sector documents collected at information providers' premises									
Document type	**Information provider**								
	BCC	BF	CAB	HM	ML	SCF	SC	SMC	W	Total
Advice services	6	0	3	3	0	0	0	0	0	12
BME (Black Minority Ethnic) organisations (inc. refugees & asylum seekers)	4	0	2	0	0	4	0	1	0	11
Educational	17	0	0	0	0	2	0	0	0	19
Environment	2	0	0	0	0	0	0	1	0	3
Financial help; credit unions	4	0	0	0	0	0	0	0	0	4
Health & sports	18	0	1	0	0	5	0	0	0	24
Home energy saving	1	0	0	0	0	0	0	0	0	1
Jobs	5	0	3	0	0	3	0	0	0	11
Leisure, arts, festivals	0	0	0	0	0	1	0	0	0	1
Pets	0	0	0	0	1	0	0	0	0	1
Politics	3	0	0	0	0	1	0	4	0	8
Religion & spirituality	6	2	0	0	0	0	0	6	0	14
Safety	2	0	0	0	0	0	0	0	0	2
Social services	1	0	0	0	0	0	0	0	0	1
Total	**69**	**2**	**9**	**3**	**1**	**16**	**0**	**12**	**0**	**112**

Abbreviations and dates of collection of documents: BCC: Broomhall Community Centre (11.11.2005); BF: Broomhall Forum (24.11.2005); CAB: Citizens Advice Bureau (14.11.2005); HMC: Hanover Medical Centre (12.12.2006); ML: Mobile Library from Sheffield City Council Library, Archives and Information Services located at Exeter Drive, section A (04.06.2007); SC: Stow Centre (18.08.2005); SMC: Saint Mark's Church (18.08.2005); W: Waitrose (12.12.2006).

Table 5.5 below shows the *Statutory sector (central government) documents collected at information providers' premises.*

Table 5.5 Statutory sector (central government) documents collected at information providers' premises									
Document type	**Information provider**								
	BCC	BF	CAB	HMC	ML	SCF	SC	SMC	W	Total
Cabinet Office	0	0	0	0	0	1	0	0	0	1
Environment	1	0	0	0	0	0	0	0	0	1
Health & sports	28	0	0	14	0	1	0	1	0	44
HM Treasury	0	0	0	0	1	0	0	0	0	1
Home energy saving	4	0	0	0	0	0	0	0	0	4
HM Inland Revenue	0	1	0	0	0	0	0	0	0	1

	BCC	BF	CAB	HM	ML	SCF	SC	SMC	W	Total
Leisure, arts, festivals	5	1	0	0	0	0	0	0	0	**6**
Radio	1	0	0	0	2	0	0	0	0	**3**
Safety	13	0	2	0	0	0	0	1	0	**16**
UK Online Centres	1	0	0	0	0	0	0	0	0	**1**
Total of documents	**53**	**2**	**2**	**14**	**3**	**2**	**0**	**2**	**0**	**78**

Abbreviations and dates of collection of documents as in Table 5.4 above.

Table 5.6 below shows the *Statutory sector (Sheffield City Council) documents collected at information providers' premises.*

Table 5.6 Statutory sector (Sheffield City Council) documents collected at information providers' premises

Document type	Information provider									
	BCC	BF	CAB	HM	ML	SCF	SC	SMC	W	Total
Catering services	1	0	0	0	0	0	0	0	0	**1**
Education	4	0	0	0	1	1	0	1	0	**7**
Elected members	2	0	1	0	0	1	0	1	0	**5**
Environment	16	0	0	0	1	0	0	0	0	**17**
Funding	2	0	0	0	0	0	0	0	0	**2**
Health & sports	1	0	1	1	0	1	0	0	0	**4**
Housing	1	0	0	0	0	0	0	0	0	**1**
Information services	4	0	1	4	7	5	0	0	0	**21**
Jobs	4	0	2	0	0	0	0	0	0	**6**
Leisure, arts, festivals	5	0	0	0	2	0	0	1	0	**8**
Museums & galleries	1	0	0	0	2	0	0	1	0	**4**
Safety	2	1	0	0	0	1	0	0	0	**4**
Social security; benefits	2	0	1	0	0	0	0	0	0	**3**
Social services	4	0	0	1	2	0	0	0	0	**7**
Transport	0	0	0	1	0	2	0	0	0	**3**
Total of documents	**49**	**1**	**6**	**7**	**15**	**11**	**0**	**4**	**0**	**93**

Abbreviations and dates of collection of documents as in Table 5.4 above.

Table 5.7 below shows the *Documents from the private sector collected at information providers' premises.*

Table 5.7 Documents from the private sector collected at information providers' premises

Document type	Information provider									
	BCC	BF	CAB	HMC	ML	SCF	SC	SMC	W	Total
Educational	0	2	0	0	0	0	0	0	0	**2**
Food	0	0	0	0	0	0	0	0	3	**3**
Health & sports	4	1	0	5	0	0	0	0	0	**10**
Home energy saving	2	0	1	0	0	0	0	0	0	**3**
Information services	0	0	0	0	7	1	0	0	0	**8**
Jobs	3	0	0	0	0	0	0	0	0	**3**
Leisure; arts; festivals	4	0	0	1	3	0	0	1	0	**9**
Total of documents	**13**	**3**	**1**	**6**	**10**	**1**	**0**	**1**	**3**	**38**

Abbreviations and dates of collection of documents as in Table 5.4 above.

Table 5.8 shows a *Comparison of information providers' documents about their own organisation displayed at their premises.* See table below.

Table 5.8 Comparison of information providers' documents about their own organisation displayed at their premises	
Information provider	**No. of documents**
Broomhall Community Centre	18
Broomhall Forum	0
Citizens Advice Bureau	2
Hanover Medical Centre	1
Mobile Library (at Exeter Drive, section A)	1
Sharrow Community Forum	5
Stow Centre	2
Saint Mark Church	13
Waitrose	3

As shown in Tables 5.4 through 5.9, the Broomhall Community Centre, was the most comprehensive provider of information recorded in documents. This centre is managed and funded by the Sheffield City Council, but the management is run by individuals, and groups from the community. But the BCC is not a fully operational DII, and not even close. They only have hundreds of flyers available there for anyone who enters and wants to pick up one, but there is no proper service provision of *documental information,* or *advice,* or *help.* The place is more a local centre where people teach extracurricular activities, and a place people rent for parties, and so on.

The Broomhall Community Centre (BCC) is, nevertheless, the real soul of the neighbourhood where all communities 'feel it their own centre'. While the BBC (and for that matter other centres alike which cannot be classified properly as Documental Information Institutions, DIIs, like libraries) have hundreds of flyers in stock available free for everyone, that does not mean that people are effectively served with documental information as in libraries. That is, the BCC is not a DII as defined in this project, hence it does not satisfy people's information needs effectively as a library would do, because it is not a library, and they do not have books as a public library for people of all ages. They do not have librarians either who can give information, advice, help, etc. on a regular schedule; the BCC is a staffed by one single member who works only two hours a day, and not having the credentials as a librarian, she only gives information related to the centre (rent of the centre for events; scheduling for events and the like).

Moreover, on an even more critical note, the most negative and pressing issue and information need, for the Broomhall residents is territoriality (namely housing), and as was shown in Table 5.6, the Broomhall Community Centre (BCC) had only one single document related to housing. This is further evidence that except for the documental information provided by the Mobile Library or the advice and help by the Sharrow Citizens' Advice Bureau (SCAB), which both are limited, Broomhall residents in general terms are considerably under-provided, and the lower the social class the worse off.

The next sections report, analyse and discuss the eight major findings of this thesis.

5.2 Analysis and discussion of the issues and features of Broomhall, and the interrelationships with information needs and provision, as perceived by residents

The sections here report, analyse and discuss the eight major findings of this thesis: a) the six negative issues and the two positive features that accordingly describe the Broomhall neighbourhood, b) the translation of those eight findings into information needs, and c) the ways that information providers tried to meet those eight information needs.

The way these findings are critically presented, analysed, and discussed follows this logic: 1) first, each issue or feature is presented, 2) then, several interrelationships with information needs are made, and 3) finally, an association is made to information provision.

5.2.1 Issues, information needs, and provision about territoriality or uses of the land

The following sections present, analyse, and discuss the issues, information needs, and provision
about territoriality or uses of the land.

5.2.1.1   ISSUES ABOUT TERRITORIALITY OR USES OF THE LAND

From time immemorial territoriality and the uses of the land, also commonly associated with
human shelter or housing, have played a determinant role in human evolution. According to a
sociologist (Edgell, 1993: 52), the amount of territorial property an individual owns serves as one
prominent measure or his or her social class status.

The history of territorial privatization or privatization of the land, is the same as in the earlier forms
of accumulation of capital. However, the land is being privatized by capitalists to build not factories
like in earlier times, but upper-market residential and business developments; the expropriated
peasant and feudal classes of those days are the working, middle, and even capitalist classes of
today; the earlier Wilkinson government is today's government.

For instance, in Wilkinson's times his house was attacked by the victims of his policies of enclosures
of the commons land. But today, according to one respondent's account, apparently the developers
are attacking and setting on fire the houses of the Broomhall residents who resist the
capitalist/bourgeois class government policies and corporations (developers) to take over all of
their land and homes to build for-profit upper market Housing in Multiple Occupation:

> *"all people in the community say that [person's name omitted for security reasons] got [the
> house of this person] attacked, petrol bombed by developers because [this person... gender
> omitted for security reasons] always complained... you know developers have millions of
> pounds for development and they want to take over the community, but you know, the
> community can stop them, technically, by getting petitions, complain to the council, by getting
> signatures, and that is what [gender omitted for security reasons] was doing, getting
> signatures from lots of people, and writing articles in the papers, throwing shit [sic] basically
> against the developers basically, no one knows who did it but someone petrol bombed [the
> house of this person], you know there is no evidence but it's pretty obvious [that developers did
> it]" [a working class resident from section B of Broomhall] [R.I. 10].*

Perhaps this account is going too far and it may be inconceivable, but Broomhall residents are
complaining that they are being intimidated by developers to stop them from complaining to the
Council about their "regeneration" plans of "bulldozing" Broomhall old houses and build upper-
market Housing in Multiple Occupancy (HMO) for residential or business rents (Star (Sheffield),
2002b). Broomhall residents are complaining that developers are building more and more HMOs
(Housing in Multiple Occupancy) and thus pushing poor working class families away from the
neighbourhood (*Broomhall News*, 2004a; *Star (Sheffield)*, 2004b; Exposed, 2007). This is the
strategy that the capitalist developers, (backed by the Labour government, central and local, and
councillors and MPs from Conservative, Liberal, and even Green parties) are implementing
nationwide according to similar experiences of working class residents from other British cities, e.g.
Liverpool (Leeming, 2007a; 2007b; Radnedge, 2006); London (Cottage and Fredericks, 2006).

In addition, territorial privatization is not only for residential and business purposes, but also for
academic purposes and that is where Sheffield Hallam University (SHU) and the University of
Sheffield (UofS) have the same negative effect for the people in the neighbourhood like the
capitalist developers (Student Residences Strategy Team, 2004; Department of Marketing and
Communications, 2005; Sheffield Hallam University Alumni Association, 2003; *Star (Sheffield)*;
2007a). Even though their aims would have a positive impact for them, e.g. medicine, and basically
all the scientific and technological findings developed through universities.

The building of facilities for both housing and academic purposes by developers are of much benefit
for society, that is an undeniable fact. However, the problem perceived by Broomhall residents is
that most of them would never have access to live in the new fancy upper-market HMOs (Housing
in Multiple Occupancy) being built in replacement of their old and poor social housing, and the

other problem is that it is very unlikely that they would be able to afford to pay the university fees of both SHU or UofS, universities which are pushing the families out of the neighbourhood to build new classrooms, halls, teaching centres, laboratories, and so on, replacing their old and poor social housing with their new academic facilities.

This is the main issue and information need of Broomhall, which affects severely most residents of Broomhall. An information provider captures comprehensively the essence of these issues as being contradictory and conflicting amongst the different social classes within each section or amongst different sections of Broomhall:

> *"Land usage is definitely an issue in Broomhall, for instance there are many people in Broomhall who wanted to hold on green areas, playgrounds, we have the Sunny Bank Park rangers and the Friends of Lynwood Gardens who protect the Sunny Bank [Park, located at the end of Broomhall Place and off Ecclessall Road in section C of Broomhall] and the Lynwood Gardens [located in the heart of the end of Dorset and Gloucester streets of section C of Broomhall and the end of Park Crescent of section D of Broomhall just behind the Aunt Sally pub], these parks may not be in danger to fall in the hands of developers, but others are like playgrounds which are used by many kids from long time residents of Broomhall, there are some Friends of the Playgrounds of Broomhall organizations holding on to playgrounds, but they seem to be losing them and they are being taking over by developers to build homes, business and so on."* [an information provider from section A of Broomhall] [I.P.02]

This respondent highlights these features as a conflictive issue between the residents who want to hold on to their open public and green land and the developers who want to take over that land for private Housing for Multiple Occupation (HMO), or the universities for teaching halls.

The next section presents, analyses, and discusses the information needs as emerged from the issues of territoriality or uses of the land.

5.2.1.2   INFORMATION NEEDS ABOUT TERRITORIALITY OR USES OF THE LAND

What are the community information needs related to the issues about *territoriality and uses of land?* From the evidence presented above these are interpreted by the author as follows:

• Working class residents renting in social housing need information to carry out some of these activities: 1) to know about their housing benefits entitlements; 2) to know about how to protect their homes against any security threats: crime, arson, robberies, vermin, etc.; 3) to know about how to protect their homes from any safety threats: e.g. smoke alarms (*Star (Sheffield)*, (2004d); 4) to have a certainty that their homes will not be sold by the council or if they are going to be sold they need information to know all the legal proceedings of where, how and when the council is going to relocate them to new social housing; 5) working class residents do not have information needs related to the universities because whether or not these universities expand or not is basically of no consequence. Perhaps the only information need they may have may have to do with the possibility that their children may like to become students themselves and thus need information about scholarships or government loans for them to study. Some long-standing residents, like for example those from the Ruth Square & Broomspring Lane quarter which belongs to the University of Sheffield, wish they have access to information from the university or the government or both to know how to protect themselves from being evicted when the university sells the block of houses.

• Middle class residents need information to carry out some of these activities: 1) to know how to make refurbishments to their homes, e.g. obtain grants from the government; 2) to know how to protect themselves from the lobbies of both the government (included local councillors or MPs or MEPs) and housing capitalists in order to stop them from buying, or demolishing their properties; 3) to know all about these universities' expansionist plans in order to try to protect their properties from being bought, or demolished by the universities. Other secondary needs have to do with how to have some communication with universities' authorities in order to making them aware of certain nuisances being caused by their students, e.g. student life at night; students not collecting their rubbish bins, and so on.

• Capitalist class residents need information to carry out some of these activities: 1) to know
how to buy more properties to develop them to offer them for rent or for sale as profitable
Housing in Multiple Occupation (HMO); 2) to know how to lobby the government, e.g. in order
to buy properties for example from conservation areas or restricted areas, or from citizens; 3) to
know how to carry out jobs for the universities, e.g. building halls, flats, labs, research centres,
etc. in order to maximise their profits.

The next section presents, analyses, and discusses the information provision about territoriality or
uses of the land.

5.2.1.3   INFORMATION PROVISION ABOUT TERRITORIALITY OR USES OF THE LAND

The most pressing issues and thus information needs derived from them are related to
territoriality; namely housing. Hence keeping abreast of all the information related to
housing could be a matter of one day having roof and the next day being evicted:

> *"The problem now in Broomhall today is that houses are too expensive for local
> people to buy them. That's the new problem. At one time it was not a desirable area
> and the houses were very cheap. And now they are very expensive. How they find
> information? [about housing] They can go to churches, they can go to libraries, they
> can read local newspapers. Local newspapers have quite lots of information." [an
> information provider from section C of Broomhall] [I.P.04]*

The most effective information provider on housing issues from the statutory sector is the
Howden House of the Sheffield City Council.

> *"The main issue of information in Broomhall is about housing, and people tend to go to First
> Point housing office in central town in Howden House. That's pretty good. You just can turn
> up and you can speak face to face with somebody and get information and there is a free
> phone there and you can phone free through somebody in the council [Sheffield City Council]
> so I think that they provide information." [a middle class resident from section C] [R.I.02]*

However, when individuals have problems which cannot be sorted out by Howden House,
they would go to the Sharrow Citizens Advice Bureau.

> *"So it is not that "oh, I give you a bit of information on GSA," but also in all the housing issues
> involved, the housing benefits involved, if they notified their change of address and so and so.
> And what about if they have a disability, do they have a disability living allowance? We are
> very proactive in giving information to people rather than just passively responding to their
> queries." [an information provider from section C of Broomhall] [I.P.05]*

However another organisation acting somewhat like a Documental Information Institution
(DII) considers that the SCAB does not satisfy all the advice, information, and help needs
people face:

> *"To give advice to people on legal matters and so on, you have to have trained
> people... a lot of what we end up doing is at very low level, but people need that
> support, they need support for school meals, filling forms for reception places, lots of
> our families need support on that, and the Citizens' Advice Bureau wouldn't do that,
> but sometimes other things happen as well, you know, we ring the housing
> associations, we make phone calls for people and that is something that the Citizens'
> Advice Bureau could be doing." [an information provider from section B of
> Broomhall] [I.P.07]*

As has been argued throughout the thesis, social class is a determinant factor to having or
not having access to information. For instance, most middle class residents would just
telephone the agency on which information is needed:

"There are lots of ways to find information, it depends on what we need, for example if it relates to housing, we just telephone the council..." [a middle class resident from section C] [R.I. 05]

It was found that Sheffield and Hallam universities only provide exclusive information, advice and help services for the members of their own communities but not for all city wide citizens.

"The universities [University of Sheffield and Hallam University] have done very little to support Broomhall. The presence of the universities makes a huge impact in the community. If the universities wouldn't be here, not many students would come to live here, that makes a huge effect against the community." [a middle class resident from section C] [R.I. 08].

"The universities [University of Sheffield and Hallam Sheffield University] are very important drivers of the Sheffield economy, but I question whether the money is spent in Broomhall, I would imagine is a tiny fraction." [an information provider from section C of Broomhall] [I.P.05].

5.2.2 Information needs and provision relating to poverty and social, and economic inequalities

The sections here present, analyse, and discuss the issues, information needs, and provision relating to poverty, and social, and economic inequalities.

5.2.2.1 POVERTY, AND SOCIAL, AND ECONOMIC INEQUALITY ISSUES

This section presents, analyses, and discusses issues of poverty, and social, and economic inequalities. These include: a) the destitute, asylum seekers, and refugees, b) unemployment, c) debt, and d) crime.

5.2.2.1.1 The destitute, asylum seekers, and refugees

Poverty has been found as an endemic failure of the capitalist system (Green, 2000c; 2000a), and not only in present times, but also from history (Fearnley, 2001; Orwell, [1937], 1962; Engels, [1845], 2000). In the Britain of the 1830s and 1840s Victorian times, according to a Sheffield chronicler, "...the government of the day clearly classified poverty as a disease and not as an economic disaster incurred by a national recession" (Fearnley, 2001: 33). Some may relegate this argument as a historic fact of no consequence for present times, or some may even find that writer biased.

However in recent times, poverty is still a big issue for many people, perhaps not at a national level, but at least in the poor and most overcrowded areas of Broomhall, like section A, and even with worse consequences for the destitute individuals who are not even entitled to any government social security benefits as an information provider explains:

"Unemployment is not only the big issue, there are people who can't even work at all, so they can't get a wage. And there are many people like this in the area [Broomhall, particularly on section A] who are not entitled to anything because the asylum system refused them, so they are what we call them destitute. They don't have any right for anything, no accommodation. There are many destitute people. And they [are] basically living on the good will of other people. And probably they are involved in crime and all of that if anyone maybe would do if they don't have any legal means for survival. So they have come here to us many destitute people but we can only give them a very limited referral to other legal institutions. You know there has been [by the government] a lot of restrictions on immigration. Personally I don't believe everyone is having a fair hearing, and then you have the situation... [of the destitute] it's very difficult to meet the asylum criteria [of the government] as it is. So they tell them to go back, but they are terrified to go back, but they can't go back because they are going to be killed by their husbands' family so that maybe won't fit the strict criteria of asylum, you know what I'm saying?" [an information provider from section C of Broomhall] [I.P.05].

The same commentator explains that most of the destitute in Broomhall, particularly from section

A, are asylum seekers whom the government denied permission to remain in the UK. They are completely destitute entitled to no public or humanitarian social service.

> *"so I see a bigger issue of failure in the government, before asylum seekers had humanitarian protection and could remain for 3 or 4 years in the UK fully entitled to asylum rights waiting for the government to sort out their legal situation but not sending them back to their countries, but now I don't see the government is giving them any humanitarian protection. But if they claim for asylum they [government] have to give them almost immediately and they have the rights almost immediately. An under the Geneva Convention, any nation subscribing the Geneva Convention is supposed to provide asylum related to questions of violence and so on. And the UK subscribes this convention. But when they [the government] deny asylum to any one they are denying any kind of support for asylum seekers. ... the requirements are very complex and stiff. ... and I think that there are many cases where people are legitimately entitled for asylum right, but they [the government] denies it and therefore they become destitute ...the major group of asylum seekers and refugees in Broomhall is the Somali community they came to join the pre-existing Somali community in Broomhall." [an information provider from section C of Broomhall] [I.P.05].*

This argument shows how bigger political issues at the British national level affect the lives of the poor and the destitute at lower levels such as the poorest areas of Broomhall. There are also many social problems and issues related to poverty as a commentator explains (Green, 2000c; 2000a), for example, in Broomhall "there is a relationship of poverty and health" [a middle class resident from section C] [R.I. 08]. A poor working class resident on social benefits confirmed the above statements by suggesting that the government does not help the poor in the way they need it:

> *"There is nothing around here, there is nothing around here for the needy, the down and out, the alcoholics, the drug addicts, there is nothing for them to do, there is no way for them to go, and that's what we need. You know we know each other, we can work together, we know we can work together, but it's like, we need somebody, that's gonna say: 'yes, we're gonna do this' and not be fucked up like the council like happens all the time." [a working class resident from section A] [F.G.03.A].*

Another poor working class resident on social benefits, in the same focus group interview, even argued that some people, in allusion to the government and some voluntary sector organisations, treated young people like animals (meaning animals in a clear pejorative and contemptuous way as being irrational):

> *"because if we start treating these youngers [sic] as human beings, and not as animals as some people think, then we might get some good, because you know we all are human beings." [a working class resident from section A] [F.G.03.C].*

Poverty was found in the poorest areas of sections A, B, and C of Broomhall, and particularly in section A as a "big issue, there are people in benefits, they don't have money" [an information provider from section D of Broomhall] [I.P.06]. "There are therefore features of deprivation, poverty, overcrowding" adds [an information provider from section C of Broomhall] [I.P.05]. In the poorest areas of sections ABC, especially in A, thousands of people live overcrowded in the 494 flats of the Hanover Estates. And the same commentator argues that cheek by jowl, in section D, the Broomhall Park (BP), lives a "part of the community that is so well off, very privileged, cheek by jowl" [I.P.05]. However, the people from BP are not part of the Broomhall neighbourhood, at least not part of the sections A, B, and C of Broomhall. Poverty is not an issue for the people of section D, the BP.

5.2.2.1.2   Unemployment

As shown in Table 5.1 above there is a general consensus that unemployment is a major issue with pervasive negative consequences for the poor working classes of Broomhall. These are the perceptions of some residents and information providers:

> *"The first worst thing [in Broomhall] is unemployment and low income. There's not much*

employment in the area. The majority or the biggest percentage of the residents in Broomhall are unemployed." [an information provider from section C of Broomhall] [I.P.01].

"The major feature that describe this community is high unemployment. There is not enough work for people in this estate [Hanover Flats, Exeter Drive, Sheffield, S3]. There is nothing for the younger people to do so they go out and commit crime, because they get bored and that causes other problems." [a working class respondent from section A] [F.G.03.A].

"definitively employment is an issue." [an information provider from section B of Broomhall] [I.P.07]

One respondent commented on the lack of jobs and the lack of advice and information provision:

"There are not jobs. There is not advice about jobs or information." [a working class resident from section B] [F.G.02.A].

Another respondent mentioned that many people lacked jobs and face difficulties raising their children:

"I think is by providing jobs, through jobs so these workers can get the skills, so these organizations need to come and encourage. You know many parents they don't have jobs and for raise their kids is difficult." [a working class respondent from section C] [F.G.01.D].

5.2.2.1.3   Debt

The author (Muela-Meza, 2005b), in a recent paper found that a Sheffield middle class citizen – however, not from Broomhall – committed suicide by hanging himself on the 28th of July 2003 because he had a debt with banks amounting to more than £ 70, 000 pounds through 19 credit cards, several of them issued by the same bank, when he only earned £ 22, 000 pounds a year. The author (Muela-Meza, 2005b) questioned if more effective institutionalised provision of information, advice and help would have prevented this man from killing himself.

"But there is also a lot of debt in the area, due to unemployment, due to multiculturalism, and due to drugs, and drunk [sic] behaviour. That is always involved, so you need those things, you need unemployment, a good... [sic, pause] and debt as part of the area. People get to debt because because [sic double because] they have to pay basic needs and money just isn't enough, you need... there isn't enough money for their basic needs. You know, if they already smoke, or they already drink, they are not going to stop, they going to do that anyway." [a working class resident from section A] [F.G.03.A].

5.2.2.1.4   Crime

Crime is one of the major issues found in this research, but not as a causal agent affecting other issues of this report, but rather as effect of the direct or tangential effects of others like poverty.

A respondent gives a rather positive account of crime in Broomhall and Broomhill:

"there is not much crime against the person, but against properties, cars, homes, and students are very vulnerable because they bring computers and all kind of fancy things and they get stolen. So that's one of the constant problem of living in this kind of area high incidence of crimes." [an information provider from Broomhill] [I.P.03].

However those impressions do not match with the news from the press. On 10 August 2006 a writer and businessman was knifed in intended robbery on Victoria Road, section D, the Park of Broomhall:

"A brave dad today told how he tackled robbers who held him at knifepoint outside his Sheffield home. John Malcomson was attacked by two men as he placed his wheelie bin outside his house at Victoria Road, Broomhall. But he escaped with cuts to his hands, arms and leg as he wrestled the knife from one of his assailants on Tuesday evening" (*Star (Sheffield), 2006a*).

On 20 September 2004 a university lecturer was robbed at knifepoint on section D, the Park, Broomhall:

"A lecturer was robbed on a Sheffield street by two men who held a blade to his throat. The 53 year old was followed by two men as he walked home from the city centre last night and they struck in Clarkegrove Road, Broomhall." (*Star (Sheffield), 2004a*)

An old lady was also attacked and robbed in section D, the Park, Broomhall, like the recent robbery and attack on an old lady who died afterwards in hospital:

An 80 years old "woman suffered injuries to her face, hands and legs after her handbag was snatched on Collegiate Crescent, Broomhall. The thug fled towards Ecclesall Road with the bag. He was in his early 20s, stocky, of medium height and wearing a dark anorak" (*Star (Sheffield), 2006e*).

Making self complacent stereotypes about the types of criminals and crimes do not describe comprehensively the phenomena.

Drug dealing crimes are the most common in Broomhall. Between 2005 and 2006 several cannabis factories were seized (BBC News (Sheffield), 2005b; 2006). But there has been a fatal crime against Mohammed Abdu Razak Abdullahi, a Somali 19 year old man, who was killed by having been thrown to the ground from the 9th floor of the Hanover Flats on section D of Broomhall, Exeter Drive (BBC News (Sheffield), 2004; 2005a; 2006; *Star (Sheffield), 2004c*).

There have been not only attacks on the person, but also violently with fire arms (BBC News (Sheffield), 2007; Star (Sheffield), 2007d). Arson crimes are very common in different multi occupant housing, like the Hanover Flats on Exeter Drive, section A of Broomhall. In 2004 a flat was set on fire in an arson attack through the letter box and the owner died of smoke intoxication (*Star (Sheffield)*, 2004d). A mentally unstable person murdered Mrs. Ali by arson attack on her flat (Star (Sheffield), 2005a).

Therefore, in the respondent's opinion painting a positive picture of the security of the area is fine. He has the right to imagine we live in the most secure and happy world. But in the case of the police minimizing crime it is a different story, because police are supposed to be there to protect the public before crimes occur, not after. Thus these crimes show evidence of the failures of police and leave people deprived from their right to a safe environment from crime.

"the police are to a larger extent it's always as if they don't want to do the job, we had something on the street, a house that was occupied, and it was growing large amounts of weed, basically, and it smelled, it stunk, they might have had 4 crops a year, and the whole of the house was like a greenhouse basically, and... and... people told the police. Nothing we can't do about it. Well why don't you just pass by and have a smell, because you can smell it, it's obvious, at some point you'll feel the smell so bad and don't know which house is coming from because is so strong to the whole of the street, you smell it and gee was really bad. Eventually, eventually after a year, a year, they were forced, because someone phoned up, and forced them to actually do something about it because someone phoned someone higher up, and the police were caught with their trousers down [sic, and respondent laughs] basically, they went, they went to the letterbox, and it was so... so in your face, they had to do something, you know it was an embarrassment [for the police] feel like embarrassed, embarrassed to do the job [police job against drug dealing], it is almost as if they [the police] don't want to do the job [a working class resident from section A] [R.I. 07]."

Nevertheless, the same respondent mentions that the police have been less racist than in previous years:

> *"and they [the police] don't want to do the job, and now and then when things got so bad, there'll be a raid and things will settle down, then they can go back to square, and it's being like that all the time since I've live in Broomhall, I mean... it used to be the police more racist I must say" [a working class resident from section A] [R.I. 07].*

The next section presents, analyses, and discusses the information needs that emerged from the issues about poverty, and social, and economic inequalities.

5.2.2.2   INFORMATION NEEDS RELATING TO POVERTY, AND SOCIAL, AND ECONOMIC INEQUALITIES

What are the community information needs related to poverty, social, and economic inequalities? Based on the evidence presented above, there follows a discussion of the community information needs, as interpreted by the author.

• Working class individuals need information to carry out these activities: 1) to know about their entitlements such as jobseeker allowance, asylum seeker allowance, single parent allowance, etc.; 2) to know how to find jobs; 3) to know how to cope with debt; 4) to know how to cope with crime, e.g. how to deal with the police in both cases, if they are victims or crime or if they allegedly committed crime; 5) basically to know about all the necessary things to allow them to maintain themselves above the "accepted" social standards of poverty, and to prevent them from falling beyond those standards into extreme poverty, thus becoming an even heavier burden for society. Otherwise they may fall pray of crime; or of negligent abandonment of statutory social care; or commit suicide; or killing others (*Star (Sheffield)*, 2005a), etc. in order to overcome their extreme poverty condition. Thus, poor working class people will need information to know about things, only when there is still a chance for them to know, either because they are literate, or because they are able to speak for themselves in order to empower themselves. There are many cases where individuals are in an extreme poverty condition where they face the most severe mental disorders possibly due in part to extreme poverty conditions and other factors, and cannot know or find information for themselves. There is also scientific evidence that poverty is correlated with malnutrition due to the lack of nutrients such as iron on the regular diet. People lacking sufficient iron might develop anaemia, and consequently they will develop cognitive disorders for life, where even in the most positive teaching conditions they would never learn like normal individuals. Thus they will be cognitively crippled for life (Sagan, 1997; Heap, 2003; Muela-Meza, 2004b). These findings are particularly interesting because they challenge the validity of previous research. For example, Moore's (2002) model of social information needs emphasizes that "people with low levels of literacy absorbs less information than others with high literacy levels because so much of it is presented as text" (2002: 301). Whilst Moore's (2002: 301) assertion is valid, his model, nevertheless, fails to analyse the causes of people's limitations to absorb information behind his statement of the lack of literacy. He fails to correlate poverty and cognitive disorders caused by poverty found in this project as a realistic and materially rooted cause to explain why people cannot satisfy better their information needs.

• Middle class individuals need information either to try to understand the poverty phenomenon of their housing neighbours (e.g. from section B) in order to protect themselves from poor people in the case of criminals, or to try to help them to solve their problems. Although the evidence shown above indicates that basically they use information to protect themselves from the negative effects poor people present to them and their properties, rather than to help them to solve their problems, in some cases they worsen their condition; e.g. attempting to ban prostitution (Hall, 1981), attempt to ban noisy pubs (*Star (Sheffield)*, 2006f).

• The capitalist classes also need information to try to understand poor people, but more specifically to avoid the risks they represent to their capitalist businesses. For instance, since the territorial features had over-arching impacts on residents, in most cases capitalist housing developers have bluntly excluded the poor in their development plans and mentioned that the property market middle class and the more affluent (e.g. capitalist class) classes are the targets of their businesses, such as the upper market West One (see location in Figure 4.5 in Chapter 4 above or in *Broomhall News*, 2006: 4, and see pictures at Muela-Meza, 2003-2007). As a capitalist developer commented in relation to the West One complex: "we knew our target audience was going to be upper-market" (Blandy and Parsons, 2004: 12). They also challenged and lobbied and in the end circumvented, in the view of the author as he interpreted the data, the legal provisions from the government to provide "social housing" or "mixed tenure" and other protections for the poor working classes (Cabinet Office, 2001). In the view of the author, they screened out and rejected poor working class applicants, and if they did not reject them from the outset, they built expensive accommodation for middle and capitalist classes. The poor working classes, in the view of the author, were rejected by default since they could never afford to live there, e.g. in West One (Blandy, & Parsons, 2004). Poor working classes could never afford to live either in similar brand new upper-market developments around Sheffield city centre and Broomhall such as: Velocity Village, Cutlery Works, Fulcrum, AG1, Butcher Works, Cornish Square and City Walk developed by Blundells Ltd.'s *Centro* (*Exposed*, 2007: 22-23) or Finnegan Ltd.'s One Eleven (see location in Figure 4.5 in Chapter 4 above or in *Broomhall News*, 2006: 4) just across Ecclesall Road off the Hanover Flats, which redeveloped the ex Ward's Brewery and is even larger Blundells' West One.

The reader just needs to compare the pictures (see Muela-Meza, 2003-2007) of the Hanover Flats of section A (Sheffield City Council social housing particularly for poor working classes, destitute, asylum seekers, refugees, and other highly deprived groups) with the high middle and capitalist class developments like West One off the road from section B and One Eleven or Velocity just off the road from section A, and they will confirm that the high middle and capitalist class market developments have excluded completely poor working class residents, even at the slightest glimpse of their exterior design. For instance, Fulcrum development "is so good that even the architects who designed it have moved in downstairs" (*Exposed*, 2007: 22).

The next section presents, analyses, and discusses the ways in which information providers tried to meet the information needs that emerged from the issues about poverty, and social, and economic inequalities.

5.2.2.3   INFORMATION PROVISION RELATING TO POVERTY, AND SOCIAL, AND ECONOMIC INEQUALITIES

A LIS researcher found, in an MA dissertation at the Department of Information Studies at the University of Sheffield (Johnson, 1995), that there was a strong connection between unemployment and social needs, being the most critical of them information, help and advice to help them know their entitlements and statutory rights and untangle the maze of statutory sector institutions. She argued that unemployment in the UK grew from one million to three million from 1981 to 1982 which took place as an effect of the Thatcher regime's steamroller of privatization of public services, cuts in welfare benefits, decline of steel industries, and so on (Johnson, 1995). "The work of advice centres therefore became more nominated by welfare rights work and many local authorities began to establish benefits advice services, often as part of an 'anti-poverty initiative.' ... From the eighties onwards information and advice services have faced new demands of an increasingly depressing nature as a result of the contraction of the welfare state and cuts in public spending, leaving more and more people with inadequate or no means of support..." (Johnson, 1995: 4). This fact is corroborated by the perceptions of residents:

"One of the major issues is jobs. There are not jobs. There are not advice about jobs or information. Also drugs, people don't find other way to get money." [a working class resident from section B] [F.G.02.A].

"We have a credit union to help people, but it's more about education financially. And we have a tenants' association, but people don't have confidence with either." [a working class resident from section A] [F.G.03.B].

"also we are bombarded with information, you know people have televisions, we're bombarded with information, you go out on the street and there's adverts everywhere, our society is quite in new face, isn't? It gives the false impression that everything is available all you have to do is to have money, if you have it you can get anything, but if you don't, then you find the ways to get the money, that's what they do, but it isn't necessarily to get a job... they

resort to crime..." [a working class resident from section A] [R.I. 07].

5.2.3 Issues, information needs, and provision related to health

The sections here below present, analyse, and discuss the issues, information needs, and provision relating to health issues.

5.2.3.1 HEALTH ISSUES

It was found in historic documents that British poor people, working classes and the destitute of the 19th and mid 20th century suffered severe deprivation of health services (Engels, [1845], 2000; Orwell, [1937], 1962; Fearnley, 2001) . A Sheffield chronicler, (Fearnley, 2001), who spent his childhood in a social care hospice, and who conducted historical research into the living conditions of poor people, the working class, and the destitute who were confined to the workhouses hospices in Sheffield in Victorian times, the 1800s, found a cruel and crude reality where the poor, the destitute, and the pauper [sic] were punished for being paupers [sic] and he argued that they were treated by the authorities and workhouses carers with "sheer brutality", and despised by society, specially under the Poor Law of 1839 (Fearnley, 2001: 37). Being in care himself as a child, his accounts may appear to some extent biased by his own experiences. However, there are other accounts of the living conditions of the poor, and the working class people in Victorian England, and they do not differ from his. For instance Engels ([1845], 2000), in his book *The Condition of the Working Class in England: From Personal Observation and Authentic Sources* written in 1845, also depicted the paupers [sic] living in the most miserable conditions even worse than criminal prisoners:

> "The food of criminal prisoners is better, as a rule, so that the paupers frequently commit some offence for the purpose of getting into jail. For the workhouse is a jail too; he who does not finish his task gets nothing to eat; he who wishes to go out must ask permission, which is granted or not, according to his behaviour or the inspectors whim; tobacco is forbidden, also the receipt of gifts from relatives or friends outside the house; the paupers wear a workhouse uniform, and are handed over, helpless and without redress, to the caprice of the inspectors" (Engels, [1845], 2000).

People today may dismiss these arguments and consider them an historical account not applicable to current times. They may also even argue that such episodes of extreme deprivation do not exist in current times. However, nowadays there are still cases of extreme deprivation of health services provision, but taking place in different ways than those of Victorian times. The times have changed, but in both periods extreme deprivation of health services has taken place.

For instance, cases were found in this project where people under care have been deprived of adequate health provision, like for example the case of a victim of some careless staff from the private social care South Yorkshire Housing Association 911 Project charity located in Broomhall: "a chronic drinker was found dead in bed at a Sheffield residential home after night support workers failed to spot she was dying of alcohol poisoning" (*Star (Sheffield)*, 2006b). This victim whose care staff thought she was "sleeping it off" died there at the SYHA 911 Project charity, South Yorkshire HA Care and Supported Housing, at 9-11 Filey Street, section C of Broomhall, Sheffield, S10 2FF.

Certainly this is only one case of alleged negligence committed by this private health care institution and generalizations cannot be drawn from this. Nor can this be rigorously compared with the condition of the destitute in Victorian workhouses. However, by the simple fact that this case has happened, provided that *The Star* could be taken as a true and reliable information source, it may be symptomatic of the condition of other people under care. It is arguably symptomatic of a current kind of neglect the people of our times are experiencing. And this is particularly true for Broomhall where many people with alcohol related diseases are being taken care of in places like SYHA. Many more go to Broomhall from other sides of Sheffield to have free meals provided by Christian people at the Hanover Methodist Church, Broomspring Lane, or at the Sunnybank Community Centre, Williams Street, both in section C. A working class resident perceives social care neglect in these terms:

*"I see all these drunk people sitting by CostCutter, here by Broomhall Street, [section C] and it
is very sad and they live their lives of themselves and they are outcast by the community and
generally everyone just ignores them and that is sad." [a working class resident from section
B] [F.G.02.A].*

Apparently those Christian people feed the drinkers and other people out of disinterested charity.
However other working class respondents perceive that such help has hidden intentions or agendas
in trying to convert people to Christianity, or Islam, or become followers of their churches:

*"St. Thomas, the church is in Crookes, but they serve in the Sunny Bank Community. [...] but
that's the problem with all religions, you can say the same for Muslims, quite of few people
who teach the children, the Koran, but behind it all again like the Jesus Army stands where
they want to convert them, you know, bring them into their religion, and they are quite a few."
[a working class resident from section A] [R.I. 07].*

*"So it is like indoctrination, like bringing more people in, but that is not doing something for
the community. Whereas the Methodist Church [Hanover, at Broomspring Lane, section C]
they do things because they see as a need, sometimes they may suffer because there is a need
as they see a need, they will feed the drinker, and the drinker will come and spend the time in
Broomhall, so we have a problem with the street drinkers here, by the CostCutter [at
Broomhall Road in the corner of Williams Street]." [a working class resident from section A]
[R.I. 07].*

Another resident agrees with resident R.I.07's perceptions:

*"the Jesus Army don't do anything for the community, they just try to convert people to
Christianise and to love God [a working class resident from section B of Broomhall]." [R.I. 10]*

The comments of respondents 07 and 10 just mentioned shed light on broader issues related to
health. Both of them provide a strong argument relating to how the negligence of government,
private and voluntary sectors relating to adequate health services provision has to be compensated
for by religious people and churches. Furthermore, 07 highlights another aspect of the problem:
Broomhall has a severe problem of drinkers on the streets, in particular in sections C, A, and B (but
not D), because those religious people and churches attract them to feed and indoctrinate them. But
religious people and churches fail to criticise the causes of this problem.

Religious people and churches, either disinterestedly or for indoctrination purposes, play a great
role in attracting many drinkers and drug addicts to the Broomhall neighbourhood, and hence
increasing the security and health risks of residents, and particularly of children. At best, they cause
nuisances, but at worst they throw away drug needles on the streets or in children's playgrounds.
This is a big social problem and issue for the people in the neighbourhood, because within the
neighbourhood there is already a big problem of alcoholism and drug addiction. Hence religious
people and churches, by simply feeding alcohol and drug abusers –either by honest charity or
indoctrination– without criticising the government's health policies, become part of the problem.

There are other cases in the press of alleged victims of health care neglect. For example Michael
Wilkinson, according to the press, "has cerebral palsy but has lost two of his regular carers 15
months ago within weeks of each other - throwing his life into disarray. But he says over the past
few years employing a carer has become a nightmare. In order to live as full a life as possible
Michael needs to have a carer to help him with general household chores. But he has grown
increasingly frustrated at the difficulty of finding reliable and considerate employees" (*Star
(Sheffield), 2005e*). According to the charity Scope, specialist in cerebral palsy, much of the blame
for Mr. Wilkinson's problems is due to the fact that the government changed the funding rules for
disabled people and now they can buy their own care, but Scope argues that this would put more
stress and difficulties on patients as in Mr. Wilkinson's case (*Star (Sheffield), 2005e*).

Another dramatic example of alleged health care neglect is the case of 61 year old Somali
grandmother Amina Ali who "died in an arson blaze because a paranoid schizophrenic did not

receive the correct treatment. Abdirisak Hussein [another Somali] started a blaze which killed Amina Ali just hours after pleading for help from a social worker in the street" (Star (Sheffield), 2005a). Mrs. Ali died in her flat at Cliff Street, maisonettes flats in Sharrow which are located just across the road off Ecclessall Road and near the Hanover Flats. This fatal example did not take place actually within the working boundaries of this thesis, but it is arguably relevant to this study of Broomhall, since according to the press, the murderer of Mrs. Ali threatened many times at the Broomhall Sunny Bank Community Centre (section C) Mrs. Ali's husband because he belonged to the Black Adam Tribe in Somalia. It is also reported that he pleaded for mental health care at the Hanover Medical Centre, but he was not served; or at least as seen from these fatidic facts he was not served well. The defence alleged that if he would have been given adequate mental treatment and medication he might not have killed Mrs. Ali (Star (Sheffield), 2005a).

This is a very sad example of health care neglect, and whilst nothing will justify this murder's act, the arguments of his defence have some weight. Nevertheless, this murder case is too complex to be attributed solely to medical factors. Conflicts based on tribalism are the other side of this case. Some respondents made comments about this:

"I don't like people talking about tribes, I don't like it much." [a working class resident from section B] [F.G.02.C].

Another respondent elaborates on this idea:

"You know what she wants to say is that... You know that is what I like about England is that no one asks you about tribes and that is something very good even among Somali here. You know in our country no one can marry any one from other tribes because they put first the tribes and they don't marry people from other tribes even if you are beautiful or rich. So I think here that the young generations we are happy here, but in our country is very bad because of the tribalism." [a working class resident from section B] [F.G.02.B].

Thus, the alleged mental disorders of Mrs. Ali's murderer are one side of the story; his tribalism is another side, and certainly there may be some or many other sides. But another resident suggests that the fragmentation of Somali people back home due to their civil war might have been brought to the UK as they came here as asylum seekers fleeing from war:

"the other thing is fragmentation you may be aware of conflicts among the Somali community after all the Somali community arrived after the civil war so, I am presuming people from more than one side in the civil war are here." [a middle class resident from section C] [R.I. 01].

This respondent's opinion gives another view of the possible issues behind Mrs. Ali's murder. Perhaps the British policies on asylum seeking and refugees not only have adverse effects on the people being refused, namely the destitute, but also on the people being accepted. These issues show some evidence that British policies, related to integrating asylum seekers and refugees as British citizens entitled to all the wide coverage of social services are very limited.

These fatidic cases of health service provision neglect provide some evidence that the authorities' responsibilities do not stop at granting people permission to stay in the country; it should be the authorities' responsibilities at all levels –central, local, voluntary – to assure that all newcomers become adapted to British culture.

Certainly all newcomers to a new culture have their responsibilities to adapt to the new culture. But this should be a reciprocal flow or adaptation: the newcomers should adapt to British culture, and the British culture should be tolerant with the newcomers' culture. The British authorities and public servants have the responsibility to understand all the diverse cultural backgrounds of the people who live in their country and who like themselves and everybody else, also need be served by all the gamut of services they need to survive and have a happy, peaceful and prosperous life.

Nevertheless, a caveat is necessary here. After all has been said above, this thesis could not provide a sound critique of the British government by simply analysing the cases found above in the press. Nor can broad generalizations be drawn.

5.2.3.1.1 Lack of health due to lack of public green open space

Territoriality or uses of the land have a strong relation with health. More clearly the lack of health facilities has been found to have a strong connection with the lack of healthy lifestyles in Broomhall. Observation suggested that since most of the land is being privatised for upper-market Housing in Multiple Occupancy (HMO), which most of the poor working class (and some lower middle class) residents could not afford, this privatisation phenomenon has brought at the same time the problem that most of the health and sport facilities affordable for poor working classes have been replaced by upper-market ones (see for instance hundreds of photographs which show evidence of this at Muela-Meza, 2003-2007). Two residents from section C support this idea:

> *"public green space is under provided in Broomhall according to the council records, I don't know how precisely they define Broomhall for the purpose of compiling those statistics but they say there is under provision. And I really think there is under provision if you contemplate the density of houses in Exeter of twin tower flats [section A]... so there are 256 flats in each tower..." [a middle class resident from section C] [R.I. 01].*

> *"There are very little green open spaces for everyone. There is an allotment around here but there are only 20 plots and some people have more than two lots. And as for gardens some people got almost nothing and there are some others with very big gardens, it varies a lot. And the houses with multiple occupation don't have any gardens.... people from Broomhall use Devonshire park." [a middle class resident from section C] [R.I. 04].*

One respondent mentioned that there is a lack of parks and playgrounds for all the people and children:

> *"No, the building developers, they come in to do student accommodation, modernising building, but they don't regenerate the parks. Around here there are lots of children around here, and when it comes to holidays they are just walking around the streets, but if there would be something constructive like parks where they would go, so there wouldn't be broken glass, no needles [used by drug addicts], it would be nice for parks. The developers they don't do anything, I think they don't." [a working class respondent from section C] [F.G.01.B].*

There is only one playground on Hanover Street and another smaller one around the Hanover Flats, but they are not enough and they look rather old, with some benches semi-derelict.

> *"The playground may be enough for younger children, but for older children there is a quite a lot of pressure... there is a great competition between spaces for university students and to older children from the community." [a middle class resident from section C] [R.I. 04]*

5.2.3.1.2 Lack of health due to lack of free, or affordable sport facilities

Poor health is associated with a lack of engagement in sport and fitness activity. The latter was corroborated by respondents' perceptions and by observation. A lack of health was perceived as due to a lack of free or affordable sport facilities as these respondents note:

> *"there is a big issue in Sheffield to sports facilities because they are very expensive." [a middle class resident from section C] [R.I. 06].*

> *"there are many leisure facilities, theatres, cinemas, swimming pools, and so on, but you have to pay for access." [a working class resident from section A] [R.I. 07].*

> *"the worst is that there are not affordable facilities for recreation, you know sports, and recreation, there is Ponds Forge swimming pool but it's too expensive and people here cannot afford it [meaning from sections A, B, and C of Broomhall], or if you want to go to the cinema is not cheap." [an information provider from section B of Broomhall] [I.P.07].*

*"You know, there is [sic] no youth clubs. We don't have nothing [sic]. We don't have
any advice centre." [a working class resident from section A] [F.G.03.C].*

But this lack of free and affordable health and sport facilities in Broomhall is a recent phenomenon,
because even in the very recent past, Broomhall used to be better served with free or affordable
facilities. And this fact is even corroborated by a middle class resident:

*"but it would be very nice to have here in Broomhall a healthy living centre so they don't need
to go all the way up to Upperthorpe to swimming pool and gym there is more cheaper, and
you know if you want to join a gym you need to pay a yearly subscription and many people
around here, including ourselves could not afford to pay a subscription to have access on an
occasional basis, so it would be nice to have a centre like Upperthorpe, you know they have a
library, a cafe, and a swimming pool, and they have classes and I think that would be great,
whereas, yes there are gyms around here but used by a very select number of people, and that
is great. It would be great if we have something like Upperthorpe. We used to have Glossop
Road baths and they shut them down there was a swimming pool there just across the
carriageway for it is not longer there. And it would be good if one of the universities [of
Sheffield and Hallam Sheffield] would put something back in the community and even if the
university opened up their own facilities at a reasonable rate, and they opened it, but again,
they are too expensive. And Hallam [Hallam Sheffield University] haven't got any good
facilities any way." [a middle class resident from section C] [R.I. 06].*

Thus, if even a middle class resident complains about the lack of sport facilities or the expensive
fees to access them, then it could be inferred that for poor working classes on benefits, not to
mention the destitute, access to these facilities is impossible.

Furthermore, there is particularly one health and sport facility missing in Broomhall, especially
missing for the poorest working classes: the Sheffield YMCA (Young Men's Christians Association).
As shown in Table 5.1 in this chapter, the YMCA has emerged as one of the most negative issues
affecting the residents of Broomhall. Many interviewees complained that since 2001 when they sold
their facilities on Broomhall Road, (section D, the Park), to Sheffield Hallam University (SHU) (Star
(Sheffield), 2002b), they have been deprived of free and affordable access to 10, 956 square metres
of sport facilities (gym, pitches, and other services where people did aerobics, weightlifting, health
exercise, yoga, training and many other healthy activities). This was much used and needed,
particularly by poor people. To give an idea of the massiveness of 10, 956 m2 of the ex-YMCA
property on Broomhall Road compared with the twin towers of Hanover Flats, of section A which is
only 1,155 m2, see Table 4.6 (in Chapter 4).

Thus, most of the respondents, working and middle class residents and information providers alike,
criticised the YMCA for this sale and consequent deprivation.

*"for leisure facilities, the YMCA used to have a gym I think it was at Victoria Road or
Collegiate Crescent [it was located on Broomhall Road actually] but they sold it to the Sheffield
University [actually to Sheffield Hallam University Broomhall campus] and this university
demolished it and built formal classroom type buildings, I'm not sure what they built as a
replacement. And that was a quite cheap gym [the YMCA] many people used to use and now is
gone, so that is something they can't use any more." [an information provider from section A]
[I.P.08].*

*"There are quite some private companies which have set gyms one called Greens at walking
distances, literally just opposite to Waitrose you know what I mean? But again, it's private
and it's quite expensive. So my guess is that people used the YMCA and now [since the YMCA
sold the property to Sheffield Hallam University] don't use anywhere [sic]." [an information
provider from section A] [I.P.08].*

*"I know there is a Somali football team but there is no pitch to play in Broomhall, I think they
go to play to the nearest pitch which in the General Cemetery." [an information provider from
section A] [I.P.08].*

The YMCA sold to the Sheffield Hallam University the massive land on Broomhall Road where the gym mentioned above used to be. See table 5.9 below to find the *Comparative ground areas in square metres of the ex YMCA properties on Broomhall Road (section D) and the ex St. Silas Church (section C)*. In this table the reader will find that the ex YMCA premises on Broomhall Road (section D) were 24 times bigger than the new ones they bought on the ex St. Silas Church (section C) where they plan to serve Broomhall from sections A, B, and C.

Table 5.9 Comparative ground areas in square metres of the ex YMCA properties on Broomhall Road (section D) and ex St. Silas Church (section C)	
Area of ex YMCA property on Broomhall Road	Area of new YMCA property on ex St. Silas Church
10, 956 m2 (132 m frontage per 83 m depth)	450 m2 (15 m frontage per 30 m depth)

The developers destroyed the YMCA, the Solar and all of that area, but not to build flats. Some data from the literature illustrate this. The developers destroyed the YMCA, but they have built a multi million pound development for the School of Health and Social Care of the Sheffield Hallam University (SHU):

"The School of Health and Social Care is to have a new purpose-built home with state-of-the-art facilities that will enable it to provide the very best in training for the next generation of health professionals. Due for completion in September 2004, the multi-million pound development of the former YMCA building site on Broomhall Road will ensure Sheffield Hallam is well placed to meet the Government's radical agenda for tackling the national healthcare recruitment crisis" (Sheffield Hallam University Alumni Association, 2003: 9).

This news does not mention at all that the Sheffield Hallam University will create any alternative facilities for the free use of the community as the YMCA used to offer. That is, clearly this university has destroyed the only health and fitness centre the Broomhall residents used to have, but at the same time it has built other facilities which will prepare the health scientists and practitioners to cope with health problems at a higher level. This evidences a twofold problem: on the one side they adversely affect the health of the community, but on the other hand they are investing in their future provision of health services that will contribute to the health of all, not only for Broomhall residents. Nevertheless, this study did not find any evidence relating to whether, or how, Sheffield Hallam University will provide alternative fitness facilities to the community. This study aims just to present the facts as perceived by residents.

"I used to go to the YMCA gym but Hallam [Hallam Sheffield University] demolished it, I used to go there and make lots of friends there a long time ago, there used to be many things there, but you know Hallam demolished it and built a new building there for their students... you know, I think it is part of the erosion of local facilities, maybe I'm a bit sentimental but you know all over Sheffield there used to be a network of swimming baths and there are very very [sic, double "very"] few left now." [a middle class resident from section C] [R.I. 06].

5.2.3.1.3   Health issues related to drugs

Drug issues have dramatic effects on all the people involved and even on innocent non-involved people, but mainly on drug addiction victims who are victims of the illegal drug dealing crime or sheer poverty and statutory social care neglect. Drug issues have relations to many other issues. However this project did not delve into the manifold causes or effects because the author is not expert in medicine or other health related disciplines, and because that goes beyond the scope of this project. Nevertheless, this project does indeed show evidence that drug issues are perhaps the most adverse issues affecting not only the victims, but also many other people. Next are presented some discussions from residents and information providers of what they perceive to be the causes of drug addiction in Broomhall.

A working class respondent associates the problem of drug addiction with unemployment:

> *"The main cause for drugs problem is unemployment, if people had jobs they
> wouldn't be in drugs..." [a working class resident from section A] [F.G.03.B].*

On similar lines as respondent F.G.03.B, another respondent argues that poverty or unemployment
may drive people not to become drug addicts, but drug dealers:

> *"There is definitely a drug issue in this area for easy money and a lot of families are
> very worried in their families that their older sons get into drugs or as drug dealers,
> you know is easy money, but we are always encouraging them with education of the
> dangers of those issues. There are needles in the yard. There is prostitution; we have
> found evidences of prostitution in our playgrounds and car parks." [an information
> provider from section B of Broomhall] [I.P.07].*

This invites the question of why drug addiction is not alleviated, or dealt with properly by statutory
health care provision.

A working class resident complains that there are no drug rehabilitation institutions free of charge
for drug addicts:

> *"We need a drug rehabilitation house free of charge for all the people around here, we
> don't have any." [a working class resident from section A] [F.G.03.C].*

There are some drug rehabilitation institutions in Broomhall, but these are not statutory,
but private such as Phoenix House in section D, the Park. It is evident that in section A
many people have severe health problems caused by alcoholism, drug addiction, and other
factors, and across the road, in section D, the Park, there is the Phoenix House institution
that could help them, or the Counselling Services of the University of Sheffield, in
Wilkinson Street, section C. But in both cases they are private and exclusive institutions,
the first serving only people from a middle or capitalist class background, and the second
only members of the university community.

Another working class resident agrees with respondent *[F.G.03.C]* above and complains
that there are no drug rehabilitation institutions. This respondent also emphasizes that
drug addiction is a larger social public issue which is not addressed properly:

> *"...another issue is drug addicts because society divide them, separate them for no
> reason, but drug issue is not an issue on its own, it isn't, the people who takes drugs don't
> come in one group, they don't come in one category, you know drug users come not only
> from poor houses, they come from all over, they come from different nationalities, you
> have Asian people who take drugs, black people, men and women who take people,
> young people who take drugs, all people who take drugs, people religious take drugs, you
> know what I mean? There are no boundaries, and society tries to put them as they don't
> happen and put them in a little box..." [a working class resident from section A] [R.I. 09].*

Another problem that drug addiction brings to people is that the private companies have to provide
health care for drug addicts and their families. Due to the severe circumstances they are
experiencing they then become a heavier burden for other social services providers, as one
respondent comments:

> *"it's really hard, we also have drug rehabilitation unit, hostel, homeless
> accommodations on the other side [section D of Broomhall], and those children come
> here [Springfield Primary School, section B], so we have quite a lot different area of
> those very affected families. That's the Phoenix house, their children come here [to
> Springfield Primary School] and there these women hostels where their kids arrive in
> a dreadful state and those homeless accommodations and their kids come here, so
> those problems are completely different! [sic] here, you know, they come [the*

children] with lots of emotional problems, and we have to do the job of psychologists, social workers, and we can't hire psychologists because we don't have the money. It's very expensive." [an information provider from section B of Broomhall] [I.P.07]

The next section presents, analyses, and discusses the information needs that emerged from health issues.

5.2.3.2 INFORMATION NEEDS RELATED TO HEALTH ISSUES

What are the community information needs related to health issues? To summarise the evidence presented above, these are the following.

- All social classes need information to know how to improve their health, e.g. about their corresponding GP, a particular health provider or service for their particular illnesses, etc.
- Working class residents particularly need information to: 1) to know about their health benefits entitlements; and 2) to cope with alcohol and drug addiction.
- Capitalist and middle class residents need information to cope with alcohol and drug addiction.

The next section presents, analyses, and discusses the ways in which information providers tried to meet the information needs that emerged from the issues related to health.

5.2.3.3 INFORMATION PROVISION RELATED TO HEALTH ISSUES

Residents complain that there is no provision related to health issues.

"The way to break these circles [lack of health facilities or poverty] is by bringing in those advice bureaux and youth clubs, I think the youth clubs will be fantastic, a place where people can come, and talk to someone and get some advice, you know like those places of the Sunny Bank people come from all over Sheffield and those people feed them, and that's nice, but if there would be a place where they can also listen to them and help them with their drug, job and other problems." [a working class resident from section A] [F.G.03.E]

However as shown above in Tables 5.4 through 5.9, there is provision of health information, advice, and help through the Hanover Medical Centre (HMC). There is an extension service every Tuesday at the HMC from the Sharrow's Citizens Advice Bureau (SCAB). But the problem is that people want information, advice, and help services within Broomhall boundaries.

5.2.4 Issues, information needs, and provision related to politics

The sections below present, analyse, and discuss the issues, information needs, and provision relating to politics.

5.2.4.1 POLITICAL ISSUES

Politics are the thorniest issues found in this project, because it is where the social class struggle concept unfolds bringing to the surface the powerful dominating classes (capitalist and middle) and their negative effects against the weak dominated ones (working). Thus, a major organisation as described above in Table 5.1 emerged as the most negative political issue affecting the community: the Broomhall Forum (BF).

The main conflict derived from the BF has to do with funding. The BF since its foundation in 1998 has been acting as a self imposed umbrella organisation obtaining large amounts of funding from the European Union, the UK central government, regional government, and the Sheffield City Council amongst many other voluntary sources. Once they have obtained the money they have become a sort of mini "city council" within Broomhall and they unilaterally have self-assumed a role perceived by residents as dangerous because they decide who they fund and who they do not and they are not publicly accountable before any authority.

5.2.4.1.1   The Broomhall Forum (BF)

The Broomhall Forum has been perceived by residents as a non accountable organisation and they
distrust it:

> *"The Forum should be a public accountable group [Broomhall Forum, located and acting
> inside the offices of the Sheffield YMCA at 7 Broomgrove Road, Sheffield, S10 2LW, section D of
> Broomhall], it is in the process of doing it but it should do it better." [a working class resident
> from section A] [R.I. 09].*

Some others perceive it as an organisation that does not provide funding for all the people
of Broomhall when it is needed. A working class resident complains that the Broomhall
Forum denied funding to a BME (Black Minority Ethnic) organisation of Broomhall in
2004:

> *"This one [organisation's name omitted] centre applied for funding for the Broomhall
> Forum but it was denied funding. And this is the only black minority centre in the
> south of Sheffield and it was denied funding. It is Black Minority Ethnic
> organizations, BME." [a working class resident from section B] [F.G.02.A].*

A member of that organisation supported the perception of respondent F.G.02.A:

> *"The problem we are facing at the moment. The funding people, the funding bodies, they
> normally need references, a lot of documents, we have some because we are open over a year,
> you know places like the Broomhall Forum that would suppose to help with projects like ours
> it has never been there for us, from the Forum. So a lot of people in the area really are asking
> what is the Forum for and no one is answering questions. Because the Forum is suppose to
> help. Because the forum is there for the rich area..." [an information provider from section C of
> Broomhall] [I.P.01].*

A critical resident from the neighbourhood even published a letter in the *Broomhall News* to
criticise the negative role of the BF affecting the communities within the neighbourhood:

> "Letters. Dear Broomhall News, Can anyone fill us in a bit more on this "Broomhall Forum?"
> Somebody told me, maybe jokingly, it's a wholly owned subsidiary of the YMCA; someone else
> said, "No, that's Broomhall Cosmopolitan." More seriously, I think twice now we got a flyer
> through the door saying "come to our Annual General Meeting," but aside from that... Then ,
> early this summer, and just months into his office term of office, I saw a letter from the Chair
> resigning his post. Rightly or wrongly, he had some pretty strong things to say about how it fails
> to relate to the community which certainly struck a chord with me. Members of the Broomhall
> Park Association have since received rather furtively-phrased Minutes of follow-up meeting, but
> some of us ordinarily folk, this end of the neighbourhood, haven't even got that. Please, can
> somebody in-the-know tell us what is going on? And, for that matter, what exactly IS Broomhall
> Forum? What is set up to do? Who is supposed to represent? And what connection does it claim
> with the folk who live around here? Thank you. John Revill." (Revill, 2005: 3).

In addition, not only BME (Black Minority Ethnic) organisations have complained about the BF
because they do not fund their projects. Even a highly respected and valued organisation from the
voluntary sector complains because the Broomhall Forum does not fund them:

> *"We are desperately trying to get the resources to increase our level of service in Broomhall
> but we haven't been able to do so. We've talked to the Broomhall Forum to fund us because
> they have money available sitting on it and they have identified key needs, but it's very
> difficult to that community being fragmented to make a decision to where spend money. And
> they have got money sitting out for ages because they are not ready to make a decision to
> spend." [an information provider from section C of Broomhall] [I.P.05].*

According to another information provider the Broomhall Forum (BF) budget was:

"current budget is... nearly £ 500 000 over the next three and half years [from November 2005 until May 2009]" [an information provider from section D of Broomhall] [I.P.06].

The author of this project also wonders why the BF did not fund those organisations if they have had the money since 1998. According to the evidence generated, it has emerged that the BF only funds small short projects of a few hundred pounds a year, and they spend the rest of the money paying themselves huge amounts of money in salaries.

For instance, an internal document from the BF, a minute from an Annual General Meeting (which was open to the public to attend from within or outside the community) corroborates this. A member of the Broomhall Forum (BF), at the 2005 AGM presented the accounts for the period 1st April 2004 to 31st March 2005. From £37,474 pounds the BF received, £ 29, 286 pounds were spent in salaries for the BF's staff, only £ 2,252 were spent to fund community activities, and the rest was given to the YMCA because this charity company hosts the BF (Broomhall Forum, 2005: 3). That is, 78.15 % was spent on staff's salary, and only 6.0 % to fund community projects, and funding community projects is allegedly the reason for the existence of the Broomhall Forum (BF).

Therefore, it is not surprising that most Broomhall residents perceive the BF as having a considerably negative impact on the communities of the Broomhall neighbourhood. These are some of these perceptions:

"the Broomhall Forum has been for ages, but it hasn't done anything for the community." [a working class resident from section B of Broomhall] [R.I. 10].

"The people in the Broomhall Forum, Families United [user meant Family Service Unit at 86 Upper Hanover St., section C of Broomhall and closed permanently by mid 2006], with no disrespect, they seem no doing much for our people in this estate [Hanover Flats, Exeter Drive, Sheffield, S3]." [a working class resident from section A] [F.G.03.C].

the [Broomhall] Forum is concentrating only on one side of the area which is... Maybe to put it clearly... the richest side of Broomhall where they talk about doing speed bumps, but here there are a lot of things needed to be. But here there are more urgent matters to deal with but the Forum they don't address them." [an information provider from section C of Broomhall] [I.P.01].

"I think the complexity and the funding regimes of different services and the way they're organized and they way they shift from time to time hasn't helped, from the government. Once they funded Broomhall, then they lumped it with other organizations, and then back to other area, and then back to Broomhall... these funding shifts are just so complex and bureaucratic and much more than what they need to be and they [the government] complicating things it just don't help. So the Broomhall Forum if they got some money why on Earth they just don't use it and do something with it? Things like the Learning Skills of the council [Sheffield City Council] a lot of money is just wasted, not only at a community level." [an information provider from section C of Broomhall] [I.P.05].

The next section presents, analyses, and discusses the information needs that emerged from the political issues.

5.2.4.2   INFORMATION NEEDS RELATED TO POLITICAL ISSUES

Political information needs should not be assessed as a collective action of equal benefit for all, because the members of the three major classes analysed in this project have very distinctive differences and each follow very different interests from one another.

1)When working class residents need political information they are calling basically to the government for a decent and affordable house to rent, because it is very unlikely they will ever buy one in a lifetime. Supporting or not the capitalist or middle classes will not in any way improve their living conditions. But most working class residents lack sufficient understanding about the issues surrounding their lives, because their educational backgrounds are very low (Cassen and Kingdon, 2007), or because they have cognitive failures caused by for example an inadequate intake of iron due to endemic poverty (Sagan, 1997), or because of a huge number of other causes.

2)   When middle class residents call for political housing action they are basically calling on the parties involved (namely the government) to preserve their homes from the danger of demolition by the government, slum clearance policies, and so on. For those actions they need the full support of the working classes, not because by obtaining their support these will become middle class, or home owners themselves, but because their collective strength serves well their own benefit.

3)   When capitalist class members call for housing political action they are basically calling on the parties involved (namely the government and citizens of all classes especially the middle classes who most of the time serve well their interests) to give their business freedom to do business: to use brown, or green field sites or demolish old buildings in order to build, develop, or redevelop properties and obtain economic profits for their business.

The next section presents, analyses, and discusses the ways in which information providers tried to meet the information needs that emerged from political issues.

5.2.4.3   INFORMATION PROVISION RELATED TO POLITICAL ISSUES

If the issues of *territoriality or uses of the land* have emerged in Broomhall as the most pervasive and with the most adverse effects for most of its residents, particularly for poor working classes, almost as a natural consequence it also emerged that the main political issues are correlated with *territoriality or uses of the land*. As the evidence shown above related to the Broomhall Park conservation area, section D of Broomhall (Connell, 1968; Sheffield Corporation, 1974; City of Sheffield, 1989; Sheffield City Council, 2007a: 23), and the Havelock Housing Action, section C (Hall, 1981; Crook, et. al., 1976; Crook, 1983; Gibson and Dorfman, 1981), the political participation of the different individuals or groups is not geared to the collective benefit. Instead, they are motivated primarily by their private interests which they think will be well served by collective action. The political scientist James Q. Wilson (cited in Bennett, 1997: 664) in the early 1960s supported this idea by arguing that most people in the neighbourhoods, who engage in collective action to improve their housing and other conditions, do not necessarily do so by aiming consciously for the betterment of everyone through political action for social change:

> "Because of the private-regarding nature of their attachment to the community, they are likely to collaborate when each person can see a danger to him or to his family in some proposed change; collective action is a way, not of defining some broad program for the benefit of all, but of giving force to individual objections by adding them together in a collective protest." (cited in Bennett, 1997: 664).

However, since all the social classes have historically been struggling amongst themselves, the dominant classes attempting to take advantage over the dominated, as the concept of the *social class struggles* has been defined in the Methodology (Chapter 2), the political action of the people acting inside or outside Broomhall is no exception. On the same lines, a political philosopher (Demirovic, 2004) observes that the dominant classes exert their hegemony and domination through the monopolization of knowledge and information, which is of the particular interest of this research project. That is, they withhold and conceal information so the dominated classes, namely the working classes do not know what the powerful dominant and hegemonic classes (e.g. capitalist or bourgeois and middle classes) are doing allegedly to their benefit or against them:

> "As far as political domination is concerned, where knowledge [*and information, MUELA-MEZA, Z.M.]* can be monopolized, news reports and information create a considerable source of power; for those who are dominated can never know exactly what others are doing, which modes of collective behavior are developing and succeeding, and with which political reactions and decision they will have to contend" (Demirovic, 2004).

A Nobel laureate physicist concurs with that idea:

"Moreover, under existing conditions, private capitalists inevitably control, directly or indirectly, the main sources of information (press, radio, education [and libraries and other documental information institutions]). It is thus extremely difficult, and indeed in most cases quite impossible, for the individual citizen to come to objective conclusions and to make intelligent use of his political rights" (Einstein, 1949: 156-157).

How, then, do the powerful dominant classes −capitalist or bourgeois and middle classes— monopolize and conceal knowledge and information from the dominated classes? Demirovic responds to this question in these terms:

"The state [*and virtually any powerful individual or political organization, or information provider, or Institution of Documental Information*, MUELA-MEZA, Z.M.], however, defines public communication in a further sense. For the state is the sphere of political decision. Not everything that is decided is the result of previous communication. It is much more the case that politics must react to new challenges: the development of oil prices, an environmental catastrophe, currency speculation, or decisions made by international committees. In all of these cases parliament is called upon to agree to decisions made by the government. The public arena can then criticize political action after the fact. But this has no consequences. The state has won time and created facts. The possibility, bound up with the concept of the public arena - namely, to make virtually everything the object of public discussion - once again suffers irreparably from an unavoidable non-simultaneity: public discussion always comes too late" (Demirovic, 2004)

And that is what has happened, happens and will happen in Broomhall as long as the state of things continues in the way they have been found in this project.

5.2.5 Issues, information needs, and provision related to culture

The sections below present, analyse, and discuss the issues, information needs, and provision about culture.

5.2.5.1   CULTURAL ISSUES

When any issue of the Broomhall community is discussed in the light of many of the parties involved in the promotion or hampering of the development of the community, intercultural issues come into the picture. Also as some residents mentioned in this report, there is a perceptible lack of communication amongst the diverse parties involved in the Broomhall community.

As has been mentioned earlier, Broomhall is one of the wealthiest multi-cultural communities in Sheffield. Thus as might be expected in multi-cultural environments, many problems arise from this diversity, on linguistic, religious, ethnic, national, educational, or other grounds.

As far as this research goes, a real sense of unity amongst many respondents could not be found, because most of them did not like students and saw them as invaders or intruders in "their" community, not considering that they are also part of the community. The working class people are the majority of the community and they belong to the community but so do the middle and capitalist class people. These perceptions support this idea:

"Many of the ladies from Somalia they dress their clothes and local British see them threatening. And I think the local newspapers treat minorities bad." [a working class resident from section B] [F.G.02.A].

"We all come from similar roots and we come from the countries of these minorities and also we are British, so we can bring both worlds to these people. So I also think

that the media is playing a bad image to portraying bad the ethnic minorities, but
our Middle Eastern and Arabian people have input much about our cultures in
Europe and all over the world." [a working class resident from section B] [F.G.02.A].

"But no one help minorities and give them a piece of land to use it say as a youth
centre. And you know all minorities are isolated. And the British don't mix with the
ethnic minorities, these are different cultures, it is a clash of cultures, British and
minorities are very different for socializing." [a working class resident from section
B] [F.G.02.A].

"it doesn't matter how people see each other as long as they see them as human beings and
with tolerance to differences. So the big danger I see is when they see each other too much
under religion. And the government is passing laws to ban discrimination on the grounds of
religious beliefs. So people should respect everybody's religions and also the secular people
who don't have a religious belief, and see each other as human beings. I really see this
fragmentations caused by faith communities as counterproductive." [an information provider
from section C of Broomhall] [I.P.05].

However bad these issues may look, there are also some positive impressions from
individuals and their families who came as asylum seekers and refugees into the UK from
African and middle-eastern countries:

"Even if they live here in a very democratic culture many children are answering
back their parents and they are losing some good cultural things from back home.
But at the same time they are gaining some good cultural things. Like one of the
diseases from Middle East is tribalism. You are from that tribe, no I can't do
anything, I can't marry you because you are not from my tribe, your tribe is not
good. Very pathetic you know, same country, same language but with tribe problems,
you know. And this is something I like about England, because here you don't go for
the tribe, it is about your brain, how much can you apply for your mind. How much
can you get from life through your mind. So that's something I like too." [a working
class resident from section B] [F.G.02.A].

Other respondents elaborate on the positive sides of living in the UK:

"You know what she wants to say is that... You know that is what I like about
England is that no one asks you about tribes and that is something very good even
among Somali here. You know in our country no one can marry any one from other
tribes because they put first the tribes and they don't marry people from other tribes
even if you are beautiful or rich. So I think here that the young generations we are
happy here, but in our country is very bad because of the tribalism." [a working class
resident from section B] [F.G.02.B].

"I think the Broomhall community is much more fragmented than others because of historic
reasons and much has to do on faith fragmentation." [an information provider from section C
of Broomhall] [I.P.05].

5.2.5.2   INFORMATION NEEDS RELATED TO CULTURAL ISSUES

This section presents, analyses, and discusses the information needs that emerged from the cultural
issues.

From the evidence presented above it was found that the social class struggle concept cannot be
applied properly to cultural information needs. Cultural information needs are felt from individuals
irrespective of their social class. What individuals need is information that helps them to
understand and value different cultures; to be more tolerant and respectful of different cultures.

The next section presents, analyses, and discusses the ways in which information providers tried to
meet the information needs that emerged from cultural issues.

5.2.5.3 INFORMATION PROVISION RELATED TO CULTURAL ISSUES

It has emerged, through observation and the author's own participation as a library user, that the Sheffield Central Library information services are very good information providers. For more than 3 years in different periods the author has rung (or visited) the library and asked them for different queries just to see how the library would provide him with information. And during all this time they have responded with precision, pertinence, and above all, with a nice mood and patience. They have looked up information in local directories, in electronic databases and they have always given him positive answers. In most of the cases as expected they have referred him to other agencies giving him names of agencies, and telephone contacts. The treatment has always been nice, kind, obliging and respectful regardless of the type of query.

But in the case of cultural provision of information the traditional documental information institutions (DIIs) such as libraries or the Citizens' Advice Bureau (CAB) do not cover all the widest range of information needs. In such a case there are intercultural gateways within the neighbourhood.

> "I don't know to what extent [name of person omitted] is a gateway too, but the fact that is a Somali shop and have a large, so you see many male Somalis coming and going, socializing, not just shopping, so you have this difference of socializing and shopping like in Coronation Street. if you watch it... people know there is a blend of shopping and socializing which doesn't exist in the giant supermarket, so I'm guessing that is another gateway, so I'm thinking of gateways of [name of person omitted], City Wide Learning, and [name of person omitted], and of course religious gateways which I wouldn't know about... there are religious groups which meet at Broomspring Centre [Broomhall Centre] and in Sunny Bank Centre or seemingly religious groups." [a middle class resident from section C] [R.I. 01].

The author tried very hard to approach some of these gateways, but had no success. Hence it could not be assessed to what extent these gateways satisfy people's information, advice, or help needs. More research is needed in that regard.

However as in the case of other disciplines, e.g. medicine, the provision of medical services through scientifically mediated GPs, hospitals and so on is not the same as that of shaman witch doctors (with due respect to shamans). Likewise, scientifically mediated information, advice and help provision through Documental Information Institutions (DIIs), e.g. libraries, CABs, are not the same as those provided by intercultural gateways which cannot be made accountable for the services they provide. Basically no one knows about their facilities, conditions, quality, extent, etc.

They might be able to serve effectively people of their own ethnic background, nationality, and so on. But that is only a supposition which is not backed by evidence. The facts instead are that these intercultural gateways providers are more prone to provide inadequate services, because they are based on a myriad of non publicly accountable ways: tribalism, kinship, religious brotherhoods, privatisation, pay-per-service, etc. Such non publicly accountable or 'underground' information providers have been found as negative activities which undermine citizenship rights (Marquand, 2004).

5.2.6 Issues, information needs, and provision related to communication

The sections below present, analyse, and discuss the issues, information needs, and provision about communication.

5.2.6.1 COMMUNICATION ISSUES

During many visits paid by the researcher to all four sections of Broomhall for more than 3 years, it was found by observation that the busiest telephone boxes were those located in the middle of section A, the Hanover Flats. And all the times there were queues of people waiting to call. They were used especially by teenagers making long calls and young adults short calls. All the other telephone boxes in sections B or C were rarely used.

Although there was a short distance from the telephone box inside Hanover Flats to the one located at the end of Hanover Street at the junction of Hanover Way where the Hanover Playground ends northbound, people preferred to wait patiently to call in the one located within section A. Whereas in section D, the Park, no telephone box could be found for the public to use, there were some inside the Sheffield Hallam University halls mainly for people related to the university.

However, the most critical issue was the language barrier for individuals whose mother tongues were other than English as some respondents noted:

"Many people don't speak English, there is a high population of Somali people in this estate and they don't speak English." [a working class resident from section A] [F.G.03.B].

"communication is a big issue here because many kids' parents don't speak English and we cannot afford having translators for all, so we basically send information in English, so we end up having a lot of parents' meeting because of language issues. Communication is a big issue here definitely. So we need bilingual support employed by the school. We pay them but with the help of the city council [Sheffield City Council] we have grants from the ethnic minorities' grants. Because we have 89% percent of children coming from ethnic minorities so we need strong support from the council [Sheffield City Council] to attain it." [an information provider from section B of Broomhall] [I.P.07].

"we value the original languages spoken at home, we value and encourage parents on that, you can see at the entrance of the school [Broomspring Primary School] we have greetings written in many languages. But we also value our children learning English and that's why we teach them only in English so they can be able to integrate in the British society and be able get a job and so on, besides that's also what their parents want. Parents are very mucho so into education and that's the easy part of the job because parents back you up and support you which you don't get much in all schools, but in this school it's very much so." [an information provider from section B of Broomhall] [I.P.07].

"We also teach English for parents, we manage to contract the teachers and we teach them here for free. At the moment we teach them once a week." [an information provider from section B of Broomhall] [I.P.07]

"The main thing is about, what could happen to the whole community, when they focus, when they would come together, to have a magnet to have shared, common interest, be this information, communication. Probably we have a communication problem." [a middle class resident from section C] [R.I. 08].

Some respondents mentioned that the English language communication barrier presented a big problem for the integration of the non English speakers to British culture:

"You know the big problem with the British integration is that the British way where all the people coming here is that everyone should be integrated in the way British way is. But in UK there are big problems where they are losing respect to elderly, the British children robe the elderly and that is a bad thing and people from our communities should not be integrated in this culture. And also the war of the UK with our taxes, so we don't want to be integrated in this culture. And see, the British media don't shows the truth and expose our minorities as bad, but in reality they are not bad. And also they portray the migrants and asylum seekers as if they come here to take all the wealth from UK, but the media lies, because no one will leave their countries just for the fun, that is a huge mistake by the media." [an upper working class resident from section B] [F.G.02.C].

5.2.6.2   INFORMATION NEEDS RELATED TO COMMUNICATION ISSUES

The next section presents, analyses, and discusses the information needs that emerged from the communication issues. To summarise the evidence presented above and the author's interpretation, these include the following.

- Working class residents need information to know, for instance, how their relatives could learn English
- Middle and capitalist classes need information to know, for instance, how to make business out of the communication needs of the working classes.

The next section presents, analyses, and discusses the ways in which information providers tried to meet the information needs that emerged from communication issues.

5.2.6.3 INFORMATION PROVISION RELATED TO COMMUNICATION ISSUES

The major communication issue is that many people do not speak English in Broomhall. That becomes a barrier to them becoming citizens. Hence, they become excluded from the major benefits of being integrated in British society.

The *Broomhall News* is perhaps the most important medium of communication amongst the Broomhall residents. However, it is a newspaper written only in English. It is a voluntary community newspaper distributed for all residents of sections A, B, and C (but not D) in Broomhall that started in 2002. On 29 May 2002 it received its first grant of £ 2400 from Awards for All England (Awards for All England, 2002); in 2003 received a grant from the South Yorkshire Community Foundation (2004).

> *"Broomhall News, everybody is waiting to come, because Broomhall News is very good at telling people what's going on in Broomhall..." [a middle class resident from section C] [R.I. 04].*

> *"The Broomhall News acts as a forum if you like for the community where they can voice their opinions. We always encourage members of the community to come forward and we also certainly provide information that is useful to everyone basically, we have lists of service which will advertise or signpost for instance health issues and so on. It's basically, provides an opportunity for the community to get its voice heard and it connects people together." [an information provider from section A of Broomhall] [I.P.02].*

5.2.7 Features, information needs, and provision related to transport

The sections below present, analyse, and discuss the features, information needs, and provision about transport.

5.2.7.1 TRANSPORT FEATURES

Broomhall is flanked by many public transport services: the tram on Glossop Road and West Street just off the limits of sections B and C; buses on Glossop Road and West street off the limits of sections B and C; buses on Ecclesall Road off the boundaries of sections A, C and D; an inner neighbourhood bus, the First M29 (First, 2003), which runs in some streets within sections C and D where most of the senior residents live; and there is the Sheffield City Council community transport provided to people with mobility disabilities upon request.

But there is not a general consensus to consider transport as a positive feature for all the residents of Broomhall. A working class respondent argues that transport, in particular the M29 is not a good service:

> *"Transport? I can only say there is only one bus M29, it's not really a good service, established service, there's no bus stops, it stops anywhere you want it to stop, and it doesn't follow the signals." [a working class respondent from section C] [F.G.01.A].*

But another working class respondent argues the contrary and considers that the only problem with transport is parking:

> *"And yes, we got good transport, we got buses, tram, we are 10 minutes away from
> the city centre, so not so many problems with transport, but we have lots of problems
> of parking, always and forever." [a working class resident from section B]
> [F.G.02.A].*

Furthermore, Sheffield and particularly Broomhall is becoming increasingly gentrified, hence
transport needs are likely to become critical and severe for older people from working class
backgrounds. Having access or not to the M29 internal line within some Broomhall streets is a
factor which makes the difference between provision or deprivation of transport services, especially
around the places where most elderly live.

There is a consensus that many users and non users of the M29 bus service value very much the
service (Broomhall News, 2004b). However, the impressions of residents of transport may depend
mainly on their age, that is on the ability of individuals to be able to walk by themselves —a
condition which is interrelated with individuals' social class (e.g. being old but owing a car),
physical, and health conditions (e.g. having disabilities preventing walking or driving a car),
amongst others.

For instance, from the literature a mobility-disabled resident complained that the M29 service has
been reduced. He gave up his car and does not have a driveway to park one, thus affecting his
mobility conditions and basically his life:

> "No car, no go ... I am a disabled pensioner who 16 months ago moved into a bungalow in
> Broomhall. Having no driveway and eligible to a free bus-pass I gave up my car. Now the bus
> service around this estate has been cut to just twice a day with no Saturday or Sunday. This is
> annoying, considering the Government wants us to give up our cars in favour of public transport
> (along with the reduction of CO_2)" (Star (Sheffield), 2007c).

Despite these not so positive aspects of transport, the public provision of this service
prevails as an overall positive feature of Broomhall.

Nevertheless, the author has found that in 1905 Sheffield was better provided than today
with 281 miles of tramways (Olive, 2002). Electrical tram lines were more ecological, but
since the 1940s Nazi blitz only four lines are running. Hence with more combustion engine
powered buses there is more contamination. However, some residents might not be aware
of historic facts like this and are opposed to any tram extension proposal (SYPTA, 2004):

> *"... no, we will never allow the plans for the tram extension in Broomhill [11]..." [an information
> provider from Broomhill] [I.P.03].*

The next section presents, analyses, and discusses the information needs that emerged relating to
transport.

5.2.7.2 INFORMATION NEEDS RELATED TO TRANSPORT

What are the community information needs related to transport? To summarise the evidence

---

[11] Broomhill is a middle upper class neighbourhood adjacent to Broomhall to the north through
Glossop Road, where the Broomhill tram line was planned in 2004 (SYPTA, 2004). Within
Broomhill boundaries is located the Hallamshire Hospital, in Glossop Road, opposite to Broomhall,
and other two hospitals are located within Broomhill behind Hallamshire. These hospitals and the
hub of health services nearby attract many people: patients, health professionals, health providers,
etc., hence, by observation could be made evident that there are many people coming and going in
this area and that there is a serious parking problem within the area and surrounding areas (like
Broomhall). Hence, in this project could not be found the reasons why the plans for a Broomhill
tram extension did not come to fruition, but a tram extension in that area would alleviate much the
traffic problems. However, those are issues related to Broomhill, not Broomhall.

presented above and the author's interpretation, these include the following.

- Working class residents need information about the M29, or other bus or tram routes timetables.
- Middle class residents need information on petrol prices; car prices, and so on.
- Capitalist classes need information on how buy and sell cars, buses, petrol stations, and so on.

The next section presents, analyses, and discusses the ways in which information providers tried to meet the information needs that emerged relating to transport.

5.2.7.3 INFORMATION PROVISION RELATED TO TRANSPORT

The major information provider on transport is the statutory sector with two main offices in the city centre, Sheffield Interchange and a small branch in Arundel Street.

The next section explains the features, information needs, and provision related to education.

5.2.8 Features, information needs, and provision related to education

The sections below present, analyse, and discuss the features, information needs, and provision relating to education.

5.2.8.1 EDUCATIONAL FEATURES

This section analyses the major educational features found.

5.2.8.1.1 The Springfield Primary School

One of the best educational institutions in Broomhall as perceived by some members of the community through the data generated in this project is Springfield Primary School. This is how a respondent from this school praises its importance:

> "I think Springfield [Primary School] is the best facility without sounding with lack of modesty. But we are the most accessible facility for the community and because they trust us they come to us with lots of issues, as bills, phone bills, and community issues, whereas in other communities they've got advice bureaus, the local church, whereas here, families tend to come here to get support. And this is quite challenging for a school because our main goal is children education, but we do a lot of family support. Our core purpose is teaching, we're here to make sure our children learn, but we end up having to support families in a lot of different ways, because if we don't do it nobody will do it". [an information provider from section B of Broomhall] [I.P.07].

The impression from this respondent [I.P. 07] may appear as inclined only towards the positive side. Indeed, this impression has also been shared by the inspectors of the Sheffield Local Education Authority:

> "Inspectors have rated a Sheffield primary school as 'good' - despite it coming in the bottom five per cent in recent national league tables. Springfield Primary in Broomhall was found to provide well for its pupils, who come from a wide range of minority ethnic groups and speak 15 different languages. It takes in children of refugees and asylum seekers, as well as children of students who have travelled to Sheffield from overseas. Many often speak little English, with over 85 per cent of the children speaking it as a second language. Many more pupils than normal at Springfield have learning difficulties, while the school also has a high turnover of youngsters. But inspectors found a very high quality of pastoral care and support which meant the children's diverse personal needs were successfully met, while there were good partnerships with parents and external agencies. Pupils felt happy, safe and secure which helped them to achieve well, and teachers were very successful in helping the children learn to speak English. The youngest children made good progress, and this trend was continued throughout the school" (Star (Sheffield), 2005c).

The aforementioned data suggests that the Springfield Primary School is one of the most positive features in the neighbourhood, and this is also confirmed by observation and by the opinions of other respondents.

5.2.8.1.2   The City Wide Learning centre

Another relevant educational institution was the City Wide Learning centre, the motto of which was "The Key to your Enlightenment." This was an educational centre inaugurated at 1.00 pm Monday afternoon on the 19th April 2004 (Broomhall News, 2004a: 3). This centre was founded and managed by a Somali group. It was "open to all, but mainly to [the] Black Ethnic Minority" (Broomhall News, 2004a: 3).

The centre was opened on some abandoned premises where there used to be betting shops according to one respondent. This substitution of betting shops for an educational centre seemed to be a positive move for the benefit of all people. But not everyone seemed to be happy with this move. There seemed to be discontent for the lack of betting shops within Broomhall amongst some residents, and an anonymous resident even call this lack of betting shops a "disgrace" through the *Broomhall News* community newspaper:

> "... most people would agree that not having a betting shop in Broomhall is a local disgrace. We've all heard pensioners complain about having to go all the way to West Street to put a bet on. There is a plucky 78 year old, crippled with arthritis, who has to set off from his Exeter Drive flat at 6 in the morning to get to the bookies with his Lotto and Lucky 7 bets" (MOD 'The Voice in the Street', 2002: 3).

This anonymous resident complaining of the lack of betting shops within Broomhall, that is, closer to the Exeter Drive flats of section A, did not specifically complain of the taking over of the betting premises by the City Wide Learning centre, because this centre was open on April 2004, and his letter was published on July 2002. But his or her opinion is presented here as a contrasting view in order to illustrate the contradictory character of the different people assessed in this project.

In this project it was not possible to trace the reasons why the betting shops were closed on the premises then taken over by the City Wide Learning centre. And it was not possible to verify if the three premises from 247 to 249 were all betting shops. For instance, in an informal chat someone told the researcher that there used to be a laundry shop in one of the three premises, but this could not be verified either.

The City Wide Learning centre was found as a positive institution, specially for larger parts of the Black and Minority Ethnic residents, and as a positive information provider from most of the residents, despite the fact that the customers of gambling shops did not appreciate it in that way.

However, it was found that the police closed the centre on the basis of alleged frauds relating to the UK's Home Office citizenship tests according to information provided by whistleblowers (Star (Sheffield), 2007b). Without warning the police seized early in February 2007 all the computers from the school and questioned four top management members of the centre at one of the police headquarters; but they were released on bail and no one was later charged. The police, a month later, returned the computers, and the school reopened without major complications.

The author, in early April 2007 (and in late stages of thesis writing), approached one of the school's staff and asked him, informally, about the closure of the centre by the police and all about the situation. That person told the researcher that it was a mistake by the police and that everything was okay back then. He also told him that the LearnDirect educational institution cancelled for good the contract with the school due to the unstable legal situation of the centre after the police closure, but he also told him that the Sheffield College branch continued the contract, and hence the centre continued offering free English courses and other course for BMEs (Black Minority Ethnic) and the general public.

In May 2007 the school remained open, but in a room at 248 Broomhall Street a new enterprise opened — a kind of reading room for BME (Black Minority Ethnic) children; particularly Somali. The author approached this teacher, but he could not give the author any details about that reading room except that he mentioned that it was independent from the City Wide Learning centre. The researcher could not read what the children read because the books were written in Somali, Arabic, Urdu, or Farsi types of languages.

By June 2007 the children's reading room closed, and a Somali telephone call and money transfer shop opened in the same room; the Dahabshill Diamond Call Centre and Money Transfer. But in the third week of August 2007 the City Wide Learning centre closed its doors to the public for good, according to the author's observation and by the information provided by a Somali manager of the Dahabshill telephone call centre shop and other Somali neighbours from around that shop.

5.2.8.1.3   The Broomhall Nursery

Another outstanding educational institution within Broomhall territories is the Broomhall Nursery. This nursery is located on Broomhall Road in section D but serves all four sections of Broomhall and city-wide residents' children.

5.2.8.1.4   The Broomhall Centre

> The Broomhall Centre, according to the documents collected, is a kind of drop-in centre for all the residents of the community. It offers many free activities and classes to the community like football classes (Broomhall Centre, 2003a); Brazilian Samba classes by the Sheffield Samba Band (Broomhall Centre, 2003b). It rents the premises for parties and all kinds of social gatherings, amongst many others.

5.2.8.2   INFORMATION NEEDS RELATED TO EDUCATIONAL FEATURES

This section presents, analyses, and discusses the information needs that emerged from the educational features. To summarise the evidence presented above and the author's interpretation, these include the following:

- Working class residents need educational information about how to enrol their children in statutory LEA schools.
- Middle class residents need educational information about how to register their children in schools, colleges, universities.
- Capitalist class residents need educational information to find out about the expansionist plans of universities and see how they could be contracted to build more academic halls, and so on.

The next section presents, analyses, and discusses the ways in which information providers tried to meet the information needs that emerged from the education features.

5.2.8.3   INFORMATION PROVISION RELATED TO EDUCATIONAL FEATURES

Depending on the level of education each school, college, university is responsible for its own provision. Nevertheless, the Local Education Authority (LEA) is the main information provider located in the Moor, city centre and some other branches elsewhere.

And from the LEA the most important information provider was the Broomhall Nursery. Besides good nursery services, the Broomhall Nursery also offered a whole range of impressive information, advice, help, and similar services provided for children under 5 years old and their parents. These are some of the perceptions of parents:

> "the government has a very good library services for children at the age of 4 called Sharrow Sure Start based in Broomhall Nursery in Broomhall Street, they offer books and reading activities for children, for free." [a working class resident from section A] [R.I. 09].

*"they are having doing very nice activities for parents and children from birth to four in
Broomhall Nursery from Sharrow Sure Start, now they are bringing little by little something
good for the community... Sharrow Sure Start is building a new building in Sharrow Road...
Oh gosh yes, it's a fantastic service [Sharrow Sure Start] they've brought for the community."
[a working class resident from section A] [R.I. 09].*

This was verified by the press:

"The centres [included the Broomhall Nursery] will provide a range of services, including
education and childcare for under fives, support for families and single parents, healthcare and
links with schools, information services and job centres" (Star (Sheffield), 2006c).

It was also verified by observation. One of the teachers from the Broomhall Nursery was seen
several times in the Hanover Flats (section A) giving support to mothers of the children attending
the Broomhall Nursery.

Nevertheless, despite all of its positive features, the Broomhall Nursery did not escape from having
apparently faced some controversial issues. For instance, in 2004, according to the press, its
management sacked some teachers:

"The most common reason for the cuts are falling pupil numbers. The Sheffield pupil population
is falling year by year, a situation which has already led to the closure or merger of some
primaries" (Star (Sheffield), 2004g).

Presumably for the same reason the Broomhall Nursery closed its branch located in Mushroom
Lane behind the Department of Psychology of the University of Sheffield and the Weston Park
Museum by the end of 2004. But parents complained that apparently the nursery management did
not consult about closure with the Local Education Authority since it was given extraordinary and
independent powers to exercise policies and budget without consulting the LEA:

"Parents believe the closure plans have been drawn up by Broomhall [Nursery] without the
knowledge of the local education authority. Since April [2004], Broomhall nursery has been
given new powers to independently run its own financial affairs. As long as places are not
removed altogether, governors and staff will feel they have the authority to close the annexe"
(Star (Sheffield), 2004e).

Nevertheless, the Broomhall Nursery emerged as a very positive institution in Broomhall, and,
although they closed the Mushroom Lane branch, that does not affect the positive evaluation being
made through respondents and observation.

However, the closure of that branch did show by inference, that the areas within and around
Broomhall, due to the expansion of Sheffield and Hallam universities and the fast paced urban
development of high rise and up market multiple occupation housing for single students and
couples without children, are losing their family character, and thus services such as the Mushroom
Lane branch of the Broomhall Nursery are being closed due to the lack of children.

5.3 Summary

This chapter is the core of the thesis. It presented the main analysis, and discussions of the major
findings.

The analysis and discussions flowed through the three major conceptual and methodological parts
of the thesis:

a)   The issues and features of the Broomhall neighbourhood that emerged from the
residents' and information providers' perceptions, from observation, and from the literature.
b)   The information needs that emerged from these issues and features.
c)   The information provision that tried to meet these information needs.

As for part a), this thesis from the onset did not plan to create a *community profile of Broomhall*. However, the issues and features of this neighbourhood can be considered for the LIS community as a community profile. This thesis did not consider creating an actual community profile of Broomhall, because these instruments are part of the planning processes of established libraries or other Documental Information Institutions (DIIs). For this thesis, the *community profiling* tool was simply used for academic purposes, not to plan or measure findings against any aims or objectives of any particular library, institution, or organisation.

As for part b), the residents of Broomhall seldom articulated their needs of information as *information needs*. The residents perceived daily life problems, issues, concerns, fears, and the like. The residents needed information, but they did not mean the concept of *information as recorded in documents*. It was the major contribution of this thesis to have served as a bridge between the issues and features perceived by residents according to the way they enjoy, or suffer under their material living conditions, and the information recorded in documents that, hopefully, would make those living conditions more enjoyable, and help them to cope better with suffering. For this, the interpretivist methodology played a key role for the researcher to help him translate residents' daily life problems, issues, concerns, fears, and the like into *information needs*.

As for part c), the voluntary sector played the main role in satisfying residents' information needs on a permanent basis acting as a Documental Information Institution, particularly the Sharrow Citizens Advice Bureau, both through their main office located in the Sharrow neighbourhood, and through the extension services they offer at the Hanover Medical Centre in Broomhall (section C). The statutory sector also played a major role in satisfying the residents' information needs, but this role was secondary when compared with the Sharrow Citizens Advice Bureau. From the local authority, the Sheffield City Council emerged as the main information provider from the statutory sector: for example the First Point service at Howden House for housing information needs (the main issue of Broomhall in this thesis); and the Library, Archives, and Information Services by linking diverse needs to other different agencies (particularly the Mobile Library that reaches Broomhall directly). From Central Government the main information provider was the Sharrow Sure Start program which provided library and information services, help, advice and other services to parents and their children up to five years old. This provision was conducted in coordination with the Sheffield City Council's Local Education Authority (in this case provided through the Broomhall Nursery located in section D), and the Library, Archives, and Information Services (through the Highfield Library located in the Sharrow neighbourhood). However, despite the excellence of this service, it was available only to parents who have children up to five years, and excluded the rest of the citizens. As for the documents delivered through letterboxes in Broomhall, those from Sheffield City Council were the most relevant to meet residents' information needs, although they were the most scarce compared to commercial flyers. Finally, the Broomhall Community Centre served as the main grey literature provider. However, only two documents were relevant to the most critical information needs throughout the thesis: those relating to issues of territoriality or uses of the land.

In general terms, the information needs of the residents of the Broomhall have not been well researched by previous researchers. Those who have conducted research into Broomhall have not considered information needs specifically, and, in general, their research projects have more been motivated by political, commercial, or ideological concerns. Hence, they have not addressed information needs motivated by the highest ethical standards of pursuing knowledge for the sake of knowledge, or to empower the people to honestly improve their living conditions, as has been the motivation of this project. Therefore, the lack of a critical and analytical research study to survey at deeper levels the problems and issues people face in their daily life, such as this project was intended to be, has prevented residents from coping with their most pressing information needs. At the same time, it has prevented information providers from really meeting their most relevant needs.

Having analysed and discussed the major findings of this project, the next chapter (Chapter 6) discusses the further research steps the researcher will take in order to make these finding available to the widest public, and the insights that emerged from this thesis and consequent suggestions for the LIS and social sciences communities.

CHAPTER 6. CONCLUSIONS AND RECOMMENDATIONS

"Nothing before had ever made me thoroughly realise, though I had read various scientific books, that science consists in grouping facts so that general laws or conclusions may be drawn from them." — Charles Darwin, Autobiography (cited in Sagan and Druyan, 1992: 41)

6.1 Introduction

This chapter summarizes the major contributions to knowledge that have emerged in this thesis, and the main conclusions and recommendations for: a) the Broomhall residents; b) LIS practitioners, and c) policy makers.

6.2 Conclusions

The major contributions to knowledge of this thesis are these.

1)   The residents of Broomhall seldom articulated their needs of information as *information needs*. The residents perceived daily life problems, issues, concerns, fears, and the like. From this study the community information needs emerged interrelated with these six community issues that respondents perceived: a) Issues of territoriality or uses of the land (e.g. housing; expansion of Sheffield and Hallam universities becoming university student villages); b) issues of poverty, social and economic inequalities (e.g. unemployment, debt, crime); c) health issues (e.g. drug addiction, lack of: green public open space, playgrounds, and sports and leisure facilities); d) political issues; e) cultural issues (e.g. multicultural, ethnic, religious, and national issues); and f) communication issues, and from these two community features: a) transport features; and b) educational features. The residents needed information related to these community issues and feature, but they did not mean the concept of *information or information recorded in documents* as employed in this study. Hence, it was one of the major contributions of this study to have served as a bridge between the issues and features perceived by residents according to the way they enjoy, or suffer under their material living conditions, and the information recorded in documents that, hopefully, would make those living conditions more enjoyable, and help them to cope better with suffering. For this, the interpretivist methodology played a key role for the researcher to help him translate residents' daily life problems, issues, concerns, fears, and the like into *information needs*.

2)   The community profiling tool has been found effective for LIS practitioners as long as they apply it with qualitative research methods, such as those employed here: analysis of documents, non-participant observation, and interviews (both individual and group-focused). The tool's effectiveness was related to the main research objectives which were to understand deeply the perceptions of people and their material living or working conditions. Furthermore, the community profiling tool using territoriality categories proved to be more effective when using observation instead of census based datasets (e.g. Creaser, 1999; Bath, et. al, 2005), because it gives practitioners first-hand primary empirical data which can always be interrelated, and enhanced with actual pictures taken in the field as in this project (Muela-Meza, 2003-2007). However, census information, and all types of documents should be reviewed and triangulated with data from observations and interviews.

3)   A deeper understanding of the *community* concept. It has emerged from the evidence presented in this project that *community* is a contradictory concept that historically has sometimes tended more to be employed as a kind of political ideology (e.g. Putnam, 1999; Green, 2001; 2000), than to be based on empirical evidence. The main contradiction has been found between its two main intrinsic forces: the socializing forces of communality as belonging

(Delanty, 2003), versus the individualizing forces of private territoriality. These forces are in contradiction and therefore cannot be combined with any other terms that resemble political ideologies such as *community cohesion* (e.g. Putnam, 1999; Green, 2001; 2000; Cromar, 2003).

4)   The project has clarified the distinction between neighbourhood and community necessary when any researcher or practitioner applied the community profiling tool to LIS or any other disciplines. As has been analysed in the previous chapters, a neighbourhood (or for that matter any other territorial locality) is a territorial entity where different human communities co-exist playing different roles determined to a considerable extent by their social class status. For any information provider the consequences of this diversity are clearly contradictory: no single documental information institution (DII) (e.g. libraries) could ever satisfy all the community information needs of their users, "that is generally considered utopian" (Louie, 1976: 170), precisely because they are contradictory (Muela-Meza, 2007) and mutually excluding (Roddy, 2005). Hence, as far as our capitalist society is divided into social classes, and dominance hierarchies (Hauser, 2006; Sagan and Druyan, 1992), where the upper classes take more advantages than the lower, then the allocation of social needs and their satisfaction will always be likewise conditioned by those social class differences. When those classes conflict, the allocation and satisfaction of those needs will therefore conflict (Heller, 1996).

5)   The evidence presented in this thesis has shown that most people confuse the meaning of community with that of neighbourhood. Some of them, who have commercial or ideological-political vested interests in the neighbourhoods, do not confuse it, but they deliberately manipulate both concepts in order to obtain some social class gain, mainly financial, and sometimes relating to power, or dominance hierarchy (e.g. capitalist and bourgeois class over middle class, and these over working class).

6)   The *social class struggles* concept emerged as being appropriate at the time to analyse the social class contradictions. It was evident how some commentators (such as Cromar, 2003, or Bryson, Usherwood, and Proctor, 2003, or Pateman, 2006) by using politically ideological terminology such as "social capital" aligned their discourse with the dominant hegemonic discourse of the capitalist class. This *social class struggles* concept was also more appropriate in terms of describing the contradictory relationships of power and domination through deprivation of information or knowledge, or the deprivation of property, and in terms of describing whether individuals do physical labour for a living (Edgell, 1993; Demirovic, 2004). It was also more appropriate than those concepts employed in non social-class or socio-economic-mediated models, such as *sense making* (e.g. as interpreted by Agada, 1999: 75). "Hence, what needs to be explained is not the presumed demise of class, but the tenacity of class-based patterns of inequality and politics, and much else besides. In the meantime, class rules and classlessness remains a dream rather than a reality" (Edgell, 1993: 122).

Next sections explain the recommendations that emerged from this thesis.

6.3 Recommendations

These recommendations are divided as follows: a) recommendations for the Broomhall residents of sections A, B, and C; b) recommendations for social sciences and LIS practitioners; and c) recommendations for policy makers.

6.3.1 Recommendations for the Broomhall residents (of sections A, B, and C)

1)As analysed in this thesis, the Broomhall neighbourhood is not a homogeneous territory. The four sections (A, B, C, and D) into which Broomhall emerged geographically divided are all distinctively and contrastingly different. Residents from sections A, B, and C considered themselves as belonging to the Broomhall neighbourhood, whereas residents from section D (the most affluent section of all) considered themselves not belonging to Broomhall, but to the Broomhall Park neighbourhood. Hence, it could be recommended that, since the residents of Broomhall and the Park have already delimited the geographical boundaries of their neighbourhoods, the residents of Broomhall (sections A, B, and C) could legally change the name of their neighbourhood. Thus, since the Manor 16th century Broom Hall mansion lies in the heart of Broomhall Park (section D), and residents from the Park care mostly for their Park neighbourhood, then residents from sections A, B, and C have no contemporary links with the Broom Hall, except those from history. Furthermore, residents from section C changed the name of Havelock Square to Holberry Gardens (when the former used to have bad reputation due to prostitution). Thus, if they honoured that street with the name of the socialist chartist Holberry (*Broomhall News,* 2005), then they might as well rename the three sections A, B, and C as Holberry Gardens, or with other names. However, there might remain all the aforementioned differences between these three sections as analysed in the study, but at least they would have a better chance to join around a common name that distinguishes them and unites them more such as *Holberry Gardens,* instead of *Broomhall.*

2)   Whether or not, the residents of the sections A, B, and C of Broomhall rename themselves as *Holberry Gardens* (or any other name they choose), they should search for all the mechanisms that allow them to establish solid and strategic alliances amongst other residents from different cultures in order to set themselves a common strategic aim for the decades to come. This aim could be to build a three-section (A-B-C) front for a true *Renaissance,* a real revival of their three-section neighbourhood, but by saving their homes, their brown field, and their playgrounds, and, if possible, by converting the current upper-market HMOs (Housing in Multiple Occupancy) into green field, so scarce in those three areas. All A-B-C sections residents, regardless of their class status, could unite on a common front (under a common name as completely separated from the Broomhall idea or the Broomhall Park), to truly take their neighbourhood into their hands (without the intervention of politicians from Broomhall Park, or council or councillors, or MPs, or MEPs). They could learn as well the stories of other residents from Liverpool, or London, who succeeded under more difficult circumstances than those of Broomhall (Leeming, 2007a; 2007b; Radnedge, 2006; Cottage and Fredericks, 2006). Once again, the middle class home-owning residents could take the lead. They should be more concerned to join forces with working class residents, because as analysed in this study, the working class residents are more likely to be relocated into other council social housing somewhere around in Sheffield. That is, because they are poor working class council tenants, they might not mind being relocated, or they might have no other choice. However, even if they might be relocated they might mind to some extent, because they might lose the convenience of living 5 to 10 minutes walk away from the city centre. However, in the case of middle class home-owning residents, they are now –according to the evidence presented in this study– at a huge risk of losing their homes. They might lose all the good things they gained when they became united in the 1970s and 1980s, and stopped the Sheffield City Council's compulsory purchasing and home demolishing (Hall, 1981; Crook, et. al., 1976; Crook, 1983; Gibson, and Dorfman, 1981), and the Sheffield Hallam University's expansionist plans (Warman, 1969).

3)   Broomhall residents from sections A, B, and C could bring to account under the rule of law all the politicians and corporate magnates from the Broomhall Park, or from the Sheffield City Council, or all partisan councillors, or MPs, or MEPs before regional, national, or even international justice tribunals, e.g. EU Tribunal of Justice at The Hague, for all their responsibilities in using the extreme poverty, living condition, and misery of the most deprived sections of Broomhall, A, B, and C, but particularly from A, the Hanover Estates as a medium for them to justify their ideological-political agendas of 'social inclusion' or 'social cohesion' or 'community cohesion' where they get funding because they include these deprived ABC sections in their plans but as analysed above they do not bring many benefits for those poor people.

4)   The residents from sections A, B, and C (either the future *Holberry Gardens* neighbourhood or other name) could seek to create the legal mechanisms to audit and make accountable all politicians and elected members in relation to several issues affecting information provision. Politicians and elected members could be brought to justice when they ostensibly have conflicts of interests, e.g. being neighbourhood-elected members, and at the same time owners of building corporations. Residents from sections A, B, and C, could create an alliance with the most trusted information providers found in this study (e.g. Sheffield City Council's Library, Archives and Information department, and the Sharrow Citizens Advice Bureau), and together bring about this change.

5)   The residents (mainly working class, and middle class who really look after the interests of working class) from sections A, B, and C should seek the mechanisms to repeal the plans led by the capitalist and bourgeois class residents and community organisations that want to demolish people's homes and build upper-market HMOs (Housing in Multiple Occupation), or any other kind of upper market businesses. Projects such as Cromar (2003); LDA Design (2005), and already approved by the Sheffield City Council (2006a) cabinet in October 2006, which consisted in 'regenerating the *heart* of Broomhall,' have been found biased in almost all aspects. For instance, the major bias is that those plans are conducted more on political and ideological grounds, and for profit, than as scientific, or professional research, because as analysed in this project, the 'real heart of Broomhall' is the Broom Hall estate which lies almost at the centre of section D of the Park (see maps on Figures 4.1. and 4.2 in Chapter 4). That is, some members of the capitalist and bourgeois class have convinced the European Commission Objective 1 funding scheme, which at least in its objectives is dedicated to fund projects to help "areas lagging behind in their development." But in reality the plan has many negative underlying issues which poor working class, (the illiterate, the destitute, the asylum seekers, the refugees who do not speak English), and even middle class literate people who are not interested on any social or general issues of the community, do not understand, or do not want to understand and get involved in. Some might be so affected by drugs, debt, cognitive failures, that they might never understand. Important issues derived from the plan include the following: a) the plan will destroy the small Hanover Playground (when there are not enough playing facilities); b) it will bring many more upper market capitalist/bourgeois HMOs (Housing in Multiple Occupation) to section C and A (when section A is the most overcrowded and smallest piece of land compared with section D, the Park); c) it will consequently bring some upper market Waitrose style shops and the small and culturally diverse corner shops might disappear, d) they say (LDA Design, 2005: 7) that the YMCA which now owns St. Silas Church will accommodate in this church the Hanover Medical Centre and youth centres, sport pitches and so on. However, this is essentially the same thing that the YMCA did in 1967 –only to sell it to Sheffield Hallam University in 2001 (Star (Sheffield), 2002b). In addition, St. Silas Church is only 4% of the size of their ex property in Broomhall Road ('at the real heart of Broomhall'). Thus if the YMCA has deprived poor Broomhall residents of 10, 956 m2 of free access to health and sports facilities it is not a convincing argument that providing only 450 m2 of pay-per-access upper market facilities in their St. Silas Church would equate to the lost services. Furthermore, if the YMCA has deprived poor people of access to 96% of health facilities in the past (even if they now compensate 'their errors' with a reduced 4% of facilities), nothing can guarantee residents that they would not sell St.Silas Church to the best bidder. Residents, just need to take a look at all the upper market developments around Broomhall (*Exposed*, 2007: 22-23), and the upper market 'regeneration' of the Devonshire Green shown in hundreds of pictures taken by the author during this study (Muela-Meza, 2003-2007).

6)   Residents from the Park might also think about joining forces with residents from the prospective *Holberry Gardens* neighbourhood (sections A, B, and C) with a view to repealing the *social capital* 'experiments' against the welfare of the poor working classes of Broomhall (e.g. Cromar, 2003). There is plenty of evidence in this project to support the arguments of why they might do so. Perhaps the residents from section D, Broomhall Park, think that by ghettoising themselves in the Park, by keeping the poor working classes out of their section, and by supporting capitalist initiatives against the poor, they would get rid of the poor. However, many years ago, Wilkinson's (Hey, 1998; Odom, 1926; Leader, 1905; Senior, 1872) experiment tried to do the same and many riots, and revolts emerged. It is suggested that Broomhall history be reviewed and learn from it. Perhaps they are greatly absorbed and engrossed in their own temporary powerful status being a capitalist or middle class member might give them. However, as seen above with the Blitz, dramatic historical events cannot be stopped when they happen. In this case the rapid privatisation (what capitalist and bourgeois class calls it 'social capital') is a social disaster in the making which might affect not only the interests of poor working classes, but also those of upper classes. For instance, one of the major issues for capitalist or middle classes is the effects of extreme privatisation by capitalist class in terms of extreme negative effects on the poor. Arguably if the police would do their job properly in Broomhall they might, for example, find out why mostly Broomhall Park residents are the object of violent attacks (e.g. *Star (Sheffield)*, 2006a). The more that people from the Park distance themselves from the poor, and the more they support capitalist-driven policies, consequently the more poor people

might feel resentful towards them. There is no police evidence here; however, it would not be surprising if those crimes were found to be committed by poor people from section A. However, the solution is not to implement an Orwellian Big Brother or a police state, but to reach a genuine and better understanding amongst social classes to achieve win-win solutions. If the rich support the poor in all respects, it is more likely that better understanding and relationships could be brought about. Nevertheless, the evidence shown and analysed in this study only indicates that things may become more divisive and conflicting. From the evidence analysed here, it is possible that in the next few years most working and middle classes could be displaced from Broomhall and all sections A, B, and C could become not *Holberry Gardens,* but *Little Manhattan with not even a speck of brown field.* Both Hallam and Sheffield universities could also have made their 1969 dream come true by taking over all of the land of sections A, B, and C (see Warman, 1969 and map on Figure 4.12 in Chapter 4). However, when the residents of the Park cannot find any working class from sections A, or B, or C to support (honestly or through biased research) their capitalist policies, including even their Conservation Areas laws, will not be able to save their land from the universities' or developers' expansionism. After all, Sheffield Hallam University, after closing their Psalter Lane campus already own a third of the Park (see map on Figure 4.13 in Chapter 4). Moreover, the council is keeping them in check with their own much sought Conservation Area act (Sheffield City Council, 2007a; 2007b), because they cannot even put up a satellite dish in their own properties, because 'it affects the historic character of their own house.' Thus, it is foreseeable that when capitalist or middle class residents cannot truly conserve their own mansions they might have to sell them as happened in Hanover Square (McClarence and Rogerson, 1988). However, even if capitalist and middle classes cooperate with the poor, certainly social class struggles will not disappear (these could remain as long as society keeps itself organised through the division of classes and dominance hierarchy). However, at least perspectives aimed at cooperating strategically, truly and honestly in favour with the poor would be to the benefit of the three classes involved in the four sections of Broomhall analysed here.

6.3.2 Recommendations for social sciences and LIS practitioners

1)Social scientists, LIS practitioners, and Sheffield information providers (including Sheffield City Council's Library, Archives and Information department and the Sharrow Citizens Advice Bureau) should create legal mechanisms to audit and make accountable all politicians and elected members relating to several issues affecting information provision. Politicians and elected members should be brought to justice when they ostensibly have conflicts of interests. It is recommended that in this they consult most of the residents from sections A, B, and C as analysed in this project.

2)   LIS practitioners should try to implement locally what is known nationally as the legal deposit, and request all public organizations funded with public funds to deposit all of their internal documental information in the Sheffield libraries and archives. This is because there are many organizations that act like fiefdoms (e.g. Broomhall Forum; Broomhall Cosmopolitan Centre, Ltd.; Broomhall Park Residents Associations; YMCA). Hence, all information providers should be made accountable before the law in the Freedom of Information Act, because many NGOs act like information fiefdoms and strongholds that, rather than give access to information, tend to conceal and monopolize it. Not to mention that this issue is even worse with informal 'underground' gatekeepers that might act as information providers.

3)   This project promotes an institutional approach to the provision of information recorded in documents: it should be the responsibility of central and local government to provide all the different sources of information recorded in documents for the Broomhall residents, but in an institutionalized manner. Moreover, this information should be provided as a free and public service for the neighbourhood, because many organizations in the neighbourhood use information as a commodity of power, most of them not being accountable democratically to the people. Many people come and go from organizations, organizations come and go, but only institutions remain through time. In this regard, public libraries depend of public funding and they are steady, fixed, long standing institutions, which at least in principle are open free for all.

4)   The local government should take over the Broomhall Centre management and build a branch public library in its building, as it was suggested from different interviewees.

5)   From the data generated in this project, it emerged that Sheffield libraries were the least used information provider. Public libraries in Sheffield, or at least those near to Broomhall at a walking distance: the Central Library on Surrey Street in the city centre; further downhill at Highfield on London Road and up the hill at Broomhill at Tapton Road, do not have themselves a *community profile*, either city wide in the case of the Central Library, or locally in the case of the other two. They do have a mobile library that circulates city wide and it includes a route through Broomhall. However, as stated in a letter from the librarian of this service, they do not provide special services based on particular communities' needs. They only provide the same stock of books for all the users of Sheffield, regardless of their particular community needs.

6)   The evidence generated in this project suggests, in line with Rendón Rojas' (2005) theoretical concept of *Documental Information Institution (DII)*, that the more efficient information providers are those institutionalized (e.g. as in Rendón Rojas' (2005) *DII)*, financed by the tax payers, managed by professional *documental information professionals (e.g. librarians; advice providers)* separated and protected from any political upheavals (Marquand, 2004), and provided by the state and other statutory institutions as part of the social services for citizens through the public arena (Demirovic, 2004; Marquand, 2004), like health services, and any other social services. This recommendation is being fulfilled to some extent already, but it has emerged from the data that since the 1970s and 1980s there has been a very negative shift towards the privatization of all social services included those relating to documental information. Hence, the proponents of the deinstitutionalization of the documental information infrastructure also play an adverse role in impoverishing the public arena and the provision of vital social services by the state and statutory institutions. Some (Martin, 1989; Cronin, 1981; 1992a) do it in favour of capitalist neoliberal ventures, and some (Black and Muddiman,1997) do it 'apparently' against capitalist neoliberalism by envisioning some nostalgic return to past *community librarianship* aimed at 'bringing back' libraries to the community and by positing post-modern *'de-territorializing'* ideologies (rather than real natural and socio-historical facts or phenomena). However, either apparently in favour or against capitalist neoliberalism, both forces play in favour of the deinstitutionalisation of the documental information infrastructure, with disastrous consequences in terms of inadequate provision of information for the neighbourhood communities as has been evidenced in previous chapters of this study.

7)   LIS (as well as any other science) should proceed scientifically, instead of politically, or ideologically. That is, by allowing empirically generated data, evidence, facts, and findings to guide scientific and LIS practice, and put political, and ideological agendas at bay and away from LIS, and any other scientific realm. This is because, as some scientists put it, "politics is not a science" (Sagan, 1997: 433), that politicians do not know much about scientific matters (Feynman, 2001), and that science cannot be reduced to demagogical democratism and the whims of politicians (Penrose, 2004). Thus, politicians should not be allowed to interfere in LIS or any other scientific matters.

8)   What is at stake is the dismantling of the documental information infrastructure (Schiller, 1996; Marquand, 2004), and LIS practitioners should be very careful when they try to bring their political ideologies into LIS scientific practice. Throughout the boundaries of the Broomhall neighbourhood, only one leaflet about housing was collected in only one of the different facilities assessed (at the Broomhall Community Centre). This was at a time when housing and territorial issues emerged as having the most pressing and adverse effects on residents. This is evidence that community and voluntary sector have no idea of the value of documental information (Deacon and Golding, 1991) (with the exception of the Sharrow Citizens Advice Bureau), and that statutory sector libraries do not have a legal framework to systematically collect, organise, preserve, and disseminate the communities' documental information, the communities' documental heritage; the people's memory.

9)   Only those statutory sector documental information institutions like libraries, and archives have the capacity to preserve people's documental memory (although they might also

have it to destroy it, e.g. Báez 2006; 2007), precisely because institutions outlive individuals, especially politicians who come and go from office.

10)   Thus, LIS practitioners, based on the evidence presented in this project might decide to conduct research to find ways of preserving people's documental memory; communities' documental heritage. Broomhall poor working class and formally uneducated people (and some less formally educated middle class) cannot take intelligent decisions about the pressing issues dramatically affecting their daily lives precisely because political ideologies from all walks of life (statutory, voluntary, and professional) have been one way or the other impoverishing the people's memory of information recorded in documents (Muela-Meza, 2005c; Schiller, 1996; Marquand, 2004). An author (Báez, 2006; 2007) criticises this phenomenon as being a deliberate people's 'killing of the cultural memory' or '*memoricide*' orchestrated by powerful groups to subdue weak and large groups of society.

6.3.3 Recommendations for policy makers

1) The European Parliament should review the Objective 1 social fund scheme which in the UK is based in Sheffield, and that in Broomhall is mainly managed by the Broomhall Forum, YMCA, and Broomhall Cosmopolitan Centre, Ltd. It should conduct an investigation into why those organisms in receipt of funding do not actually spend it on the deprived communities of Broomhall.

2) Sheffield and Hallam universities emerged as classist universities, since academics have been considered here as middle class members. Universities only or primarily serve their academic communities and exclude the rest of the citizens. Middle class academics already have a great advantage over illiterate and non-formally educated working classes, and still their universities provide them with better services. The author corroborates this fact because he has used the University of Sheffield's information and advice services and compared them with non-university, statutory or voluntary services. The recommendation is that the universities of Sheffield (Sheffield, Hallam, etc.) and for that matter universities all across the United Kingdom should grant free and free of charge access to all of their services. This is because as a LIS commentator notes: "the specialization of information provision has created an environment within which no single organization can satisfy most needs –a user accessing one agency will often have to be referred to another. However, what is particularly interesting is the extent to which many organizations are progressing from basic awareness and referral liaison to more ambitious forms of joint working, those activities will enable them to collectively offer an enhanced service to the community" (McDowell, 1992: 233). Furthermore, by doing this, Sheffield, Hallam and other universities mighty be perceived positively by residents of Broomhall and across Sheffield as doing something positive for the communities by providing information, advice, and help services. Not negatively as they have been perceived by most interviewees of this study.

The next section will explain the limitations of this thesis.

6.4 Limitations of this study

The author of this project acknowledges a number of limitations that might be taken into account by the reader of this thesis relating to its concepts, methodologies, methods, findings, discussions, conclusions, and recommendations.

1)   The limitation of being a foreign student in the UK. This limitation might be the most important to be considered in this thesis. The author is a Mexican national and citizen, being born in Mexico and having lived almost all of his life in Mexico except for some stays of few years abroad to study for example in Sheffield. The first time he ever came to the UK was on 29 August 2003 when he enrolled at the University of Sheffield as a PhD student at its Information Studies Department. If the author has fallen short in understanding all the multiple complexities of the British culture, economics, politics, and so on, beyond the sound possibilities provided by the academic discourse, the author acknowledges this caveat. The

author hopes that the reader might assess this research project on the grounds of its scientific, and academic value (including its limitations), and not based on the author's nationality.

2)   Another apparent limitation is that the project at times appeared to be trying to look for a sense of justice in every bit of information analysed. However, the researcher acknowledges that this, rather than a limitation, is more inherent to the scientific research endeavour which historically has fought against all oppressive authorities, against all odds, and so on (cf. Chapter 2; Sagan, 1997: 47; Feynman, 2001: 104; Sokal and Bricmont, 1999: 207). It could be said that more than a search for justice, this project was a quest for knowledge, understanding, and scientific truth purely on academic grounds, and whenever people's expressions appeared to be contrasting (regardless of their class), the author tried impartially and disinterestedly (as a scientist would put it, Feynman, 2001: 108) to analyse and synthesize the data (perceptions, expressions, interpretations, even the author's) appealing all the time to a sense of academic ethics, integrity, humility, and honesty. Nevertheless, some authors (Fleissner and Hofkirchner, 1998: 207) consider that the search for justice and wisdom are essential elements that should be implicit in social research and critique, and they also criticise that justice and wisdom are missing from the new catchwords of the so called "information society."

3)   Finally, the ultimate limitation of this study is the nature of the study in itself. A PhD study is ultimately a process for the researcher to obtain a doctoral degree, and hence it is limited by academic and time constraints. The author became overwhelmed by so many documents, both printed and digital, that, regretfully, not all of the data could be incorporated in the thesis. The whole research process was one of constant self-correction and change in which things that one day were considered interesting might have become on another day inadequate –in the light of new observations in the field, or deeper understanding of the respondents' perceptions, or literature reviewed. In this way the author compiled an electronic document nearly 1,000 pages long, representing an electronic draft of all the drafts he made of the thesis.

6.5 Summary

This chapter has stated the major conclusions of the thesis, as well as its recommendations for the Broomhall respondents, information providers and policy makers.

Chapter 7 discusses the further research steps the research will conduct in order to make these finding available to the widest publics, and the insights that emerged from this thesis suggested for the LIS or social sciences communities.

Chapter 7. Further research

"Societies will, of course, wish to exercise prudence in deciding which technologies –that is, which applications of science—are to be pursued and which not. But without funding basic research, without supporting the acquisition of knowledge for its own sake, our options become dangerously limited." – Carl Sagan, *The Dragons of Eden: Speculations on the Evolution of Human Intelligence* (Sagan, 1978: 245).

"That is, if we investigate further, we find that the statements of science are not of what is true and what is not true, but statements of what is known to different degrees of certainty: 'It is very much more likely that so and so is true than that is not true', or 'such and such is almost certain but there is still a little bit of doubt'; or – at the other extreme—'well, we really don't know.' Every one of the concepts of science is on a scale graduated somewhere between, but at neither end of, absolute falsity or absolute truth." — Nobel laureate, Richard Phillips Feynman, *The Pleasure of Finding Things Out,* (Feynman, 2001: 248).

7.1 Introduction

This chapter presents the broad recommendations for further research that emerged from this project. These are the further research steps the researcher intends to follow in order to disseminate the findings of the research, and themes for further research that the author and other researchers might pursue in the future.

7.2 Steps for communication of the findings of this thesis

These are some of the steps the researcher intends to follow in order to communicate widely the findings of this study:

1. In order to increase the readership of the research findings, the author will explore the possibility of publishing them in book format through a commercial publisher. Not for the sake of making a profit, but to reach a public audience that could only access it through commercial venues. For instance, the book *Public Library and Community Analysis* by Satyanarayana (1997), which was of paramount importance for this thesis, was originally a LIS PhD thesis from India, and then communicated in book format by a commercial publisher. Thus, the researcher could access this valuable thesis only through the commercial services of Amazon.co.uk. Therefore, that may be the only logic behind the idea of assessing the possibilities of communicating this thesis through commercial publishers.

2.   In addition, the researcher will present the findings of the thesis through international conference papers. He will also publish articles in international journals –especially open access journals where users can access the content free of charge. Moreover, he will continue developing in the near future the lines of research that emerged from this thesis, and consequently he will continue communicating its future findings.

3. Moreover, the researcher will try to create or join international networks of academic research with those authors whose current projects were found to be compatible and relevant to this thesis, about lines of research that gave birth to this thesis, as well as those that emerged afterwards. For instance, he might contact these authors in order to create or join networks related to *community profiling tool* or *community analysis* applied in LIS: (e.g. Cooper, et. al, 1993; Satyanarayana, 1997; Sarling and Van Tassel, 1999; Westbrook, 2000; 2001; Galluzzi,

2001; and Long, 2006). Also of interest are networks relating to *community profiling tool* from different social sciences other than LIS: with Roger Green (e.g. 2000a; 2000c), and Hawtin, Hughes, and Percy-Smith (1994).

7.3 Themes for further research

These are some of the themes for further research that the author and other researchers might pursue in the future:

1. The continuation of the study towards the creation of an *integral analytical model for Library and Information Science or The Eratosthenes Research Spirit model for LIS.* In the last few years the author (Muela-Meza, 2008; 2007; 2006a; 2005b; 2005c; 2004b) has been working towards the creation of this model, to be used as a theoretical framework for LIS practitioners and researchers. This model would combine (or 'triangulate') concepts from the natural sciences, the social sciences, and humanities, in order to obtain a comprehensive, and integral analysis of LIS phenomena. This model in progress assumes that LIS research phenomena should not be studied only from a LIS theoretical perspective, but also from perspectives other than LIS. This thesis is a clear example of the configuration of the historically grounded model, in that it has been inspired by Eratosthenes (ancient Greece, 246 BC). Eratosthenes was a classical librarian or LIS practitioner and researcher, geographer, poet, humanist, and scientist. However, the author came to know about him from authors other than LIS authors: for example, US astronomer Carl Sagan (2001), Armenian-Mexican astronomer Shahen Hacyan (1986), and Italian philosophers Giovanni Reale and Dario Antiseri (2004a).

2.   Further research into the informal information networks of people who act like/as if they were gateways to information. As explained in Chapter 5 relating to the provision of information of cultural information needs, the traditional documental information institutions (DIIs) such as libraries, or the Citizens' Advice Bureau (CAB) did not satisfy adequately the widest range of cultural information needs. In such a case there are intercultural gateways within the neighbourhood which might satisfy community's cultural information needs. From data several names of these gateways who might act as information providers emerged. However, these gateways are residents of the neighbourhood who might have small shops, but they did not have any premises as documental information institutions have (e.g. libraries, and Citizens Advice Bureau). Hence, even though the author was aware that they might be acting as information providers of a gateway type, he had no success in approaching them. This was due, according to findings analysed and discussed in Chapter 5, to the fact that these providers provided information in selective ways based on tribalism, kinship, religious brotherhoods, ethnic background, and nationality. Hence, the author did not have any of those characteristics that could make him become a viable candidate to be served by these selective 'underground' and informal information providers of gateway type. Hence, since the services of these 'underground' providers were not open for all citizens, and they socially excluded people, it was not possible to assess to what extent, quality, and professionalism they satisfied people's information, advice, or help needs. However, in this study emerged that the information these 'underground' might provide is open to question, and might have more negative impact on the users being served. As for Broomhall, they emerged as a very closed informal network, less publicly accountable, and more prone to provide inadequate services, because basically no one knows about their facilities or where they provide them, or the conditions, quality, extent, or professionalism of how they provide them. Thus, such non publicly accountable gateways or 'underground' information providers have been found as negative activities which undermine human and citizenship rights (e.g. Marquand, 2004). Nevertheless, this study was not focused on assessing *per se* the provision of information through gateways, as others have focused (e.g. Agada, 1999). However, more research is needed on how to approach 'underground' informal gateways who claim to act as information providers, but actually act as hurdles to information provision in relationship to the application of community profiling and the analysis of community information needs.

3. Further research into the surrounding issues of provision of information via the unsolicited postings that people receive through their letterboxes. As explained in Table 5.3 in Chapter 5, 72 documents were received through the author's letterbox from 16 September 2006 to 16 March

2007 while he lived in Broomhall. Of these: a) 55 are related to commercial information (19 are related to fast food takeaway shops and 15 about supermarkets: CostCutter from Broomhall and Somerfield from Broomhill); b) 11 from voluntary sector; and c) 5 from statutory sector, Sheffield. Given the nature of this grey literature and elusive documents, the author could not establish which of these documents can be considered useful for the residents and which 'rubbish unsolicited post,' because any of them could be either useful or useless by different residents. Hence, this could be a research theme for further research by LIS practitioners if they wanted to find out: a) what are the types of documents households receive in a given neighbourhood and on a given period; b) the quality of information provided; c) if residents find useful the information received; d) if the written information through leaflets, and booklets is enough in itself to inform residents, considering that some commentators have found that that information is not enough in itself, and that instead, the assumption that this information might inform families was considered as "simplistic and potentially dangerous" (Mitchell and Sloper, 2002: 78).

4.   Further research into the controversial issues on the privatization of information provision in publicly funded institutions. All the interviewees of this study, except one (a working class respondent, R.I.07, from section A), did not have any problem or complaint regarding the borrowing of books to borrow books through the Sheffield public libraries, and they did not pay any fare to borrow them. From the perceptions of interviewees it was apparent that they did not have any problems or complaints related to book borrowing. However, there are some new laws within the European Union relating to intellectual property and copyright, which have become controversial issues relating to the privatization of information provision in publicly funded institutions. Due to these laws EU citizens are paying extra taxes to read in publicly funded libraries or other documental institutions. For instance, a study from the Copy/South Research Group, *The Copy/South Dossier : Issues in the Economics, Politics, and Ideology of Copyright in the Global South* (Story, Darch, and Halbert (Eds.), 2006), in which the author of this thesis collaborated, found that the British government, at central and local levels, in compliance with European Union EU1992/100 directive, is taxing all the books bought and lent –checked out for home reading– throughout all the public libraries in the country. This directive has been enforced throughout the EU since 1992. However, a LIS researcher notes that in the UK this tax has been enforced in similar terms as in the European directive since 1978 through the British copyright law (Gimeno Perelló, 2007b). Hence, through this British 1978 copyright law and EU1992/100 directive, every time a book is lent to a user through any British public library –or through any other library from any other EU country– the taxpayers have to pay an extra tax to the copyright holders of that book on top of the regular taxes they already pay to the government. It was not found through the literature how much British taxpayers pay to copyright holders through the British government; however, Spanish taxpayers pay them € 1 euro per each book lent through their public libraries (Muela-Meza, 2005c). In addition, a LIS researcher (Gimeno Perelló, 2007b) found in an European-wide study that such EU100/1992 directive has been the main cause in the UK for the reduction of 30% of book lending in 2003 as compared with previous decade: "At the same time, the number of book loans in the British libraries descended until 30% in 2003 in relation with the previous decade: from 563 million loans in 1993 they descended to 406 million in 2003. These are direct consequences of the application of the European Directive [100/1992 on Intellectual Property taxes on library book lending]" (Gimeno Perelló, 2007b). Allegedly this tax is exacted from libraries in order to give an extra incentive to authors for their creativity, however, most of that money is collected by copyright holders (Story, Darch, and Halbert (Eds.), 2006). In addition, from the scarce money authors get, only the most checked out books as home loans get the maximum benefit: "In the UK, during the 2002-2003 period, 67% of the British authors obtained a profit of less than 143 Euros, whilst a 1.3% obtained the maximum benefit stipulated by the Law: 8, 663 Euros" (Gimeno Perelló, 2007b). Hence, further research relating to the negative issues of the copyright law as the new mechanism of privatization of the publicly funded documental information institutions is needed. For common citizens, these negative issues are generally hidden from their consideration; therefore, it is suggested that LIS practitioners conduct further research in this area; because publicly funded libraries and another documental information institutions: a) have an endemic problem of not having enough budget to acquire all the information their users need (Gimeno Perelló, 2007a; Rikowski, 2007); b) that money that the government pays to copyright holders could be invested in libraries to keep them open, better staffed and stocked, or

to build new ones, c) copyright law has become a sensible barrier to access to information through publicly funded documental information institutions (Story, Darch, and Halbert (Eds.), 2006; Muela-Meza, 2006a; 2005c).

7.4 Summary

This chapter has presented the broad recommendations for further research that emerged from this project: a) those further research steps that the researcher might follow, b) themes of research that the researcher might follow, and c) themes of research that the researcher suggests to the international academic community to follow.

This study has not tried to prove any theory, or methodology, or method, or tool, or anything. It has simply tried to understand a particular phenomenon, namely, the issues and features, information needs and provision of the people of the Broomhall neighbourhood through the application of the community profiling tool of analysis, and the implications for policy makers, the profession, and the human development based in a particular territory, a particular place in time: Broomhall. The research has been conducted with reflexivity, with humility, with analytical and critical rigour, without any vested interests at all. The aim has only been to understand the phenomena and advance the scientific endeavour and understanding, and most of all to foster the spirit of community. By writing this thesis, which will eventually be more widely communicated, that is, made public, (e.g. through libraries, or papers, or conferences), it will foster the spirit of community. As an author puts it: "without communication there is no community, because through it reality is made common to everyone, at its diverse levels and forms" (Sander Villarino, 1992: 39). Thus this thesis will made common to everyone who can access it and read it. If at times, the findings and discussions emerged as only having negative and critical implications, then the reader is advised to be critical and sceptical of the content of this thesis, and is invited to corroborate the evidence submitted here for public debate and scrutiny. If they do so, then they will –hopefully– understand why the picture of this phenomenon emerged as it did.

As a final remark, not exactly related to the phenomena researched here, the author also recommends that British, European, US, and all academic sponsors from around the world, sponsor academic research, like the author's sponsor, the Mexican CONACYT, for the sake of knowledge itself, 'for the pleasure of finding things out' (Feynman, 2001) on whichever subjects. Academic research funding should be should be encouraged and carried out for academic purposes with non-vested commercial, corporate, ideological-political interests (Sagan, 1978: 245). Academic inquiry should also be completely free from any pressure (ideological-politico, commercial, corporate, etc.). Researchers can research purely theoretical or practical research, but it is recommended that they also try to conduct research incorporating social transformation, for a betterment of all humans (not only dominant classes), all other species, and a better material and cosmic balance, as this doctoral research thesis has tried to accomplish.

In the remaining pages of the thesis the reader will find: a) the Bibliography; and b) the Appendices.

BIBLIOGRAPHY

Agada, J. (1999). "Inner-city gatekeepers: an exploratory survey of the information use environment." *Journal of the American Society for Information Science, 50 (1), 74-85.*

Amorós i Fontanals, J. (2000). *InfoPrat: Proyecto de Servicio de Información a la Comunidad. (Realizado sobre la base de la Biblioteca Antoni Martí del Prat de Llobregat) (InfoPrat: Project of Information Service to the Commmunity (Conducted on the basis of the Antoni Marti del Prat de Llobregat Library).* Prat de Llobregat, Catalunya, Spain: Biblioteca Antoni Martí del Prat de Llobregat. (Unpublished report provided by its author). [Online] http://eprints.rclis.org/13370/1/2000.Amoros-Fontanals.J.InfoPrat.pdf . [Accessed 10 May 2008].

Arksey, H. & Knight, P. (1999). *Interviewing for Social Scientists. An Introductory Resource with Examples.* London: Sage Publications.

Awards for All England. (2002). *Broomhall News award.* Sheffield, UK: Yorkshire and the Humber Awards for All. [Online] http://www.c-f.org.uk/cgi-fund/a4a/england/moredetails.pl?urn=AAE/2/010040523 . [Accessed 03 October 2006].

Backhouse, R. (1986). *Taking books to people: a practical community profile.* London: London Borough of Greenwich.

Báez, F. (2006). *La Hoguera de los Intelectuales: Ensayos (The Stake of Intellectuals: Essays).* Valencia, Venezuela: Universidad de Carabobo.

Báez, F. (2007). "Bibliotecas en guerra (Libraries at war)." In: Gimeno Perelló, J., López López, P. & Morillo Calero, M.J. (Coords). (2007). *De Volcanes Llena: Biblioteca y Compromiso Social (Full of Volcanoes: Library and Social Commitment).* Gijón, Asturias, Spain: Editorial Trea, 215-237.

Bambery, A. (1983). *A Walk around the Broomhall estate, Sheffield.* Sheffield, UK: Victorian Society. Illustrated, typewritten. [Available at the Sheffield Central Public Library; Sheffield Local Studies].

Bath, P.A. (et. al). (2005). "Use of graph theory to identify patterns of deprivation and high morbidity and mortality in public health data sets." *Journal of the American Medical Informatics Association, 12,* (630-641).

Batho, G.R. (1968). "The Broomhall area as a conservation area." *The Sheffield Spectator.* July 1968.

BBC - Action Desk Sheffield. (2005). *WW2 People's War. An Archive of World War Two Memories —Written by the Public, Gathered by the BBC.* Sheffield, UK: BBC, 03 October. [Online] http://www.bbc.co.uk/ww2peopleswar/ . [Accessed 04 October 2005].

BBC - Action Desk Sheffield. (2006). *WW2 People's War. An Archive of World War Two Memories —Written by the Public, Gathered by the BBC.* Sheffield, UK: BBC, 23 January. [Online] http://www.bbc.co.uk/ww2peopleswar/stories/18/a8766318.shtml. [Accessed 24 January 2006].

BBC News (Sheffield). (2003). "Shooting victim targeted twice." *BBC News (Sheffield).* [Online] http://news.bbc.co.uk/go/pr/fr/-/2/hi/uk_news/england/south_yorkshire/3309957.stm . [Accessed 22 December 2004].

BBC News (Sheffield). (2004). "Police name body found by flats." *BBC News (Sheffield), 23* December. [Online] http://news.bbc.co.uk/go/pr/fr/-/2/hi/uk_news/england/south_yorkshire/4117115.stm . [Accessed 23 December 2004].

BBC News (Sheffield). (2005a). "Fresh appeal over city flat death." *BBC News (Sheffield),* 17 January.   [Online]   http://news.bbc.co.uk/go/pr/fr/-/2/hi/uk_news/england/south_yorkshire/4181963.stm . [Accessed 17 January 2005].

BBC News (Sheffield). (2005b). "Strong smell leads to drugs haul." *BBC News (Sheffield),* 01 February.   [Online]   http://news.bbc.co.uk/go/pr/fr/-/2/hi/uk_news/england/south_yorkshire/4226799.stm . [Accessed 01 February 2005].

BBC News (Sheffield). (2006). "Raids uncover cannabis factories." *BBC News (Sheffield),* 16 August.   [Online]   http://news.bbc.co.uk/go/pr/fr/-/2/hi/uk_news/england/south_yorkshire/4798937.stm . [Accessed 16 August 2006].

BBC News (Sheffield). (2007). "Inquiry as woman shot in the face." *BBC News (Sheffield),* 29 April. [Online] http://news.bbc.co.uk/go/pr/fr/-/2/hi/uk_news/england/south_yorkshire/6605349.stm . [Accessed 29 April 2007].

Beal, C. (1976). Information *Provision in Sheffield : Report of a Study Carried out in 1976-1977.* Rev. ed. Sheffield, UK: University of Sheffield, Centre for Research on User Studies.

Beal, C. (1985). *Community Profiling for Librarians.* Sheffield: Centre for Research on User Studies.

Beal, C. (1979). "Studying the public's information needs." *Journal of Librarianship,* **11** (2). In: Satyanarayana, M. (1997). *Public Library and Community Analysis.* New Delhi, India: Reliance Publishing House; Dr. S.K.Bhatia.

Bedfordshire County Library. (1975). *A Community Profile Prepared by the South Bedfordshire District Library Team as the first report in a 3-part study of the Leighton Buzzard Library and Community.* Bedfordshire County, UK: Leighton Buzzard Library and Community.

Bennett, L. (1997). "Urban redevelopment and grassroots action in Chicago and Sheffield: themes, variations and uncertain legacies." *International Journal of Urban and Regional Research,* **21** (4), 664-676.

Black, A. & Muddiman, D. (1997). *Understanding Community Librarianship: The Public Library in Post-modern Britain.* Aldershot, UK: Avebury.

Blandy, S. & Parsons, D. (2004). "Affordable Housing and the Private Residential Market." *FIG (International Federation of Surveyors) Regional Conference.* Jakarta, Indonesia, October   3-7,   2004.   [Online] https://www.fig.net/pub/jakarta/papers/ts_07/ts_07_6_blandy_parsons.pdf . [Accessed 17 November 2005].

Borough of Sunderland Department of Recreation and Libraries. (1986). *Handbook on Community Profiling.* Sunderland, UK: Borough of Sunderland Department of Recreation and Libraries.

Bradley, J. (1993). "Methodological issues and practices in qualitative research." *Library Quarterly,* **63** (4), pp. 431-449.

Breen, L.J. (2007). "The researcher 'in the middle': negotiating the insider/outsider dichotomy." *The Australian Community Psychologist,* **19** (1), 163-174.

Broomhall Centre. (2003a). *Saturday Morning Football.* Sheffield, UK: Broomhall Centre. [Flyer available at the Broomhall Centre, Broomspring Lane, Sheffield, UK S10 2FD].

Broomhall Centre. (2003b). *Sheffield Samba Band.* Sheffield, UK: Broomhall Centre. [Flyer available at the Broomhall Centre, Broomspring Lane, Sheffield, UK S10 2FD].

Broomhall Forum. (1999). *Broomhall Community Survey: Report of the Findings of a Community Survey Carried out by Residents of Broomhall in the Summer of 1999* (a 13 pages report). Sheffield, UK: Broomhall Community Forum.

Broomhall Forum. (2005). *Annual General Meeting, 27 September at Broomhall Centre.* Sheffield, UK: Broomhall Forum.

Broomhall News. (2002). *Broomhall News: Connecting the Community,* (14).

Broomhall News. (2004a). "Still more flats?" *Broomhall News: Connecting the Commmunity,* April (29), p. 1.

Broomhall News. (2004b). *Broomhall News: Connecting the Community,* (30).

Broomhall News. (2004c). *Broomhall News: Connecting the Community,* (32).

Broomhall News. (2005). *Broomhall News: Connecting the Community, (38).*

Broomhall News. (2006). *Broomhall News: Connecting the Community,* (42). [Online] http://broomhallgateway.googlepages.com/broomhallnewsmarch2006number.pdf . [Accessed 29 May 2007].

Broomspring Writers Group. (2002). *Broomsprings: Short Stories, Poems, Novels in Progress. [Writers Write Readers Paint the Pictures].* Rotherham, UK: WEA, Rotherham; B & B Press (Parkgate).

Bryman, A. (2006). "Paradigm peace and the implications for quality." *International Journal of Social Research Methodology,* **9** (2), 111-126.

Bryson, J, Usherwood, B & Proctor, R. (2003). *Libraries must also be buildings? New Library Impact Study.* Sheffield: University of Sheffield. [Online] http://cplis.shef.ac.uk/New%20Library%20Impact%20Study.pdf . [Accessed 14 October 2003].

Budnick, V.M. (2006). *Perceptions of Library Students versus Library Professionals Toward the Homeless Patron: A Comparative Study.* Chapel Hill, North Carolina, USA: University of North Carolina at Chapel Hill. [Research paper for the Master of Science in Library Science submitted to the faculty of the School of Information and Library Science]. [Online] http://etd.ils.unc.edu/dspace/bitstream/1901/254/1/vanessabudnick.pdf . [Accessed 15 April 2006].

Cabinet Office. (2001). *A New Commitment to Neighbourhood Renewal: National Strategy Action Plan. Report by the Social Exclusion Unit.* London: Cabinet Office, Social Exclusion Unit.

Caidi, N. & Allard, D. (2005). "Social inclusion of newcomers to Canada: An information problem?" *Library and Information Science Research,* **27** (3), 302-324.

Calva González, J.J. (1991). "Una aproximacion a lo que son necesidades de informacion." *Investigación Bibliotecológica,* **5** (11), 33-38.

Calva González, J.J. (2004). *Las Necesidades de Informacion: Fundamentos Teoricos y Metodos (Information Needs: Theoretical Foundations and Methods).* Mexico: National Autonomous University of Mexico (UNAM), Centro Universitario de Investigaciones Bibliotecologicas (CUIB) (University Library and Information Science Research Centre).

Capurro, R. (1996). "On the genealogy of information." In: Kornwachs, K, & Jacoby, K. Eds. *Information. New Questions to a Multidisciplinary Concept.* Berlin: Akademie Verlag, pp. 259-270.

Cassen, R. & Kingdon, G. (2007). *Tackling Low Educational Achievement.* York, UK: The

Joseph Rowntree Foundation; London School of Economics. [Online] http://www.jrf.org.uk/bookshop/eBooks/2063-education-schools-achievement.pdf . [Accessed 22 June 2007].

Chagari, S. (2005). "Information capability building : role of information literacy programmes: A study." *World Library and Information Congress: 71th IFLA General Conference and Council, "Libraries - A voyage of discovery,"* August 14th - 18th 2005. Oslo, Norway: IFLA. [Online] http://www.ifla.org/IV/ifla71/papers/043e-Chagari.pdf . [Accessed 15 April 2006].

Chambers Dictionary. (2003). *Chambers Dictionary.* 9th ed. Beccles, Suffolk, UK: BCA.

Cisterna Cabrera, F. (2005). "Categorización y triangulación como procesos de validación del conocimiento en investigación cualitativa." (Categorisation and triangulation as processes of validation of knowledge in qualitative research). *Theoria,* **14** (1), 61-71.

City of Sheffield. (1989). *Broomhall Conservation Area.* Sheffield, UK: Planning Division, Department of Land & Planning, July 1989. [Map available at the Sheffield City Council Central Library, Surrey Street, Sheffield 1].

Cocker, J. et al. (2012) "Wickerman (lyrics)." In: *Pulp Wiki.* London: Pulp Wiki. [Online] http://www.pulpwiki.net/Pulp/Wickerman .

Connell, J. (1968). *Interim Report on the Proposal to Designate the Broomhall Area as a Conservation Area Submitted to the Sheffield City Council .* Sheffield, UK: Typewritten by the author at 43 Victoria Road, Broomhall Park, Sheffield, S10. [Available at the Sheffield City Council Central Library, Surrey Street, Sheffield, S1].

Cooper, S.M. (et. al). (1993). *Community Analysis Methods and Evaluative Options: The CAMEO Handbook.* Richmond, VA, USA: The Library of Virginia. [Online] http://skyways.lib.ks.us/pathway/cameo/index.htm [Accessed 2 February 2005].

Cottage, P. & Fredericks, P. (2006). "Tenants' victory over housing privatization." *Socialist Worker,* 7 October, (2021), p. 3.

Creaser, C. (1999). "A study of branch library catchments in two London boroughs." *Journal of Documentation,* **55** (2), 121-143.

Cromar, P. (2003). *Broomhall Cosmopolitan Centre. A Sustainable Regeneration Opportunity. Feasibility Study.* Sheffield, UK: Cromar & Hackett Ltd.

Cronin, B. (1981). "From paradigm to practice: the logic of promotion." *Aslib Proceedings.* 33, (10).

Cronin, B. (1992a). "Market research: introductory notes." In: Cronin, B. (1992b). *The Marketing of Library and Information Services 2.* London: Aslib.

Cronin, B. (1992b). The Marketing of Library and Information Services 2. London: Aslib.

Crook, T. (et. al). (1976). *Havelock: The Case for Priority Treatment. A Report Presented to the City of Sheffield Metropolitan District Council for the Purposes of Section 36 of the 1974 Housing Act.* Sheffield, UK: Broomhall Community Group, 5 Fitzwilliam Row, Sheffield S3.

Crook, T. (1983). *Havelock Housing Action Area, Achievements After Five Years : The Resident.* Sheffield, UK: Department of Town and Regional Planning University of Sheffield.

Curtis, M. (1972). *The Public Library and its Community: a Study of the Purposes of the Public Library in the Community with Special Reference to Non-Users, Including Case Studies of Residents of Sheffield Carried out in the Summer of 1972.* Sheffield, UK: University of Sheffield [M.A. Dissertation in Librarianship].

Czerwinski, B. (2005). "Days Gone By - the Sheffield Blitz." In: BBC - Action Desk Sheffield. (2005). *WW2 People's War. An Archive of World War Two Memories —Written by the Public, Gathered by the BBC*. Sheffield, UK: BBC, 03 October. [Online] http://www.bbc.co.uk/ww2peopleswar/ . [Accessed 04 October 2005].

de la Garza Toledo, E. (1999). "Epistemología de las teorías sobre modelos de producción." ("Epistemology of the theories about the models of production)." In: De la Garza Toledo, E. (Comp.). *Los Retos Teóricos de los Estudios del Trabajo hacia el Siglo XXI (The Theoretical Challanges of the Labour Studies towards the 21st Century)*. Buenos Aires: CLACSO (Consejo Latinoamericano de las Ciencias Sociales) (Latin American Council of the Social Sciences). [Online]. http://docencia.izt.uam.mx/egt/publicaciones/capituloslibros/index.htm . [Accessed 28 May 2006].

de la Garza Toledo, E. (2000). "El papel del concepto de trabajo en la teoría social del siglo XX." ("The role of the labour concept in the social theory of the XX century." In: de la Garza Toledo, E. (coord.). *El Tratado Latinoamericano de Sociología del Trabajo (Latin American Treatise of the Sociology of Labour)*. Mexico: COLMEX; FLACSO; UAM; FCE.

de la Garza Toledo, E. (2001). "La epistemología crítica y el concepto de configuración: Alternativas a la estructura y función estándar de la teoría." ("The critical epistemology and the concept of configuration: alternatives to the structure and standard function of theory)." *Revista Mexicana de Sociología (Mexican Journal of Sociology)*, (1) [Online]. http://docencia.izt.uam.mx/egt/publicaciones/articulos/index.htm . [Accessed 28 May 2006].

de la Garza Toledo, E. (2002). "La configuración como alternativa del concepto estándar de la teoría." ("The configuration as an alternative to the standard concept of theory"). In: Valencia García, G., de la Garza Toledo, E. & Zemelman Merino, H. (2002). *Epistemología y Sujetos: Algunas Contribuciones al Debate (Epistemology and Subjects: Some Contributions to the Debate)*. México: UNAM; Plaza y Valdés. [Online]. http://docencia.izt.uam.mx/egt/publicaciones/capituloslibros/index.htm . [Accessed 28 May 2006].

de la Garza Toledo, E. (2006). "Neoinstitucionalismo, ¿Alternativa A La Elección Racional?: Una Discución Entre La Economía Y La Sociología." ("Neoinstitutionalism, Alternative To The Rational Election: A Discussion Between Economy And Sociology"). In: de la Garza, Enrique (coord.) *Teorías Sociales y Estudios del Trabajo: Nuevos Enfoques (Social Theories and Studies of Labour: New Approaches)*. Barcelona: Anthropos, Biblioteca de Comunicación Científica, (Col. Cuadernos A, Núm. 24). [Online]. http://docencia.izt.uam.mx/egt/publicaciones/capituloslibros/index.htm . [Accessed 18 September 2006].

de la Garza Toledo, E. (Comp.) (1999). *Los Retos Teóricos de los Estudios del Trabajo hacia el Siglo XXI (The Theoretical Challenges of Labour Studies towards the 21st Century)*. Buenos Aires: CLACSO (Consejo Latinoamericano de las Ciencias Sociales) (Latin American Council of the Social Sciences). [Online]. http://docencia.izt.uam.mx/egt/publicaciones/capituloslibros/index.htm . [Accessed 28 May 2006].

Deacon, D.N. & Golding, P. (1991). "The voluntary sector in the information society: a study in division and uncertainty." *Voluntas: International Journal of Voluntary and Non Profit Organisations*, **2** (2), 69-88.

Delanty, G. (2003). *Community*. London; New York: Routledge.

Delanty, G. (2005). *Social Science: Philosophical and Methodological Foundations*. Second Edition. Berkshire, UK; NY: Open University Press; McGraw Hill Education, (Collection: Concepts in the Social Sciences).

Demirovic, A. (2004). "Hegemony and the paradox of public and private." *Transversal: EIPCP Multilingual Webjournal*. June number. [Online] http://eipcp.net/transversal/0605/demirovic/en

. [Accessed 28 August 2006].

Denscombe, M. (2002). *Ground Rules for Good Research: A 10 Point Guide for Social Researchers.* Maidenhead, Berkshire, UK: Open University Press; McGraw Hill Education.

Denscombe, M. (2003). The *Good Research Guide. For Small-scale Social Research Projects. 2nd. ed.* Maidenhead, UK: Open University Press.

Denzin, N.K & Lincoln, Y.S. (Eds). (2000). *Handbook of Qualitative Research. 2nd ed.* Thousand Oaks, California, USA; London; New Delhi: Sage Publications.

Department of Marketing and Communications. (2005). "Green light from council for student village." *Overview Newsletter: for Everyone who Works at the University of Sheffield,* (12), pp: 4-5.

Edgell, S. (1993). *Class.* London; New York: Routledge.

Einstein, A. (1949). "Why socialism." *Monthly Review.* In: Einstein, A. (2005). *Ideas and Opinions.* London: A Condor Book; Souvenir Press.

Einstein, A. (2005). *Ideas and Opinions.* London: A Condor Book; Souvenir Press.

Engels, F. ([1845], 2000). *The Condition of the Working Class in England: From Personal Observation and Authentic Sources.* Pacifica, CA: Marxist Internet Archive. [Online] http://www.marxists.org/archive/marx/works/1845/condition-working-class/index.htm . [Accessed 14 October 2003].

Ewart, L. (2004). *"How's my Profile?" An Exploration of Community Profiling in Public Library Authorities.* Sheffield, UK: Department of Information Studies, University of Sheffield. [M.A. dissertation in Librarianship]. [Online] http://dagda.shef.ac.uk/dissertations/2003-04/External/Ewart_Laura_MALib.pdf . [Accessed 18 September 2005].

Exposed. (2007). "Property, the changing face of Sheffield: An exposed guide to the latest line of city centre apartments from Blundells Centro." *Exposed: Sheffield and South Yorkshire's Ultimate Entertainment + Listings Guide,* July issue.

Fearnley, A.R. (2001). *Our Daily Bread.* Sheffield, UK: Juma.

Feynman, R.P. (2001). *The Pleasure of Finding Things out: The Best Short Works of Richard P. Feynman.* London: Penguin Books.

First. (2003). *Sheffield. Your Guide to High Frequency Bus Travel. Network Guide.* Rotherham, UK.

Floridi, L. (2002). "On defining library and information science as applied philosophy of information." *Social Epistemology,* **16** (1), 37-49.

Floridi, L. (2004). "Afterword. LIS as applied philosophy of information: A reappraisal." *Library Trends,* **52**, (3), 658-665.

Fleissner, P. & Hofkirchner, W. (1998). "The making of the information society: driving forces, 'Leitbilder' and the imperative for survival. *BioSystems. (46), pp. 201-207.*

Ford, N. (1987). "Research and practice in librarianship: a cognitive view." In: Katz, B. & Kinder, R. (Eds). *Current Trends in Information: Research and Theory.* NY: The Haworth Press, pp. 21-47.

Forsetlund, L. & Bjorndal, A. (2001). "The potential research-based information in public health: identifying unrecognised information needs." *BMC Public Health,* **1** (1). [Online] http://www.biomedcentral.com/1471-2458/1/1 . [Accessed 2 February 2005].

Frías, J.A. & Borrego, A. (2004a). "Más allá de la cantidad: la incorporación de los métodos cualitativos a la investigación en información y documentación." (Beyond quantity: the incorporation of qualitative methods in information and documentation research). In: Frías, J.A. & Ríos Hilario, A.B. (2004b). *Metodologías de Investigación en Información y Documentación (Methodologies of Research in Information and Documentation)*. Salamanca, Spain: Ediciones Universidad de Salamanca (Series: Aquílafuente, No. 80), pp. 193-212.

Frías, J.A. & Ríos Hilario, A.B. (2004b). *Metodologías de Investigación en Información y Documentación (Methodologies of Research in Information and Documentation)*. Salamanca, Spain: Ediciones Universidad de Salamanca (Series: Aquílafuente, No. 80).

Galluzzi, A. (2001). "Analisi di comnita: uno strumento per la planifcazione dei servizi." ("Community analysis: an instrument for planning services."). *Bollettino AIB*, **41**, (2), 175-188.

Geographers' A-Z Map Company, Ltd. (2002). *A-Z Premier Street Map of Sheffield*. Sevenoaks, Kent, UK: Geographers' A-Z Map Company, Ltd.

Gericke, E.M. (1997). "Serving the unserved in the year 2000." *63rd IFLA General Conference – Conference Programme and Proceedings*. August 31 – September 5.]. [Online]. http://www.ifla.org/IV/ifla63/63gere.htm [Accessed 23 December 2004].

Gibson, T. & Dorfman, M. (1981). *The Planning For Real Report. Part 2: Participation & Commitment In North Birkenhead And Sheffield (Broomhall)*. Sheffield, UK: No publisher.

Gimeno Perelló, J. (2007a). "El conocimiento no es una mercancía (Knowledge is not a commodity)." In: Gimeno Perelló, J., López López, P. & Morillo Calero, M.J. (Coords). *De Volcanes Llena: Biblioteca y Compromiso Social (Full of Volcanoes: Library and Social Commitment)*. Gijón, Asturias, Spain: Trea, pp.129-157.

Gimeno Perelló, J. (2007b). "En las bibliotecas de la Unión Europea hay que pagar por leer." (In the libraries of the European Union it is mandatory to pay to read). *Librinsula. Weekly Bulletin of the National Library of Cuba "Jose Marti"*, **4** (175), 11 May. [Online] http://www.bnjm.cu/librinsula/2007/mayo/175/documentos/documento535.htm . [Accessed 12 May 2007].

Gimeno Perelló, J., López López, P. & Morillo Calero, M.J. (Coords). (2007). *De Volcanes Llena: Biblioteca y Compromiso Social (Full of Volcanoes: Library and Social Compromise)*. Gijón, Asturias, Spain: Editorial Trea.

Glaser, B.G. & Strauss, A.L. (1967). *The Discovery of Grounded Theory; Strategies for Qualitative Research*. Chicago: Aldine Pub. Co.

Glitz, B. (1998). *Focus Groups for Libraries and Librarians*. New York: Forbes. Cited in: Glitz, B., Hamasu, C. & Sandstrom, H. (2001). "The focus group: a tool for programme planning, assessment and decision-making —an American view." *Health Information and Libraries Journal*, (18), 30-37.

Glitz, B., Hamasu, C. & Sandstrom, H. (2001). "The focus group: a tool for programme planning, assessment and decision-making —an American view." *Health Information and Libraries Journal*, (18), 30-37.

Golafshani, N. (2003). "Understanding reliability and validity in qualitative research." *The Qualitative Report*, **8** (4), 597-606. [Online] http://www.nova.edu/ssss/QR/QR8-4/golafshani.pdf . [Accessed 20 April 2009].

Google Earth. (2007). *Satellite Mapping System*. [Online] Mountain View, California, USA: Google Inc.; (The GeoInformation Group; Europa Technologies; TeleAtlas). [Accessed 26 May 2007].

Gorman, G.E. & Clayton, P. (1997). *Qualitative Research for the Information Professional: A Practical Handbook*. London: Library Association Publishing.

Gorman, G.E. & Clayton, P. (2005). *Qualitative Research for the Information Professional: A Practical Handbook*. 2nd ed. London: Facet.

Gracián, B. ([1647] 1993). *El Arte de la Prudencia: Oráculo Manual (The Art of Worldly Wisdom: Oracle Manual)*. Mexico: Planeta.

Green, G. (2000). *Social Capital, Health and Economy in South Yorkshire Coalfield Communities*. Sheffield, UK: Sheffield Hallam University, Centre for Regional Economic and Social Research.

Green, G. (2001). *Capital Accounting for Neighbourhood Sustainability*. Sheffield, UK: Sheffield Hallam University, Centre for Regional Economic and Social Research.

Green, R. & Farrington, P. (1996a). "The social worker as a professional advocate: working with clients claiming benefits." *Practice: A Journal of the British Association of Social Workers,* **9** (1), 49-58.

Green, R. & Gilchrist, A. (1994). "Getting to know a community." In: Harris, V. (Ed). *Community Work Skills Manual*. Newcastle, UK: Association of Community Workers. Section 7, pp.1-11.

Green, R. & Turner, A. (1999). "Challenging the power of professionals: involving the community in tackling poverty." In: Payne, H. & Littlechild, B. (Eds). *Ethical Power and the Abuse of Power in Social Responsibility: Leave no Stone Unturned*. London: J. Kingsley.

Green, R. (1996a). *Marginal Inclusion? A Survey of Refugees in the London Borough of Redbridge*. Essex, UK: Redbridge Refugee Forum. [Online] http://web.archive.org/web/*/http://www.refugeeforum.org/Marginal%20inclusion.pdf . [Accessed 30 October 2004].

Green, R. (1996b). *Mental Health Needs on a North East London Housing Estate*. London: Waltham Forest Mind.

Green, R. (1996c). *The Rosedale Estate: A Community Needs Survey*. Hertfordshire, UK: Rosedale Free (Baptist) Church.

Green, R. (1997). *Community Action Against Poverty: A Poverty Profile of the Kingsmead Estate in Hackney*. London: Kingsmead Kabin.

Green, R. (2000a). "Applying a community needs profiling approach to tackling service user poverty." *British Association of Social Workers,* **30** (287-303).

Green, R. (2000b). *Barriers To Accessing Support: Perspectives On Mental Health Needs Of The Asian Communities In North Hertfordshire; A Research Report For The Mann Project*. Hertfordshire, UK: Ravidassia Community Centre, Hitchin, North Hertfordshire.

Green, R. (2000c). *Marginalised Groups and Community Development: Inclusion through Community Needs Profiling*. Hertfordshire, UK: University of Hertfordshire. [Ph.D. Thesis in Social Work].

Green, R. (Ed). (2005). *Voices from the Mead: People's Stories on the Kingsmead Estate*. Suffolk, UK: Arima Publishing.

Greig, S., Parry, N. & Rimmington, B. (2003). "Promoting sustainable regeneration: learning from a case study in participatory HIA." *Environmental Impact Assessment Review,* **24** *(2004) 255-267.*

Hacyan, S. (1986). *El Descubrimiento del Universo (The Discovery of the Universe)*. Mexico: Fondo de Cultura Economica (Low-price Culture Collection), (Collection Science from Mexico, No. 6).

Hall, I.B. (2006). "Irene B. Hall's (nee Gleed) Story." In: BBC - Action Desk Sheffield. (2006). *WW2 People's War. An Archive of World War Two Memories —Written by the Public, Gathered by the BBC.* Sheffield, UK: BBC, 23 January. [Online] http://www.bbc.co.uk/ww2peopleswar/stories/18/a8766318.shtml . [Accessed 24 January 2006].

Hall, J.P. (1981). *West Indians and Libraries: An Enquiry into the Needs of West Indian Community in Sheffield and the Potential Role of the Public Library in Helping Satisfy some of Those Needs, with Particular Reference to the Havelock Area of the City.* Sheffield, UK: University of Sheffield [Master of Arts dissertation in Librarianship].

Hanover Tenants Association. (2005). *Minutes of the 13 June 2005 Regular Meeting.* Sheffield, UK: Hanover Tenants Association.

Harman, R. & Minnis, J. (2004). *Sheffield.* New Haven; London: Yale University Press, (Series: Pevsner Architectural Guides).

Harris, V. (Ed). (1994). *Community Work Skills Manual.* Newcastle, UK: Association of Community Workers. Section 7.

Harrison, M. (1982). *A Community Profile of Long Eaton.* Long Eaton, UK: Long Eaton Library.

Hauser, M. D. (2006). *Moral Minds: How Nature Designed our Universal Sense of Right And Wrong.* New York: Ecco; Harper Collins.

Hawking, S. (1988). *A Brief History of Time: From the Big Bang to the Black Holes.* NY: Bantam Books.

Hawtin, M., Hughes, G. & Percy-Smith, J. (1994). *Community Profiling: Auditing Social Needs.* Buckingham, UK; Bristol, PA, USA: Open University Press.

Heap, B. (2003). "Can we end hunger?" In: Swain, H. (Ed.). *Big Questions in Science.* London: Vintage, pp. 180-185.

Heller, A. (1996). *Una Revisión de la Teoría de las Necesidades (A Revision of the Theory of Needs)*, 1st ed. Barcelona: Editorial Paidós Ibérica (Series: Contemporary Thinking No. 47).

Hey, D. (1998). *A History of Sheffield.* Lancaster, UK: Carnegie Publishing.

Hill, D. (et. al). (2002). *Marxism against Postmodernism in Education Theory.* Lanham, MD: Lexignton Books.

HMSO. (1990). *Planning (Listed Buildings and Conservation Areas) Act 1990 (c. 9).* London: Controller of HMSO being the Queen's Printer of Acts of Parliament; The Queen's Printer of Acts of Parliament The Stationery Office Limited. [Online] http://www.opsi.gov.uk/ACTS/acts1990/Ukpga_19900009_en_1.htm . [Accessed 15 November 2004].

Huberman, A. M. & Miles, M. B. (2002). *The Qualitative Researcher's Companion.* Thousand Oaks, California: Sage Publications.

Hull, B. (2003). "Information and Ccommunication Technology and social exclusion: the roles of libraries." *Telematics and Informatics,* **20,** 131-142.

Hunter, J. (1998). *The Effectiveness of Mobile Library Provision in Urban Communities which*

Have Lost Static Libraries: A Case Study. Sheffield, UK: University of Sheffield [M.A. Librarianship Dissertation]. [Online] http://dagda.shef.ac.uk/dissertations/1997-98/hunter.pdf . [Accessed 21 April 2004].

Ilyenkov, E.V. (1960). *The Dialectics of the Abstract & the Concrete in Marx's Capital* . Moscow; Pacifica, CA, USA: Progress Publishers; Evald Ilyenkov Archive. [Online] http://www.marxists.org/archive/ilyenkov/works/abstract/index.htm . [Accessed 14 September 2005].

Ilyenkov, E.V. (1977). *Dialectical Logic: Essays on its History and Theory*. Moscow; Pacifica, CA, USA: Progress Publishers; Evald Ilyenkov Archive. [Online] http://www.marxists.org/archive/ilyenkov/works/essays/index.htm . [Accessed 14 September 2005].

Jenkins, C. (1990). "Bohemian rhapsodies." *West Side*. October 1990, p. 80-81.

Johnson, R. (1995). *Community Information Providers as Agents of Change: A Study in Sheffield*. Sheffield, UK: University of Sheffield [M.Sc. Dissertation in Information Management].

Jones, S.J. (1998). "Subjectivity and class consciousness: the development of class identity." *Journal of Adult Development,* **5** (3), 145-162.

Jootun, D. (et. al). (2008). "Reflexivity: promoting rigour in qualitative research." *Nursing Standard,* **23** (23), 42-46.

Jordan, P. & Walley, E. (1977). *Learning About The Community: A Guide For Public Librarians*. Leeds, UK: School of Librarianship, Leeds Polytechnic.

Kalyane, V. L. & Devarai, Rajashekhar S. (1994). "Empathy in public librarianship: a subjective and qualitative analysis". *Indian Journal of Information, Library and Society,* 7, (1-2), 87-104. [Online] http://eprints.rclis.org/archive/00001421/ . [Accessed 8 April 2005].

Kaniki, A.M. (1989). *Agricultural Information Needs in Zambia: A Study of a Two-way Information Flow*. Pittsburgh, PA: University of Pittsburgh [PhD thesis].

Kaniki, A.M. (1995). "Exploratory study of information needs in the Kwa-Ngwanase (Natal) and Qumbu (Transkei) communities of South Africa." *South African Journal of Library and Information Science,* **63**, (1), 9-18.

Kaniki, A.M. (2001). "Community profiling and needs assessment." In: Stilwell, C., Leach, A. & Burton, S. (Eds.). (2001). *Knowledge, Information and Development: an African Perspective. Scottsville,* South Africa: School of Human and Social Studies, University of Natal (Pietermaritzburg), pp. 187-199 (Research Series No. 1).

Katz, B. & Kinder, R. (Eds). (1987). *Current Trends in Information: Research and Theory*. NY: The Haworth Press.

Kinnell, M. (Ed.) (1992). *Informing Communities: The Role of Libraries and Information Services*. Newcastle, UK: CSG Publishing.

Kitzinger, J. (1995). "Qualitative research: Introducing focus groups." *BMJ*. (311), 299-302.

Krueger, R.A. & King, J.A. (1998). *Involving Community Members in Focus Groups*. Thousand Oaks, California: Sage Publications (Series: The Focus Groups Kit No. 5).

Krueger, R.A. (1998). *Moderating Focus Groups*. Thousand Oaks, California: Sage Publications (Series: The Focus Groups Kit No. 4).

Labaree, R.V. (2002). "The risk of 'going observationalist': negotiating the hidden dilemmas of being an insider participant observer." *Qualitative Research, 2* (1), 97-122.

Larkin, M., Watts, S. & Clifton, E. (2006). "Giving voice and making sense in interpretative phenomenological analysis." *Qualitative Research in Psychology, 3,* 102-120.

Lawal, M. (2009). "Reconciling methodological approaches of survey and focus group." *Nurse Researcher, 17* (1), 54-61.

LDA Design (2005). *The Vision: Broomhall Community Centre, Ltd.* London: LDA Design, Ltd.; Broomhall Community Centre, Ltd.

Leach, A. (1999). "The provision of information to adults in rural KwaZulu-Natal, South Africa, by non-governmental organisations." *Libri, 49*, p. 71-89.

Leader, R.E. (1905). *Sheffield in the Eighteenth Century, 2nd Ed.* Sheffield, UK: Sir WC Leng; Daily Telegraph Offices.

Leeming, C. (2007a). "Saved from demolition." *The Big Issue in the North: Working not Begging,* 3-9 September (686), p.4.

Leeming, C. (2007b). "The buildings are rotting before our very eyes." *The Big Issue in the North: Working not Begging,* 8-14 January (652), pp: 14-17.

Lenin,V.I. ([1908], 1964). *Materialism and Empirio-criticism: Critical Comments on a Reactionary Philosophy.* 3rd. rev. ed. Moscow : Progress Publishers.

Linley, R. & Usherwood, B. (1998). *New Measures for the New Library: A Social Audit for Public Libraries.* Sheffield, U.K.: The University of Sheffield; DIS/CPLIS. [British Library Research & Innovation Centre Report 89]. [Online] http://cplis.shef.ac.uk/newmeasures.pdf . [Accessed 15 November 2003].

Lofthouse, A. (2001). *Then & Now: The Sheffield Blitz, Operation Crucible.* Sheffield, UK: ALD Design & Print.

Long, S.A. (2006). "Recovery and renewal: libraries lead the way in post-Katrina New Orleans." *New Library World, 107* (1230/1231), 552-554.

Louie, R.L. (1976). *A Community Profile Approach Toward Expanding Public Library Services: Communication Survey Procedures Reaching Chinese Americans in the Los Angeles Chinatown Community and Obtaining their Information-Seeking Patterns.* California: University of Southern California. [PhD thesis in library science].

Madden, A.D. (2000). "A definition of information." *Aslib Proceedings, 52* (9), 343-349.

Manzi, S. (1993). Portsmouth North Community Profile. Portsmouth: SSRIU.

Marcella, R. & Baxter, G. (2000). "The impact of social class and status on citizenship information need: the results of two national surveys in the UK." *Journal of Information Science, 26*, (4), 239-254.

Marquand, D. (2004). *Decline of the Public: The Hollowing-out of Citizenship.* Cambridge, UK; Malden, MA, USA: Polity.

Martin, W. J. (1989). Community Librarianship: Changing the Face of Public Libraries. London : Bingley.

Marx, K. & Engels, F. ([1845-1846] 1976a). *The German Ideology. Critique of Modern German Philosophy According to its Representatives Feuerbach, B. Bauer and Stirner, and of German Socialism According to its Various Prophets.* In: Marx, K. & Engels, F. (1976a). *Karl Marx and Frederick Engels Collected Works. Vol. 5.* London: Lawrence & Wishart; Moscow: Progress

Publishers; Institute of Marxism-Leninism Moscow. (Marx and Engels: 1845-47).

Marx, K. ([1867], 1974). *Capital: A Critical Analysis Of Capitalist Production. Volume 1*. London: Lawrence & Wishart; Moscow: Foreign Languages Publishing House.

Marx, K. & Engels, F. (1976a). *Karl Marx and Frederick Engels Collected Works. Vol. 5*. London: Lawrence & Wishart; Moscow: Progress Publishers; Institute of Marxism-Leninism Moscow. (Marx and Engels: 1845-47).

Marx, K. y Engels, F. (1976b). *Karl Marx and Frederick Engels Collected Works. Vol. 6*. London: Lawrence & Wishart; Moscow: Progress Publishers; Institute of Marxism-Leninism Moscow. (Marx and Engels: 1845-48).

Maslow, A. (2005). *El Hombre Autorrealizado: Hacia una Psicología del Ser (Toward a Psychology of Being)*, 16th ed. Barcelona: Editorial Kairós.

Mason, J. (2002). *Qualitative Researching*. 2nd edition. London: Sage Publications.

Mautner, T. (Ed.). (2000). *The Penguin Dictionary of Philosophy*. London: Penguin Books.

McClarence, S. & Rogerson, N. (1988). Sheffield Walkabout. Sheffield, UK: Sheffield City Libraries.

McDowell, O. (1992). "Inter-agency cooperation." In: Kinnell, M. (Ed.) (1992). *Informing Communities: the Role of Libraries and Information Services*. Newcastle, UK: CSG Publishing, p. 231-250.

McElvenney, R. (et. al). (2005). "Recollections of an evacuee." In: BBC - Action Desk Sheffield. (2005). *WW2 People's War. An Archive of World War Two Memories —Written by the Public, Gathered by the BBC*. Sheffield, UK: BBC, 03 October.

McGuire, S.M. (1981). *A Community Profile of the Handsworth Area of Sheffield: With some Observations on the Aims and Activities Involved in Profiling and Suggestions for Action to be Taken on the Basis of the Profile*. Sheffield, UK: University of Sheffield. [M.A. Dissertation in Librarianship].

McManus, K.M. (1987). *Trade Union Information Needs: a Critical Study of the Library at Merseyside Trade Union Community and Unemployed Resource Centre*. MA in Librarianship. Sheffield: University of Sheffield.

Mellon, C. A. (1990). *Naturalistic Inquiry for Library Science: Methods and Applications for Research, Evaluation, and Teaching*. New York: Greenwood Press.

Miles, M.B. & Huberman, A.M. (1994). *Qualitative Data Analysis: An Expanded Sourcebook*. 2nd ed. Thousand Oaks, CA; London; New Delhi: Sage Publications.

Miller, D.A.J. (1977). *An Analysis of a Project Undertaken by Sheffield City Libraries on the Compilation of Community Profiles*. Sheffield, UK: University of Sheffield [M.A. Dissertation in Librarianship].

Milne, E. (2004). *Closing the Gap. A Framework for Neighbourhood Renewal in Sheffield*. Sheffield,   UK: Sheffield   First   for   Health.   [Online] http://www.sheffieldfirstforhealth.net/meetings/docs/sffhagenda230104d.pdf . [15 April 2004].

Mitchell, K. & Branigan, P. (2000). "Using focus groups to evaluate health promotion intervention." *Health Education*, **100**, (6), 261-268.

Mitchell, W. & Sloper, P. (2002). "Information that informs rather than alienates families with disabled children: developing a model of good practice." *Health and Social Care in the Community*, **10** (1), 74-81.

MOD 'The Voice in the Street.' (2002). "Letter to *Broomhall News.*" In: *Broomhall News.* (2002). *Broomhall News: Connecting the Community.* (14).

Moore, N. (2002) "A model of social information need." *Journal of Information Science,* **28** (4), 297-303.

Morales Campos, E. & Ramírez Leiva, E. (coords) (1992). *Edición Conmemorativa del X Aniversario del Centro Universitario de Investigaciones Bibliotecológicas. Vol. 1. En Torno a la Investigación Bibliotecológica (Commemorative Edition of the 10*[th] *Anniversary of the University Centre of Library and Information Science Research. Vol. 1. About the LIS Research).* Mexico: Mexico, SEP, Consejo Nacional para la Cultura y las Artes; UNAM, Dirección General de Bibliotecas, Centro Universitario de Investigaciones Bibliotecológicas.

Moran, R.A. & Butler, D.S. (2001). "Whose health profile?" *Critical Public Health,* **11,** (1), 59-74.

Morgan, D.L. (1988). *Focus Groups as Qualitative Research (Sage University Paper Series on Qualitative Research Methods, Vol. 16).* Newbury Park, CA, USA: Sage.

Morgan, D.L. & Scannell, A.U. (1998). *Planning Focus Groups.* Thousand Oaks, California: Sage Publications (The Focus Groups Kit No. 2).

Muddiman, D. (2000a). "Images of exclusion: user and community perceptions of the public library." In: Muddiman, D. (et. al). (2000b). *Open To All? : The Public Library And Social Exclusion. Vol.3. Working Papers.* London: Resource (Library and Information Commission Research Report No. 86).

Muddiman, D. (et. al). (2000b). *Open To All? : The Public Library And Social Exclusion. Vol.3. Working Papers.* London: Resource (Library and Information Commission Research Report No. 86).

Muela-Meza, Z.M. (1995). "Breve introducción a las bibliotecas públicas mexicanas." (A brief introduction to Mexican public libraries). Research paper for the College of Library and Information Science, School of Philosophy and Letter, Autonomous University of Nuevo Leon (Mexico). [Online] http://eprints.rclis.org/view/people/Muela-Meza,_Zapopan_Mart=n.html . [Accessed 24 February 2007].

Muela-Meza, Z.M. (1999a). "Los servicios de referencia de las bibliotecas UACJ, panacea para sus males de información : primera de tres partes." (The reference services of the UACJ libraries, a panacea for all of your ills: first of three parts). *Gaceta Universitaria de la UACJ.* 14(116) 12, University Autonomous of Ciudad Juarez (Mexico). [Online] http://eprints.rclis.org/view/people/Muela-Meza,_Zapopan_Mart=n.html . [Accessed 24 February 2007].

Muela-Meza, Z.M. (1999b). "Los servicios de referencia de las bibliotecas UACJ, panacea para sus males de información : segunda de tres partes." (The reference services of the UACJ libraries, a panacea for all of your ills: second of three parts). *Gaceta Universitaria de la UACJ.* 14(119) 2, University Autonomous of Ciudad Juarez (Mexico). [Online] http://eprints.rclis.org/view/people/Muela-Meza,_Zapopan_Mart=n.html . [Accessed 24 February 2007].

Muela-Meza, Z.M. (1999c). "Los servicios de referencia de las bibliotecas UACJ, panacea para sus males de información : tercera de tres partes." (The reference services of the UACJ libraries, a panacea for all of your ills: third of three parts). *Gaceta Universitaria de la UACJ.* 14(120) 12, University Autonomous of Ciudad Juarez (Mexico). [Online] http://eprints.rclis.org/view/people/Muela-Meza,_Zapopan_Mart=n.html . [Accessed 24 February 2007].

Muela-Meza, Z.M. (2001a). "Impulsemos en serio el desarrollo de las bibliotecas públicas mexicanas." (Let us really promote the development of the Mexican public libraries). In: *Proceedings of the First Mexican National Congress of Public Libraries and Documental Centres: Future and Perspectives of Library and Information Services.* Saltillo, Coahuila, Mexico. [Online] http://eprints.rclis.org/view/people/Muela-Meza,_Zapopan_Mart=n.html . [Accessed 24 February 2007].

Muela-Meza, Z.M. (2001b). "Let us really promote the development of the Mexican public libraries." *Library Juice,* **4** (25). [Online] http://eprints.rclis.org/view/people/Muela-Meza,_Zapopan_Mart=n.html . [Accessed 24 February 2007].

Muela-Meza, Z.M. (2001c). "Ley de acceso a la información pública, bibliotecarios y archivistas (Mexican freedom of information act, librarians and archivists)." *El Heraldo de Chihuahua* (3 August 2001), Organización Editorial Mexicana (OEM). [Online] http://eprints.rclis.org/archive/00003599/02/informationact.pdf . [Accessed 24 February 2007].

Muela-Meza, Z.M. (2002a). "¿Dónde quedaron los administradores del acceso a la información en la nueva Ley de Acceso a la Información?" ("Why have the information access experts been left out from the debate of the new Mexican Freedom of Information Act"). In *Proceedings Foros de Consulta Popular Sobre el Derecho al Acceso a la Información*, Monterrey, Nuevo León (Mexico). [Online] http://eprints.rclis.org/view/people/Muela-Meza,_Zapopan_Mart=n.html . [Accessed 24 February 2007].

Muela-Meza, Z.M. (2002b). "Estrategias para construir un nuevo paradigma de recursos humanos en las bibliotecas públicas mexicanas." (Strategies to build a new paradigm of human resources in Mexican public libraries). In *Proceedings of the Second Mexican National Congress of Public Libraries: Strategies and Projects for Development.* Guadalajara, Jalisco, Mexico, pp. 168-172. [Online] http://eprints.rclis.org/view/people/Muela-Meza,_Zapopan_Mart=n.html . [Accessed 24 February 2007].

Muela-Meza, Z.M. (2003-2007). *Master File Compilation of Maps, Pictures and other Documents Related to Broomhall, Sheffield, UK for the Author's PhD Research Project.* Sheffield, UK: Personal file of the author. [Online] http://picasaweb.google.com/zapopanmuela . [or] http://broomhallgateway.googlepages.com/ . [Accessed 17 May 2007].

Muela-Meza, Z.M. (2003a). "An introduction to the applicability of qualitative research methodologies to the field of Library and Information Sciences." unpublished paper. [Online, preprint version] http://eprints.rclis.org/archive/00008489/ . [18 January 2007]. For a postprint version of this paper see: Muela-Meza, Z. M. (2006b). "Una introducción a las metodologías de investigación cualitativa aplicadas a la bibliotecología." ("An introduction to the qualitative research methodologies applied to librarianship."). *BiblioDocencia : Revista de Profesores de Bibliotecología (Library Teaching: Journal of Librarianship Professors),* **2** (12), 4-12. [Online] http://eprints.rclis.org/archive/00006732/ . [Accessed 28 July 2006].

Muela-Meza, Z.M. (2003b). "Un acercamiento a las barreras políticas en las bibliotecas públicas mexicanas. (An approximation to the political barriers in the Mexican public libraries)." In *Proceedings Third Mexican National Congress of Public Libraries: "Celebrating the 20 Years of the Mexican National Network of Public Libraries."* Durango, Durango, México. [Online] http://eprints.rclis.org/view/people/Muela-Meza,_Zapopan_Mart=n.html . [Accessed 24 February 2007].

Muela-Meza, Z.M. (2004a). "Liberación de la información como condición de la liberación del acceso a la información. (Liberation of information as a condition for the liberation of the access to information)." In *Proceedings of the First Social Forum of Information, Documentation, and Libraries." Programs of Alternative Action from Latin America towards the Society of Knowledge."* Buenos Aires, Argentina, August 2004. http://eprints.rclis.org/archive/00003623/ [Accessed 14 March 2005].

Muela-Meza, Z.M. (2004b). "Una introducción a la crítica de los desafíos teóricos y prácticos que

enfrentan los integrantes de los repositorios públicos de conocimiento en el fenómeno de la
Sociedad de la Información (An Introduction to the critique of the theoretical and practical
challenges which face the stakeholders of the repositories of public knowledge in the phenomenon
of the Information Society)." *Pez de Plata, Bibliotecas Públicas a la Vanguardia. Revista de
Opinión para el Desarrollo de las Bibliotecas Públicas. (Pez de Plata –Silver Fish– Chilean Peer
Reviewed Journal for the Development of Public Libraries)*, **1** (2), 1-45. [Online]
http://eprints.rclis.org/archive/00003577 [Accessed 24 September 2004].

Muela-Meza, Z.M. (2005c). "La era del Estado empresarial versus el dominio público informacional
y cognitivo." ("The age of the corporate State versus the informational and cognitive public
domain"). *Razón y Palabra: Primera Revista Electrónica en América Latina Especializada en
Tópicos de Comunicación.* (44), April-May. [En línea] http://eprints.rclis.org/archive/00003658/ .
[Accesed 12 July 2005].

Muela-Meza, Z.M. (2005a). "A community profile of the Broomhall community of Sheffield, UK."
Delivered at *Presentation given as a requirement to upgrade from the Master of Philosophy
student to the Doctor of Philosophy Degree student status. MPhil/PhD, Department of
Information Studies, University of Sheffield.* Sheffield, UK: Department of Information Studies,
University of Sheffield. [Online] http://eprints.rclis.org/archive/00004870/ . [Accessed 31 October
2005].

Muela-Meza, Z.M. (2005b) "Information needed to cope with crisis in the lives of individuals and
communities: an assessment of the roles public libraries and voluntary sector agencies play in the
provision of such information." *Information for Social Change.* (21), 13-26. [Online]
http://eprints.rclis.org/archive/00003616/ [Accessed 30 August 2005].

Muela-Meza, Z.M. (2006a). "Por una crítica al copyright y al rol de policías del copyright de los
bibliotecarios. (For a critique to copyright and police role of copyright librarians)." Paper presented
in the *Second Social Forum of Information, Documentation, and Libraries*, held at the Instituto de
Investigaciones Antropológicas de la Universidad Nacional Autónoma de México (UNAM)
(Institute of Anthropological Research of the Mexico National Autonomous University (UNAM)),
Mexico City, Mexico, 7 and 8 September. [Online] http://eprints.rclis.org/archive/00006986/ .
[Accesed 30 August 2006].

Muela-Meza, Z.M. (2006b). "Una introducción a las metodologías de investigación cualitativa
aplicadas a la bibliotecología (An introduction to the applicability of qualitative research
methodologies to the library and information science field)." *BiblioDocencia: Revista de Profesores
de Bibliotecología (Library-Teaching: Journal of Professors in Library and Information Science)*,
2 (12) 4-12. [Online] http://eprints.rclis.org/archive/00006732/ . [Accessed 27 July 2006].

Muela-Meza, Z.M. (2007). "Contradicciones eticas de las responsabilidades sociales de la
bibliotecologia. (Ethical contradictions of the social responsibilities of Library and Information
Science)." In: Gimeno Perelló, J., López López, P. & Morillo Calero, M.J. (Coords). *De Volcanes
Llena: Biblioteca y Compromiso Social (Full of Volcanoes: Library and Social Compromise).*
Gijón, Asturias, Spain: Trea, pp. 417-444. [Online] http://eprints.rclis.org/archive/00007942/ .
[Accessed 14 November 2006].

Muela-Meza, Z.M. (2008). "Introducción al pensamiento crítico y escéptico en las ciencias de la
información documental" (An Introduction to the critical and sceptical thinking in the sciences of
information recorded in documents)." *Crítica Bibliotecológica: Revista de las Ciencias de la
Información Documental (Library & Information Science Critique: Journal of the Sciences of
Information Recorded in Documents)*, **1** (1), 14-41. [Online]
http://critica.bibliotecologica.googlepages.com. [Accessed 30 November 2008].

Murray, R. (2002). *How to Write a Thesis*. Maidenhead, Berkshire, UK; Philadelphia,
USA: Open University Press.

NHS Sheffield PCT. (2006). *Sheffield Director of Public Health Report 2006*. Sheffield,

UK: NHS Sheffield PCT. [Online]
http://www.publichealthsheffield2006.nhs.uk/resources/ . [Accessed 17 January 2007].

Nicholas, D. (2000). *Assessing Information Needs: Tools, Techniques and Concepts for the Internet Age. 2nd ed.* London: Aslib, The Association for Information Management.

North West Museums Service. (2002). "Community Profiling: Guidance Notes." Cheshire, UK: Regeneris Consulting. [Online]
http://www.inspiringlearningforall.gov.uk/uploads/Community%20Profiling%20Guidan.pdf .
[Accessed 21 October 2004].

Odom, R.W. (1926). *Hallamshire Worthies.* Sheffield, UK: JW Northend.

Office for National Statistics. (2006). *National Statistics: Neighbourhood Statistics.* Newport, UK: Office for National Statistics. [Online] http://neighbourhood.statistics.gov.uk/dissemination/ . [Accessed 7 August 2006].

Olive, M. (2002). *A Short History of Sheffield.* Sheffield, UK: Sheffield City Council, Libraries, Archives and Information, Sheffield Central Public Library, Sheffield Local Studies Library. [Available at the Sheffield Central Public Library].

Oliver, P. (2004). *Writing your Thesis.* London; Thousand Oaks, Calif.; New Delhi: Sage Publication.

Ordnance Survey. (1849-1899). *Map of Derbyshire and Yorkshire, 1st ed. 1849-1899.* Edinburgh: Digimap, Edina, University of Edinburgh, [Mapped Extent: 432414, 385152-435035, 387772; Map Series: County Series 1:10560 1846-1969; Counties in view: Derbyshire, Yorkshire; Published dates:1855 – 1895]. [Online through Digimap geographical information system (GIS) Edina through the University of Sheffield Libraries] [Accessed 10 January 2006].

Orwell, G. ([1937], 1962). *The Road To Wigan Pier.* Harmondsworth : Penguin / Secker and Warburg.

Oxford University Press. (2004). *Concise Oxford English Dictionary, 11th Edition.* Oxford: Oxford University Press; Focus Multimedia [CD-ROM].

Pateman, J. (2000). "Public libraries and social class." In: Muddiman, D. (et. al). (2000b). *Open To All? : The Public Library And Social Exclusion. Vol.3. Working Papers.* London: Resource (Library and Information Commission research report 86).

Pateman, J. (2006). "Social exclusion to community cohesion." *Library and Information Update,* **5** (3), 41-43.

Patton, M.Q. (1990). *Qualitative Evaluation and Research Methods.* Newbury Park, CA: Sage. Cited in: Linley, R. And Usherwood, B. (1998). *New Measures for the New Library: A Social Audit for Public Libraries.* Sheffield, U.K.: The University of Sheffield; DIS/CPLIS (British Library Research & Innovation Centre Report 89).

Payne, H. & Littlechild, B. (Eds). (1999). *Ethical Power and the Abuse of Power in Social Responsibility: Leave no Stone Unturned.* London: J. Kingsley.

Penrose, R. (2004). *The Road to Reality: A Complete Guide to the Physical Universe.* Chatham, Kent, UK: BCA.

Penzhorn, C. (2002). "The use of participatory research as an alternative approach for information needs research." *Aslib Proceedings,* **54**, (4), 240-250.

Petit, M. (1998). "From libraries to citizenship: study on young users in low-income neighbourhoods of French cities." *64th IFLA General Conference,* Amsterdam, August 16-21, 1998.

[Online] http://www.ifla.org/IV/ifla64/078-155e.htm . [Accessed 7 July 2005].

Policy Research Institute. (2004). *Compass for MS-Windows. The Community Profiling Software.*
Leeds, UK: Leeds Metropolitan University, Policy Research Institute. [CD-ROM, demo version].

Putnam, R. (1999). *Bowling Alone.* New York: Simon & Shuster.

Quinn, C., (et. al). (2008). "The experience of providing care in the early stages of dementia: An
interpretative phenomenological analysis." *Aging & Mental Health,* **12** (6), 769-768.

Radnedge, A. (2006). "You are not regenerating my house." *Metro (of London),* 28 September, p.
21.

Reale, G & Antiseri, D. (2004a). *Historia del Pensamiento Filosófico y Científico. Tomo Primero.
Antiguedad y Edad Media (History of the Philosophical and Scientific Thought. Ancient times and
Middle Ages. Vol. I).* 3rd ed. Barcelona: Herder.

Reale, G & Antiseri, D. (2004b). *Historia del Pensamiento Filosófico y Científico. Tomo Tercero.
Del Romanticismo hasta Hoy (History of the Philosophical and Scientific Thought. From
Romanticism until Today. Vol. 3).* 3rd ed. Barcelona: Herder.

Rendón Rojas, M.A. (2005). *Bases Teóricas y Filosóficas de la Bibliotecología. 2ª ed. (Theoretical
and Philosophical Foundations in Library and Information Science,* 2nd ed.*).* Mexico: UNAM,
Centro Universitario de Investigaciones Bibliotecológicas (Sistemas Bibliotecarios de Información y
Sociedad) (Mexico National Autonomous University, University Library and Information Science
Research Centre (Series: Library and Information Science Systems and Society).

Revill, J. (2005). "Letter to *Broomhall News." Broomhall News.* September 2005, (38).

Rice-Lively, M.L. (1997). "Recording fieldwork data in information organizations." In: Gorman,
G.E. & Clayton, P. (1997). *Qualitative Research for the Information Professional: A Practical
Handbook.* London: Library Association Publishing, pp. 177-197.

Rikowski, G. (2002). "Marxist educational theory after postmodernism." In: Hill, D. (et. al).
Marxism against Postmodernism in Education Theory. Lanham, MD, USA: Lexignton Books, pp.
16-32.

Rikowski, R. (2007). "Globalización, bibliotecas, información y compromiso social (Globalization,
libraries, information, and social commitment)." In: Gimeno Perelló, J., López López, P. & Morillo
Calero, M.J. (Coords). (2007). *De Volcanes Llena: Biblioteca y Compromiso Social (Full of
Volcanoes: Library and Social Compromise).* Gijón, Asturias, Spain: Trea, pp. 159-212.

Rizq, R. & Target, M. (2009). "'The power of being seen:' An interpretative phenomenological
analysis of how experienced counselling psychologists describe the meaning and significance of
personal therapy in clinical practice." *Counselling Psychology Review,* **24** (3 & 4), 66-85.

Roddy, K. (2005). "Community profiling." *Library and Information Update,* **4** (5), 40-41.

Rogers, A. (2003). "Knowing your patch." In: Rogers, A., Smith, M.K. & Winstanley, L. (2003).
Approaching Community. Foundation Studies Unit 4 . London: YMCA George Williams College.
[Online] http://www.ymca.ac.uk/fs/support/approaching_community_pdf.pdf . [Accessed 23
December 2004].

Rogers, A., Smith, M.K. & Winstanley, L. (2003). *Approaching Community. Foundation Studies
Unit 4 .* London: YMCA George Williams College. [Online]
http://www.ymca.ac.uk/fs/support/approaching_community_pdf.pdf . [Accessed 23 December
2004].

Rugg, G. & Petre, M. (2004). *The Unwritten Rules of PhD Research.* Berkshire, UK; NY: Open

University Press.

Sagan, C. & A. Druyan. (1992). *Shadows Of Forgotten Ancestors: A Search For Who We Are.* London: BCA.

Sagan, C. (2001). *Cosmos.* Barcelona: Planeta

Sagan, C. (1980). *Broca's Brain: Reflections on the Romance of Science.* New York: Ballantine Books.

Sagan, C. (1997). *El Mundo y sus Demonios: La Ciencia como una Luz en la Oscuridad : (The Demon-Haunted World: Science as a Candle in the Dark).* Mexico; Barcelona: Editorial Planeta.

Sagan, C. (1978). *The Dragons of Eden: Speculations on the Evolution of Human Intelligence.* Nueva York: Ballantine Books.

Sametz de Walerstein, L. (1991). *Vasconcelos el Hombre del Libro: La Epoca de Oro de las Bibliotecas (Vasconcelos the Man of the Book: The Golden Era of Libraries).* Mexico: Universidad Nacional Autonoma de Mexico; Instituto de Investigaciones Bibliograficas (Mexico National Autonomous University; Institute of Bibliographic Research).

Sander Villarino, S. (1992). "¿Qué es la biblioteca? (What is the library?)." In: Morales Campos, E. & Ramírez Leiva, E. (coords) (1992). *Edición Conmemorativa del X Aniversario del Centro Universitario de Investigaciones Bibliotecológicas. Vol. 1. En Torno a la Investigación Bibliotecológica (Commemorative Edition of the 10th Anniversary of the University Centre of Library and Information Science Research. Vol. 1. About the LIS Research).* Mexico: Mexico, SEP, Consejo Nacional para la Cultura y las Artes; UNAM, Dirección General de Bibliotecas, Centro Universitario de Investigaciones Bibliotecológicas (Mexico, Ministry of Public Education, National Council for Culture and Arts; Mexico National Autonomous University, General Directorate of Libraries, University Library and Information Science Research Centre), pp. 33-42.

Saquilán, V.M. (2005). *Estudio acerca de las Representaciones Sociales del Rol del Bibliotecario en Usuarios de la Biblioteca Central de la Universidad Nacional Mar del Plata (Study about the Social Representations of the Role of Librarians in Users of the Central Library at the National University Mar del Plata).* Mar del Plata, Argentina: Department of Documentation, Faculty of Humanities, National University of Mar del Plata [Undergraduate Dissertation in Documentation].

Sarling, J. H. & Van Tassel, D.S. (1999). "Community analysis: research that matters to a North-Central Denver community." *Library and Information Science Research,* **21** (1), 7-29.

Satyanarayana, M. (1997). *Public Library and Community Analysis.* New Delhi, India: Reliance Publishing House; Dr. S.K.Bhatia.

Schiller, H.I. (1996). *Information Inequality: the Deepening Social Crisis in America.* New York; London: Routledge.

Senior, J. (1872). *Owd Shevvild and its Celebrities,* 2nd ed. Sheffield, UK: J. Morton, Cambridge Street.

Sheffield City Council. (2005). *Sheffield Neighbourhoods Information System.* Sheffield, UK: Sheffield City Council. [Online] http://www.sheffield.gov.uk/EasySite/lib/serveDocument.asp?doc=99207&pgid=112589 . [Accessed 07 June 2007].

Sheffield City Council. (2006a). *Broomhall Local Centre Masterplan.* Sheffield, UK: Sheffield City Council. [Online] http://www.sheffield.gov.uk/your-city-council/council-meetings/cabinet/agendas-2006/agenda-11th-october/broomhall-centre-masterplan . [Accessed 07 October 2006]/

Sheffield City Council. (2006b). *Sheffield's City Council Community Profiling Project*. Sheffield, UK: Sheffield City Council. [Online] http://www.sheffield.gov.uk/index.asp?pgid=66035 . [Accessed 15 October 2006].

Sheffield City Council. (2007a). *Broomhall Conservation Area Appraisal, Consultation Draft, June*. Sheffield, UK: Urban Design and Conservation Team; Forward and Area Planning Team.

Sheffield City Council. (2007b). *Broomhall Conservation Area Management Proposals, Consultation Draft, June*. Sheffield, UK: Urban Design and Conservation Team; Forward and Area Planning Team.

Sheffield Corporation. (1974). *Broomhall Conservation Area*. Sheffield, UK: Town Planning. [Map available at Sheffield City Council Central Library, Surrey Street, Sheffield 1].

Sheffield Hallam University Alumni Association. (2003). "Health and social care. Flagship development for the school." *Hallmark. The Magazine for Former Students of Sheffield Hallam University*. [Online] http://www.shu.ac.uk/alumni/hallmark/16/16.pdf . [Accessed 21 April 2004].

Silverman, D. (2005). *Doing Qualitative Research: A Practical Handbook*. 2nd edition. London: Sage Publications.

Silverman, D. (2000). *Doing Qualitative Research: A Practical Handbook*. 1st edition. London: Sage Publications.

Smith, G. (2002). "Community research: a practitioner's perspective on methods and values." *Journal of Community Work and Development*. [Online], **1** (3), 31-48. http://homepages.uel.ac.uk/G.Smith/communityresearch.pdf. [Accessed 15 November 2003].

Smith, J.A. (2004). "Reflecting on the development of interpretative phenomenological analysis and its contribution to qualitative research in psychology." *Qualitative Research in Psychology*, **1**, 39-54.

Sokal, A. y Bricmont, J. (1999). *Imposturas Intelectuales (Intellectual Impostures)*. Barcelona: Ediciones Paidós Ibérica.

South Yorkshire Community Foundation. (2004). *2003 Yearbook*. Sheffield, UK: South Yorkshire Community Foundation.

Standing, M. (2009). "A new critical framework for applying hermeneutic phenomenology." *Nurse Researcher,* **16** (4), 20-30.

Star (Sheffield). (2002a). "Intimidation claim over flats." *Star (Sheffield)*, 15 May. [Online] http://www.sheffieldtoday.net . [Accessed 03 February 2004].

Star (Sheffield). (2002b). "YMCA settles down to changing role in city." *Star (Sheffield)*, 11 October.

Star (Sheffield). (2003). "Outrage as far-right party targets school." *Star (Sheffield)*, 10 February. [Online] http://www.thestar.co.uk/ViewArticle.aspx?SectionID=58&ArticleID=236661 . [Accessed 20 March 2004].

Star (Sheffield). (2004a). "Lecturer 53 robbed at knifepoint." *Star (Sheffield)*, 20 September. [Online] http://www.thestar.co.uk/template/ViewArticle.aspx?SectionID=58&articleid=858367 . [Accessed 21 September 2004].

Star (Sheffield). (2004b). *"Families fight flats increase." Star (Sheffield). October 28, p. 13.*

Star (Sheffield). (2004c). "Flats fall riddle." *Star (Sheffield)*, December 22. [Online] http://www.thestar.co.uk/viewarticle.aspx?sectionid=58&articleid=909372 . [Accessed 22 December 2004].

Star (Sheffield). (2004d). "Householder collapsed in burning flat." *Star (Sheffield)*, 05 May. [Online] http://www.thestar.co.uk/template/ViewArticle.aspx?SectionID=58&articleid=785368 . [Accessed 05 May 2004].

Star (Sheffield). (2004e). "Parents fear nursery will be shut by staff." *Star (Sheffield)*, 20 May. [Online] http://www.thestar.co.uk/ViewArticle.aspx?SectionID=58&articleid=793986 . [Accessed 17 September 2004].

Star (Sheffield). (2004f). "Parking scheme aims to relieve congestion." Star (Sheffield). September 17 [Online] http://www.sheffieldtoday.net/ViewArticle2.aspx?SectionID=58&ArticleID=857382 . [Accessed 17 September 2004].

Star (Sheffield). (2004g)."Sheffield teachers face sack." *Star (Sheffield)*. 26 March. [Online] http://www.sheffieldtoday.net/ViewArticle2.aspx?SectionID=58&ArticleID=763799 [Accessed 26 March 2004].

Star (Sheffield). (2005a). "Danger patient pleaded for help." *Star (Sheffield)*. March 24. [Online] http://www.sheffieldtoday.net/ViewArticle2.aspx?SectionID=58&ArticleID=980780 . [Accessed 24 March 2005].

Star (Sheffield). (2005b). "School's fury over British National Party propaganda." *Star (Sheffield)*, 12 January. [Online] http://www.sheffieldtoday.net/ViewArticle.aspx?SectionID=58&articleid=918092 . [Accessed 12 January 2005].

Star (Sheffield). (2005c). "School's joy over rating." *Star (Sheffield)*, 29 December. [Online] http://www.thestar.co.uk/template/ViewArticle.aspx?SectionID=58&articleid=1297555 . [Accessed 29 December 2005].

Star (Sheffield). (2005d)." Tobacco and alcohol abuse issues." *Star (Sheffield)*, 24 October.

Star (Sheffield). (2005e)."Recruiting carers is a problem says charity." *Star (Sheffield)*, April 13. [Online] http://www.sheffieldtoday.net/ViewArticle2.aspx?SectionID=58&ArticleID=996962 . [Accessed 13 April 2005].

Star (Sheffield). (2006a). "Knifepoint ordeal putting out bin." *Star (Sheffield)*, 11 August. [Online] http://www.thestar.co.uk/template/ViewArticle.aspx?SectionID=58&articleid=1689706 . [Accessed 11 August 2006].

Star (Sheffield). (2006b). *"Staff thought drinker 'was sleeping it off'."* *Star (Sheffield)*, 21 August. *[Online] http://www.thestar.co.uk/template/ViewArticle.aspx?SectionID=58&articleid=1709480 . [Accessed 22 August 2006].*

Star (Sheffield). (2006c). "Centres of attention for youngsters." *Star (Sheffield)*, 28 January. [Online] http://www.thestar.co.uk/template/ViewArticle.aspx?SectionID=58&articleid=1331462 . [Accessed 28 January 2006].

Star (Sheffield). (2006d). "Fury as British National Party wins votes in four suburbs." *Star (Sheffield)*, 05 May. [Online] http://www.sheffieldtoday.net/ViewArticle.aspx?SectionID=58&articleid=1484817 . [Accessed 05 May 2006].

Star (Sheffield). (2006e). "Hoodie gang killed my mum." *Star (Sheffield),* 14 December. [Online]
http://www.thestar.co.uk/template/ViewArticle.aspx?SectionID=58&articleid=1929368 .
[Accessed 14 December 2006].

Star (Sheffield). (2006f). "Noise row pub couple hit back." *Star (Sheffield),* 11 October 2006.
[Online] http://www.thestar.co.uk/template/ViewArticle.aspx?SectionID=58&articleid=1814729 .
[Accessed 11 October 2006].

Star (Sheffield). (2007a). "Architects working on two-campus university." *Star (Sheffield),* 09 May.
[Online] http://www.thestar.co.uk/template/ViewArticle.aspx?SectionID=60&articleid=2860815 .
[Accessed 09 May 2007].

Star (Sheffield). (2007b). "Centre reopens after citizenship tests raid." *Star (Sheffield),* 23 April.
[Online] http://www.sheffieldtoday.net/ViewArticle.aspx?SectionID=58&articleid=2721800 .
[Accessed 23 April 2007].

Star (Sheffield). (2007c). "People must get to city more easily. No car, no go..." *Star (Sheffield),* 12
February. [Online]
http://www.thestar.co.uk/template/ViewArticle.aspx?SectionID=2249&articleid=2042690 .
[Accessed 12 February 2007].

Star (Sheffield). (2007d). "Two held over gun attack." *The Sheffield Star (Sheffield),* 24 May.
[Online] http://www.thestar.co.uk/template/ViewArticle.aspx?SectionID=5730&articleid=2901773
. [Accessed 24 May 2007].

Stilwell, C., Leach, A. & Burton, S. (Eds.). (2001). *Knowledge, Information and Development: an
African Perspective.* Natal, South Africa: School of Human and Social Studies, University of Natal
(Pietermaritzburg) (Series: Research Series No. 1).

Stone, S. (1985). *Community Profiling.* Sheffield, UK: University of Sheffield, Centre for Research
on User Studies; British Library Board (Series: CRUS Guide No. 9).

Story, A., Darch, C. y Halbert, D. (Eds.) (2006). *The Copy/South Dossier : Issues in the Economics,
Politics, and Ideology of Copyright in the Global South.* Canterbury, Kent, UK: Copy/South
Research Group. [Online] http://www.copysouth.org or
http://eprints.rclis.org/archive/00006278/ . [Accessed 19 May 2006].

Strauss, A.L. & Corbin, J.M. (1990). *Basics of Qualitative Research : Grounded Theory Procedures
And Techniques.* Newbury Park, California, USA: Sage Publications.

Student Residences Strategy Team. (2004). *The University of Sheffield's Student Residences
Strategy: A Vision for the Future.* Sheffield, UK: Student Residences Strategy Team.

Swain, H. (Ed.). (2003). *Big Questions in Science.* London: Vintage.

SYPTA. (2004). *Supertram Extensions, Broomhill Area Proposals.* Sheffield: South Yorkshire
Passenger Transport Executive.

Thorpe, S. (2001). *Cómo Pensar como Einstein. Maneras Simples de Resolver Problemas
Imposibles (How to Think like Einstein. Simple Ways to Break the Rules and Discover your
Hidden Genius).* Bogota, Colombia: Grupo Editorial Norma.

Usherwood, B. (1989). *The Public Library as Public Knowledge.* London: Library Association.

Usherwood, B. (1992). "Community information." In: Kinnell, M. (Ed.) (1992). *Informing
Communities: The Role of Libraries and Information Services.* Newcastle, UK: CSG Publishing, pp.
17-40.

Usherwood, B., Wilson, K. & Bryson, J. (2005). "Relevant repositories of public knowledge?

Libraries, museums and archives in the 'information age'." *Journal of Librarianship and Information Science,* **37** (2), 89-98.

Valencia García, G., de la Garza Toledo, E. & Zemelman Merino, H. (2002). *Epistemología y Sujetos: Algunas Contribuciones al Debate (Epistemology and Subjects: Some Contributions to the Debate).* México: UNAM; Plaza y Valdés. [Online]. http://docencia.izt.uam.mx/egt/publicaciones/capituloslibros/index.htm . [Accessed 28 May 2006].

Vickers, J.E. (1990). *Saving our Heritage: A History of the First Twenty Years of the Hallamshire Historic Buildings Society.* Sheffield, UK: JEV Publications.

Vincent, J.(1986). *An Introduction To Community Librarianship.* London: Association of Assistant Librarians.

von Baeyer, H.C. (2004). *Information. The New Language of Science.* London: Phoenix.

Warman, C.R. (1969). *Sheffield: Emerging City.* Sheffield, UK: City Council, Town Planning Committee; The City Engineer and Surveyor and Town Planning Officer; City of Sheffield Printing Department.

Warwickshire County Library. (1991). *Community Profile of Bedworth.* Warwick, UK: Warwickshire County Library.

Wengraf, T. (2001). *Qualitative Research Interviewing : Biographic Narrative And Semi-Structured Methods.* London; Thousand Oaks, Calif; New Delhi: SAGE Publications.

Westbrook, L. (1994). "Qualitative research methods: a review of major stages, data analysis techniques, and quality controls." *Library and Information Science Research,* **16**, 241-254.

Westbrook, L. (2000). "Analysing community information needs: a holistic approach." *Library Administration and Management,* **14** (1), 26-30. [Online] http://wilsontxt.hwwilson.com/pdfhtml/01879/2qh9a/bs0.htm. [Accessed 23 December 2004].

Westbrook, L. (2001). "Understanding faculty information needs in a special education setting: method and results of a community analysis." *Knowledge Quest,* **30**, (2), 39-42.

Wheeler, J.L. & Goldhor, H. ([1962], 1970). *Administracion Practica de Bibliotecas Publicas (Practical Management of Public Libraries).* Mexico: Fondo de Cultura Economica (Low-price Culture Collection).

Whitehead, J. & Rowan, T. (2005). *Know your Community: A Best Practice Guide for Public Libraries.* London: Museums, Libraries and Archives (MLA).

Williamson, K., Schauder, D. & Bow, A. (2000). "Information seeking by blind and sight impaired citizens: an ecological study." *Information Research,* **5**, (4). [Online] http://informationr.net/ir/4-3/paper59.html . [Accessed 15 November 2003].

Wilson, T.D. (1981). "On user studies and information needs." *Journal of Documentation.* 37, 3-15.

Wilson, T.D. (1994). "Information needs and uses: fifty years of progress?" In: Vickery, B.C. (Ed.). *Fifty years of information progress: a Journal of Documentation review.* London: Aslib, pp. 15-51. [Online] http://informationr.net/tdw/publ/papers/1994FiftyYears.html . [Accessed 25 April 2005].

Worcester, L. & Westbrook, L. (2004). "Ways of knowing: Community Information-Needs Analysis." *Texas Library Journal,* **80** (3), 102-107.

APPENDICES

Appendix 1. Invitation letter to residents or information providers of Broomhall to take part in this PhD research project

Sheffield [Date]
[Organisation; Institution, if any]
[Address, if available] [Name of resident/information provider]

Re: **BROOMHALL: INVITATION TO TAKE PART IN A RESEARCH PROJECT**

Dear [surname of prospective interviewee],

I am a research student in the Department of Information Studies at the University of Sheffield doing doctoral research into the information needs of and issues being faced by the residents of Broomhall and the roles of information providers regarding these needs and issues. I am not a member of staff of this university, or of any political party, company, or any private or public organisation. My research is completely academic and only for the sake of fostering the public knowledge in an independent, critical and rigorous way. It is my hope that from its results the quality of life of the residents from these communities may be improved and public policy may be informed. I am conducting a series of interviews in this community. I became aware of you by a reference from [name of other resident/information provider; if known], and through my literature review and a pilot project I have conducted from 2003 to 2004 [if this is the case], and as part of my research I would very much like to hear your opinions. Could you help me with this community research? If you can, I would like to arrange an appointment with you as soon as possible to carry it out. These interviews are simply an opportunity for me to ask you a few questions, and then listen to your opinions. Your answers will provide the raw material for my research. The answers will be completely anonymous and no one's responses will be identified personally. I hope you will share your opinions openly and honestly.

The meeting is informal, and will last no more than an hour.

I need your help and I hope you will take part. Please contact me if you can take part and if you would like any more information.

May I thank you in anticipation of your cooperation.

Mr. Zapopan Martín Muela-Meza, PhD Student
Department of Information Studies, University of Sheffield
Tel: (0114) 222 63 43
Fax: (0114) 278 0300
E-mail: Zapopan.muela@sheffield.ac.uk
E-mail: zapopanmuela@gmail.com
Web: http://www.shef.ac.uk/is/research/phd.html

Letter created by the author and approved on 30.08.2005 by my supervisors: Professor Nigel Ford, n.ford@sheffield.ac.uk, Tel: (0114) 2222637 and Briony Train, Lecturer, b.train@sheffield.ac.uk, Tel: 0114 2222653, the Department of Information Studies Research Committee, and the University of Sheffield Ethical Committee.

Appendix 2. Guide for individual and focus groups interviews to Broomhall residents (non prompted)

Instrument:	**Guide for individual and focus groups interviews to Broomhall residents (prompted; this guide was not given to respondents and was withheld from their sight during the interview to avoid bias; the prompts were only used to encourage the respondent to talk, sometimes they were used, sometimes they were not)**
Designed by:	Zapopan Martín Muela-Meza, PhD candidate, Department of Information Studies, University of Sheffield. Final version 30 August 2005.
Project:	*An Application of Community Profiling to Analyse the Information Needs and the Community Issues Affecting the People in Broomhall, Sheffield, and to Evaluate the Roles of their Information Providers http://www.shef.ac.uk/is/research/phd.html*
Supervisors:	Professor Nigel Ford and Briony Train, Lecturer

Ethical Note:

Dear respondent,

May I remind you an ethical note from the letter I sent you before: the answers will be completely anonymous and no one's responses will be identified personally or disclosed to any third parties. I hope you will share your opinions openly and honestly.

Questions:

1. What are the major features which describe the Broomhall community?
2. What do you think is the best and the worst thing about living in this community?
3. What are and have been the major needs, or issues or concerns you experience, or face in the community?
4. Where do you go to find facts to have a better understanding, or to find solutions to your needs, or issues, or concerns?
5. How well your needs are satisfied or your issues or concerns are alleviated from the people or institutions you sought for help?
6. What has worked and what hasn't worked and why?
7. Is there anything else you would like to add?

May I thank you in anticipation of your cooperation.

Mr. Zapopan Martín Muela-Meza
PhD Student
Department of Information Studies
University of Sheffield
Tel: (0114) 222 63 43
Fax: (0114) 278 0300
E-mail: Zapopan.muela@sheffield.ac.uk
E-mail: zapopanmuela@gmail.com
Web: http://www.shef.ac.uk/is/research/phd.html

Instrument approved on 30.08.2005 by my supervisors: Professor Nigel Ford, n.ford@sheffield.ac.uk, Tel: (0114) 2222637 and Briony Train, Lecturer, b.train@sheffield.ac.uk, Tel: 0114 2222653, the Department of Information Studies Research Committee, and the University of Sheffield Ethical Committee.

Appendix 3. Guide for individual interviews to Broomhall information providers (non prompted)

Instrument:	**Guide to interview Broomhall information providers (non prompted)**
Designed by:	Zapopan Martín Muela-Meza, PhD candidate, Department of Information Studies, University of Sheffield. Final version 30 August 2005.
Project:	*An Application of Community Profiling to Analyse the Information Needs and the Community Issues Affecting the People in Broomhall, Sheffield, and to Evaluate the Roles of their Information Providers* *http://www.shef.ac.uk/is/research/phd.html*
Supervisors:	Professor Nigel Ford and Briony Train, Lecturer

Ethical Note:

Dear respondent,

May I remind you an ethical note from the letter I sent you before. The answers will be completely anonymous and no one's responses will be identified personally or disclosed to any third parties. I hope you will share your opinions openly and honestly.

Questions:

1. What are the major features which describe the Broomhall community you (or your organisation/institution) serve?
2. What do you think is the best and the worst thing for the people living in this community?
3. What are and have been the major needs, or issues or concerns you think people experience, or face in the community?
4. How do you (or does your organisation/institution) contribute with those people to find facts, or to have better understanding, or to find solutions to their needs, or issues, or concerns?
5. How well their needs are satisfied or their issues alleviated with your help (or with the help from your organisation/institution) when they have sought you (them) for help?
6. What has worked and what hasn't worked and why?
7. Is there anything else you would like to add?

May I thank you in anticipation of your cooperation.

Mr. Zapopan Martín Muela-Meza
PhD Student
Department of Information Studies
University of Sheffield
Tel: (0114) 222 63 43
Fax: (0114) 278 0300
E-mail: Zapopan.muela@sheffield.ac.uk
E-mail: zapopanmuela@gmail.com
Web: http://www.shef.ac.uk/is/research/phd.html

Instrument approved on 30.08.2005 by my supervisors: Professor Nigel Ford, n.ford@sheffield.ac.uk, Tel: (0114) 2222637 and Briony Train, Lecturer, b.train@sheffield.ac.uk, Tel: 0114 2222653, the Department of Information Studies Research Committee, and the University of Sheffield Ethical Committee.

Appendix 4. Guide for individual and focus groups interviews to Broomhall residents (prompted)

Instrument:	**Guide for individual and focus groups interviews to Broomhall residents (prompted; this guide was not given to respondents and was withheld from their sight during the interview to avoid bias; the prompts were only used to encourage the respondent to talk, sometimes they were used, sometimes they were not)**
Designed by:	Zapopan Martín Muela-Meza, PhD candidate, Department of Information Studies, University of Sheffield. Final version 30 August 2005.
Project:	*An Application of Community Profiling to Analyse the Information Needs and the Community Issues Affecting the People in Broomhall, Sheffield, and to Evaluate the Roles of their Information Providers* *http://www.shef.ac.uk/is/research/phd.html*
Supervisors:	Professor Nigel Ford and Briony Train, Lecturer

Ethical Note:

Dear respondent,

May I remind you an ethical note from the letter I sent you before: the answers will be completely anonymous and no one's responses will be identified personally or disclosed to any third parties. I hope you will share your opinions openly and honestly.

Questions:

1   What are the major features which describe the Broomhall community?
Prompts: for example:
Population
ethnic minorities
languages
women
children and young people
elderly
people with disabilities
Culture
Festivals
Ethnic traditions
Land usage
Industry
Shops
Housing
Leisure facilities
Open spaces
Public services
Health services
Communications and transport: radio, TV, newspapers
Housing
Schools
Information services provision
Family
Friends
Community leaders

Advice centres
Churches
Libraries
Any other?

2   What do you think is the best and the worst thing about living in this community?
Prompts: Either they would be best or worst these issues could be:
Safety
Transport
Housing
Health

3   What are and have been the major needs, or issues or concerns you experience, or face in the community?
Prompts: For example:
Health issues
Social and economic issues
Employment opportunities
Any other?

4   Where do you go to find facts to have a better understanding, or to find solutions to your needs, or issues, or concerns?
Prompts: Or who do you ask for help? For example:
Relatives
Friends
Community leaders
Church leaders
Advice centres; e.g. Citizen's Advice Bureau
Libraries
Any other?

5   How well your needs are satisfied or your issues or concerns are alleviated from the people or institutions you sought for help?
6   What has worked and what hasn't worked and why?
7   Is there anything else you would like to add?

May I thank you in anticipation of your cooperation.

Mr. Zapopan Martín Muela-Meza
PhD Student
Department of Information Studies
University of Sheffield
Tel: (0114) 222 63 43
Fax: (0114) 278 0300
E-mail: Zapopan.muela@sheffield.ac.uk
E-mail: zapopanmuela@gmail.com
Web: http://www.shef.ac.uk/is/research/phd.html

Instrument approved on 30.08.2005 by my supervisors: Professor Nigel Ford, n.ford@sheffield.ac.uk, Tel: (0114) 2222637 and Briony Train, Lecturer, b.train@sheffield.ac.uk, Tel: 0114 2222653, the Department of Information Studies Research Committee, and the University of Sheffield Ethical Committee.

Appendix 5. Guide for individual interviews to Broomhall information providers (prompted)

Instrument:	**Guide to interview Broomhall information providers (prompted; this guide was not given to respondents and was withheld from their sight during the interview to avoid bias; the prompts were only used to encourage the respondent to talk, sometimes they were used, sometimes they were not)**
Designed by:	Zapopan Martín Muela-Meza, PhD candidate, Department of Information Studies, University of Sheffield. Final version 30 August 2005.
Project:	*An Application of Community Profiling to Analyse the Information Needs and the Community Issues Affecting the People in Broomhall, Sheffield, and to Evaluate the Roles of their Information Providers* *http://www.shef.ac.uk/is/research/phd.html*
Supervisors:	Professor Nigel Ford and Briony Train, Lecturer

Ethical Note:

Dear respondent,

May I remind you an ethical note from the letter I sent you before. The answers will be completely anonymous and no one's responses will be identified personally or disclosed to any third parties. I hope you will share your opinions openly and honestly.

Questions:
1   What are the major features which describe the Broomhall community you (or your organisation/institution) serve?

Prompts: for example:
Population
ethnic minorities
languages
women
children and young people
elderly
people with disabilities
Culture
Festivals
Ethnic traditions
Land usage
Industry
Shops
Housing
Leisure facilities
Open spaces
Public services
Health services
Communications and transport: radio, TV, newspapers
Housing
Schools
Any other?

2   What do you think is the best and the worst thing for the people living in this community?

Prompts: Either they would be best or worst these issues could be:
Safety
Transport
Housing
Health
Any other?

3 What are and have been the major needs, or issues or concerns you think people experience, or face in the community?

Prompts: For example:
Health issues
Social and economic issues
Employment opportunities
Any other?

4 How do you (or does your organisation/institution) contribute with those people to find facts, or to have better understanding, or to find solutions to their needs, or issues, or concerns?

5 How well their needs are satisfied or their issues alleviated with your help (or with the help from your organisation/institution) when they have sought you (them) for help?

6 What has worked and what hasn't worked and why?

7 Is there anything else you would like to add?

May I thank you in anticipation of your cooperation.

Mr. Zapopan Martín Muela-Meza
PhD Student
Department of Information Studies
University of Sheffield
Tel: (0114) 222 63 43
Fax: (0114) 278 0300
E-mail: Zapopan.muela@sheffield.ac.uk
E-mail: zapopanmuela@gmail.com
Web:http://www.shef.ac.uk/is/research/phd.html

Instrument approved on 30.08.2005 by my supervisors: Professor Nigel Ford, n.ford@sheffield.ac.uk, Tel: (0114) 2222637 and Briony Train, Lecturer, b.train@sheffield.ac.uk, Tel: 0114 2222653, the Department of Information Studies Research Committee, and the University of Sheffield Ethical Committee.

Appendix 6. Information provision through the letter boxes of Broomhall homes (at least in section C), from 16 September 2006 to 16 March 2007 (full description of 74 documents)

Appendix 6. Information provision through the letter boxes of Broomhall homes (at least in section C), from 16 September 2006 to 16 March 2007 (full description of 74 documents)				
No.	Title of document	Type of document	Publisher	Date of provision
1.	New Tanning Studio	Commercial flyer (fashion related)	Consol Suncenter	2006. 09.15
2.	£7.50 a month	Commercial flyer (Internet & cable TV related)	Sky TV	2006. 09.15
3.	Somerfield, giving you what you want	Commercial flyer (supermarket related)	Somerfield	2006. 09.15
4.	CostCutter, wow unbeatable value	Commercial flyer (supermarket related)	CostCutter	2006. 09.15
5.	New Wongs Kitchen, Chinese & English hot meals to take away	Commercial flyer (takeaway fast food shop)	Wongs Kitchen	2006. 09.15
6.	What's on at the Broomhall Centre, adult education classes, groups & youth programme from September 11th 2006	Community & voluntary sector flyer (educational related)	Broomhall Centre	2006. 09.15
7.	Oasis (takeaway)	Commercial flyer (takeaway fast food shop)	Oasis	2006. 09.16
8.	We'll beat your car insurance renewal!	Commercial flyer (insurance related)	Churchill	2006. 09.18
9.	New Roots, Shop for Justice	Commercial flyer (organic community shop)	New Roots	2006. 09.18
10.	Most wanted Tex Mex pizza	Commercial flyer (takeaway fast food shop)	Domino's Pizza	2006. 09.18
11.	*A-Z Guide to Public Services 2006/7*	Statutory sector book; directory to Sheffield City Council	Sheffield City Council	2006. 09.19
12.	Your Sheffield, Putting You in the Picture, Winter/Spring 2007	Statutory sector booklet (public service accountancy related)	Sheffield City Council	2006. 09.19

186

13.	Friends, Food & Fun	Community & voluntary sector flyer (religions & spirituality related)	Wycliffe Church	2006. 09.21
14.	Noodle Inn Authentic Chinese Restaurant	Commercial flyer (restaurant related)	Noodle Inn	2006. 09.23
15.	Wallop! Don't get hit by your car insurance renewal	Commercial flyer (insurance related)	Prudential	2006. 09.25
16.	Elif, the Ultimate Takeaway	Commercial flyer (takeaway fast food shop)	Elif	2006. 09.25
17.	Da Vinci's pizzas kebabs burgers	Commercial flyer (takeaway fast food shop)	Da Vinci's	2006. 09.28
18.	*The Sheffield Weekly Gazette & Motors Today.co.uk (West)*	Commercial newspaper (news & publicity related)	www. Sheffieldtoda y. Co.uk	2006. 09.28
19.	CostCutter	Commercial flyer (Supermarket related)	CostCutter	2006. 10.01
20.	Southern Fried Chicken (takeaway)	Commercial flyer (takeaway fast food shop)	Southern Fried Chicken	2006. 10.02
21.	It's official... women are better drivers!	Commercial flyer (insurance related)	Sheilas Wheels	2006. 10.03
22.	Inside...the 3p sachet that saved Amos' life	Community & voluntary sector flyer (poverty & children)	UNICEF	2006. 10.03
23.	Persia (takeaway)	Commercial flyer (takeaway fast food shop)	Persia	2006. 10.04
24.	Street Force, Broomspring Lane Area, Bring out your Rubbish Day Wednesday 11 October '06	Statutory sector flyer (environmental related)	Sheffield City Council and Elected Members of Broomhill/ Central/ Nether Edge Area Panel	2006. 10.04
25.	Folk Concert 4 Palestine	Political organisation flyer (solidarity related)	Sheffield Palestine Solidarity Campaign	2006. 10.05
26.	24 Self Video	Commercial flyer (video entertainment related)	24 Self Video	2006. 10.09

27.	Sky TV from £7.50	Commercial flyer (Internet & cable TV related)	Sky TV	2006. 10.11
28.	It's a girl thing	Community & voluntary sector flyer (health related)	Cancer Research UK	2006. 10.11
29.	A taste of the Rockies in Sheffield	Commercial flyer (alcoholic drinks related)	Coors fine light beer	2006. 10.21
30.	Pizza Panda, voted No. 1 Pizzeria in Sheffield (takeaway)	Commercial flyer (takeaway fast food shop)	Pizza Panda	2006. 10.21
31.	Cheesy Bites pizza	Commercial flyer (takeaway fast food shop)	Pizza Hut	2006. 10.21
32.	TV to suit your tastes	Commercial letter (Internet & cable TV related)	Sky TV	2006. 10.21
33.	Rewrite the Future	Community & voluntary sector booklet (educational related)	Save the Children	2006. 10.21
34.	Broomhall Muslim/Christian Dialogues	Community & voluntary sector flyer (religions & spirituality related)	Broomhall Centre	2006. 10.21
35.	Somerfield, giving you what you want	Commercial flyer (supermarket)	Somerfield	2006. 10.25
36.	Hillside Animal Sanctuary	Community & voluntary sector flyer (farm animal related)	Hill Top Farm, Norwich	2006. 10.25
37.	*News S10*	Statutory sector newspaper on transport about the S10 district (news related)	Sheffield City Council	2006. 10.25
38.	UK Mama, African/Caribbean Restaurant & Takeaway	Commercial flyer (takeaway fast food shop)	UK Mama	2006. 11.06
39.	CostCutter	Commercial flyer (supermarket related)	CostCutter	2006. 11.13
40.	African & Caribbean Xmas Multi-Cultural Party, Sunday 10th December 2006 at Broomhall Centre	Commercial flyer (social party related)	UK Mama & Friends of Africa and Caribbean UK	2006. 12.06
41.	Somerfield, giving	Commercial flyer	Somerfield	2006.

				12.07
	you what you want	(supermarket related)		
42.	The cost of a boiler breakdown could really add up	Commercial flyer (Plumbing; boilers; gas)	British Gas	2007. 01.03
43.	Cheese feast pizza now at its 80's price	Commercial flyer (takeaway fast food shop)	Pizza Hut	2007. 01.03
44.	Have an interest free year	Commercial flyer and application form (credit cards related)	MBNA Visa credit card	2007. 01.03
45.	Consultation on A Full Planning Application (Erection of rear lobby to Public House, Springfield Tavern 182-184, Broomspring Lane, Sheffield, S10 2FE	Statutory sector official letter (home building public consultation related)	Sheffield City Council, Development, Environment and Leisure	2007. 01.03
46.	Stylish looks for Winter	Commercial booklet (health related)	Specsavers Opticians	2007. 01.07
47.	Family Martial Arts	Commercial flyer (health & sports related)	Family Martial Arts	2007. 01.07
48.	Home broadband from Orange	Commercial flyer (Internet related)	Orange	2007. 01.07
49.	CostCutter	Commercial flyer (supermarket related)	CostCutter	2007. 01.07
50.	Somerfield, giving you what you want	Commercial flyer (supermarket related)	Somerfield	2007. 01.07
51.	Kebab World and Pizza (takeaway)	Commercial flyer (takeaway fast food shop)	Kebab World and Pizza	2007. 01.07
52.	Pisa Pizza (takeaway)	Commercial flyer (takeaway fast food shop)	Pisa Pizza	2007. 01.07
53.	Your Sheffield, Putting You in the Picture, Winter/Spring 2007	Statutory sector booklet (public service accountancy related)	Sheffield City Council	2007. 01.07
54.	Home Energy Action Team (HEAT), Sheffield Roadshows	Community & voluntary sector flyer (home energy saving related)	HEAT	2007. 02.01
55.	Da Vinci's pizzas kebabs burgers	Commercial flyer (takeaway fast food shop)	Da Vinci's	2007. 02.03
56.	Cheese feast pizza now at its 80's	Commercial flyer (takeaway fast food	Pizza Hut	2007. 02.06

	price	shop)		
57.	Da Vinci's pizzas kebabs burgers	Commercial flyer (takeaway fast food shop)	Da Vinci's	2007. 02.07
58.	Join the Sky entertainment experience today	Commercial flyer (Internet & cable TV related)	Sky TV	2007. 02.13
59.	Somerfield, giving you what you want	Commercial flyer (supermarket related)	Somerfield	2007. 02.13
60.	Oasis (takeaway)	Commercial flyer (takeaway fast food shop)	Oasis	2007. 02.13
61.	Learning and Skills Open College	Community & voluntary sector flyer (educational related)	Learning and Skills Open College	2007. 02.13
62.	Mohammad Azim's Focus	Political party flyer	Liberal Democrats Party	2007. 02.20
63.	We'll beat your car insurance renewal!	Commercial flyer (insurance related)	Churchill	2007. 02.21
64.	Save up to 40% on your heating bills with a new boiler	Commercial flyer (Plumbing; boilers; gas)	British Gas	2007. 02.21
65.	Somerfield, giving you what you want	Commercial flyer (supermarket related)	Somerfield	2007. 02.21
66.	Somerfield, giving you what you want	Commercial flyer (supermarket related)	Somerfield	2007. 02.26
67.	3 months free central heating breakdown cover!	Commercial flyer (supermarket related)	Help Link UK Ltd.	2007. 02.26
68.	Tandoori spice pizza	Commercial flyer (takeaway fast food shop)	Pizza Hut	2007. 02.26
69.	Somerfield, giving you what you want	Commercial flyer (supermarket related)	Somerfield	2007. 03.04
70.	Pizza Pan & Grills	Commercial flyer (takeaway fast food shop)	Pizza Pan & Grills	2007. 03.07
71.	CostCutter, wow unbeatable value	Commercial flyer (supermarket related)	CostCutter	2007. 03.09
72.	Get a nice surprise from BT, instead.	Commercial flyer (Telephone & Internet related)	BT	2007. 03.15
73.	Isn't it about time you had more time?	Commercial flyer (domestic cleaning services related)	Domestic Cleaning Service	2007. 03.16
74.	Somerfield, giving you what you want	Commercial flyer (supermarket related)	Somerfield	2007. 03.16

Dr. Zapopan Muela (Zapopan Martín Muela-Meza, Chihuahua, MEXICO, 29 April 1969), PhD, MLS, BA in LIS. **Education:** PhD in Information Studies at the University of Sheffield, UK (degree conferred on 1st July 2010) thanks to a high academic excellence scholarship from the Mexican National Science and Technology Council (CONACYT) and the University of Sheffield. Master in Library Science, State University of New York at Buffalo, NY, USA (2002) thanks to a high academic excellence scholarship from the U.S. Department of State Information Agency, Fulbright, Laspau, COMEXUS, and SUNY Buffalo. Undergraduate degree in Library Science (1998) at the Nuevo Leon Autonomous University (UANL). **Professional experience:** Lecturer at the Nuevo Leon Autonomous University (Universidad Autónoma de Nuevo León, UANL) since 21st January 2008 until June 2011 at the Faculty of Philosophy and Letters, and from July 2011 to present at the Faculty of Sport Organisation (FOD), undergraduate and postgraduate lecturer and Head of the Library "Ing. Cayetano Garza Garza.": a) Founder, Director and Editor in Chief of Library and Information Science Critique: An International Peer Reviewed Journal of Information Recorded in Documents, http://sites.google.com/site/criticabibliotecologica/liscritique ; b) Director and Editor in Chief of the Documental Information Bulletin at the Faculty of Philosophy and Letters at UANL. http://sites.google.com/site/cinfodocuanlffyl/boletininformaciondocumental. **Publications:** These are my recent publications: >>**Books**>> Muela, Z. (2016). *This is Broomhall, Sheffield, UK: A Marxist, Class & Qualitative Community Profiling for Information Needs and Providers.* Seattle, WA, USA: CreateSpace an Amazon.com Company. ISBN-13: 978-1495955464 , ISBN-10: 149595546X. >>**Author of this PhD thesis**>> Muela, Zapopan Martín. (2010). *An Application of Community Profiling to Analyse Community Information Needs, and Providers: Perceptions from the People of the Broomhall Neighbourhood of Sheffield, UK.* Sheffield, UK: University of Sheffield, Department of Information Studies. [PhD Thesis]. Accessible in open access through my personal archive E-LIS: http://eprints.rclis.org/handle/10760/14659 . You can also access to the official bibliographic record at the University of Sheffield Library <http://find.shef.ac.uk/primo_library/libweb/action/dlDisplay.do?vid=SFD_VU2&afterPDS=true &institution=44SFD&docId=44SFD_ALMA_DS21176803160001441>. >>**Co-author of these books**>> Muela, Z.M. (2007). "Ethical contradictions of the social responsibilities in librarianship." In: Gimeno Perelló, J. & López López, P. (Eds.). *Libraries and Social Compromise.* chapter 14, pp.417-444, Guijon, Asturias, Spain: Trea. [in Spanish]. Accessible in open access through E-LIS: http://eprints.rclis.org/archive/00011805/ . Story, A., Darch, C. & Halbert, D. (Eds). (2006). The Copy/South Dossier : Issues in the Economics, Politics, and Ideology of Copyright in the Global South. Canterbury, Kent, UK: The Copy/South Research Group. Accessible online in open access through E-LIS: http://eprints.rclis.org/archive/00006278/ . **Peer-reviewed journal articles (the 10 most recent ones):** Muela, Z.M. (2015). Socialization of the public information commons vs the enclosures of the informational and cognitive capitalism. *Library and Information Science Critique: Journal of the Sciences of Information Recorded in Documents.* Vol.8, No. 1, pp. 38-53. Muela, Z.M., et al. (2014). Critical and sceptical thinking on reading sport information (Pensamiento Crítico Y Escéptico En La Lectura De Información Documental Deportiva En Estudiantes De Licenciatura). *Revista Fod De Ciencias Del Ejercicio*, Vol.9, No. 9. Pp.1-14. http://eprints.rclis.org/24665/1/Muela et al 2014 RCE-FOD vol 9 no 9.pdf . Muela, Z.M. (2014). A critique to the policies of dismantling the full tenure and perpetuating renewable contracts affecting library workers. *Library and Information Science Critique: Journal of the Sciences of Information Recorded in Documents.* Vol.7, Pag.57-68. http://eprints.rclis.org/24733/1/Muela 2014 CB 7 2 working class.pdf . Muela, Z.M. (2014). "In defense of the scientific information and communication in free of charge Open Access through all of its processes of publication and reading." En Defensa De La Información Y Comunicación Científica En Open Access Gratuito En Todos Los Procesos De Publicación Y Lectura., , *Library and Information Science Critique: Journal of the Sciences of Information Recorded in Documents* Vol.7, Pag.55-65, http://eprints.rclis.org/24646/1/Muela 2014 artic C.B. 7 1.pdf . Muela, Z.M. (2013). "A critique to the capitalist policies that hamper the public scientific documentation and communication of sports" (Una Crítica A Las Políticas Capitalistas Que Obstaculizan La Documentación Y Comunicación Científica Deportiva Pública), *Revista Ciencias del Ejercicio* ercicio Fod, Vol.8, Pag.67-67. http://eprints.rclis.org/20572/1/final Muela Torres 2013 cong FOD UANL.pdf . Muela, Z.M. (2012). "Information needs for the creation of sport bibliographic instruction program." (Necesidades De Información Documental Para Creación De Programa De Instrucción Bibliográfica En Ciencias Del Ejercicio, Caso Fod, Uanl).. *Revista De Ciencias Del Ejercicio -- Fod*, Vol.7, Pag.92-101. http://eprints.rclis.org/17932/1/2012 Muela Torres nec info dep RCEFOD.pdf . Muela, Z.M. (2012). "A critique to the anti-labor trends in the sciences of information recorded in documents." (Una Crítica A Las Tendencias Anti-Laboristas En Las Ciencias De La Información Documental, , *Library and Information Science Critique: Journal of the Sciences of Information Recorded in Documents*, Vol.5, Pag.9-23. http://eprints.rclis.org/19728/1/Muela 2012 art c.b.vol.5.no.1.pdf . Muela, Z.M. (2012). The copyright system, librarians and libray associations defenders of copyright as main barriers of documental information access in libraries from underdeveloped countries. Ten theses *Library and Information Science Critique: Journal of the Sciences of Information Recorded in Documents*, Vol.5, Pag.9-28. http://eprints.rclis.org/11553/2/Muela 2005 10 theses VS copyright.pdf . Muela, Z.M. (2011). "For a critical and labour librarianship" (Por una bibliotecología crítica y laboral)." *Library and Information Science Critique: Journal of the Sciences of Information Recorded in Documents* 4 (2), pp. 63-114. http://eprints.rclis.org/bitstream/10760/16959/1/CB.Vol.4.No.2.2011.Muela.Bib-Eng.pdf . Muela , Z.M. (2011). "Sport information needs from Broomhall, Sheffield, UK." (Necesidades informacionales deportivas de Broomhall, Sheffield, Inglaterra). Un estudio cualitativo de 2003 a 2007." *Revista de Ciencias del Ejercicio - FOD ISSN: 1870-3941*. 7 (2), pp. 148-151. https://www.researchgate.net/publication/220048484 . But I have published 22 peer-reviewed articles; 11 non peer-reviewed articles; and 69 researchers have cited my publications worldwide (as of today 24 February 2016). For the full list of 146 publications access all free at E-LIS: <http://eprints.rclis.org/view/creators/Muela-Meza=3AZapopan_Mart=EDn=3A=3A.html> . **Conferences:** I have travelled to 18 countries and I have given hundreds of conferences; countries like: Argentina, Belgium, Canada, Colombia, France, Germany, India, Italy, Ireland, Luxembourg, México, Spain, Switzerland, The Netherlands, UK, Uruguay, USA, Venezuela. **Lines of research:** Critical community profiling or analysis in librarianship; qualitative research methodologies and interpretivism; information needs; critical and sceptical thinking; Marxist and critical epistemology and theory in librarianship; social commitment in librarianship; critique to the fallacious ideologies of information & knowledge society; intellectual property affecting librarianship; ethics in librarianship; librarianship education. **Honours and other academic distinctions**: a) Associate Editor for DOAJ (Directory of Open Access Journals) since May 2015; b) Laureate with the distinction of "Candidate to Become a National Researcher" for outstanding high academic merits devoted for scientific and technological research by the Mexican National System of Researchers of the National Council of Science and Technology (SNI-CONACYT), Federal Mexican Government, Mexico, 2011-present; c) Laureate with the distinction of "PROMEP-Profile (Profile of the Mexican Program for the Betterment University Professors)", for outstanding high academic merits devoted for scientific and technological research by the PROMEP Program of the Secretary of Public Education, Federal Mexican Government, Mexico, 2009-present; d) Member of the Copy/South Research Group, Canterbury, Kent, UK, 2005-to present; e) E-LIS: The International Eprints Open Archives in Library and Information Science, 2005 – Present (appointed as Editor of E-LIS for Mexico). **Other data:** Activist of Amnesty International since 2004; Activist of Greenpeace since 2004; Member of Exit Directory of Information Professionals <http://www.directorioexit.info/ficha237>; . **Contact:** E-mail: zapopanmuela@gmail.com ; https://mx.linkedin.com/in/zapopanmuela; https://www.facebook.com/zapopan.muela ; http://www.uanl.mx/universidad/persona/investigador/zapopan-martin-muela-meza.html . Full text Curriculum Vitae: http://sites.google.com/site/zapopanmuela/ .